Thucydides' Meditations on Fear

Thucydides' Meditations on Fear

Examining Contemporary Cases

Raymond Taras

ANTHEM PRESS

Anthem Press
An imprint of Wimbledon Publishing Company
www.anthempress.com

This edition first published in UK and USA 2023
by ANTHEM PRESS
75–76 Blackfriars Road, London SE1 8HA, UK
or PO Box 9779, London SW19 7ZG, UK
and
244 Madison Ave #116, New York, NY 10016, USA

British Library Cataloguing-in-Publication Data
A catalogue record for this book is available from the British Library.

Library of Congress Cataloging-in-Publication Data
A catalog record for this book has been requested.
2023936665

ISBN-13: 978-1-83998-948-3 (hbk)
ISBN-10: 1-83998-948-3 (hbk)

ISBN-13: 978-1-83998-995-7 (pbk)
ISBN-10: 1-83998-995-5 (pbk)

This title is also available as an e-book.

CONTENTS

ACKNOWLEDGMENTS

In recent years, I was the recipient of a Fulbright distinguished professor award in Australia (at the Australian National University) and of a Leverhulme guest professorship in England (at Sussex University). I am grateful for these awards which were key to unlocking suppositions, guesses, and findings in my research. I am also indebted to the Carol Lavin Bernick faculty grant award at Tulane University that helped bridge a major gap caused by the pandemic and allowed me to travel to Australia when the time was right. Tulane University's School of Liberal Arts provided a publication subvention for which I am very grateful. I especially wish to thank Dean Brian Edwards and Assistant Faculty Dean Tara Hamburg for facilitating it.

There is a backstory to the cover art. The 2010 painting by awardwinning Australian impressionist Marie Green is titled "Dark Clouds Gather." It recounts how the end of a long drought is replaced by storm clouds bringing in fairer weather. Fear has been vanquished, hope has been rekindled. Marie Green's artwork is in turn based on a famous poem written in 1911 by Australian teenager Dorothea Mackellar who pined for Australia after having briefly experienced life in England. It was simply called "My Country" and has become emblematic of that country's resilience, particularly in the face of dramatic climate changes. This backstory, including a reading by Mackellar, can be found at: https://lifeism.co/mycountry-a-poem-by-dorothea-mackellar.

AUTHOR BIOGRAPHY

Born and educated in Montréal, Québec, Raymond Taras completed postgraduate degrees at universities in Europe and began publishing scholarly books in the 1980s. He has authored or edited over twenty books, among them on the collapse of the USSR, Russia's identity in international relations, the rise of liberal and illiberal nationalisms, the internationalization of ethnic conflict, the looming threats of xenophobia and Islamophobia, a comprehensive critique of multiculturalism, the impact of fear on foreign policy, a reimagined understanding of nationhood and, recently, a multidisciplinary study of Russia's exceptionalism in international politics. He served on the faculty of universities in North America and Europe including Harvard, Stanford, Michigan, and Vermont; and at the European University Institute, Malmö, Aalborg, and Sussex. In 2013–14 he was awarded the Fulbright Distinguished Chair at the University of Warsaw, and in 2018–19 the Fulbright Distinguished Chair at the Australian National University in Canberra. He is professor of politics at Tulane University in New Orleans, Louisiana, and has been director of the World Literature Program.

INTRODUCTION

This book focuses on Greek classical historian Thucydides, his classification of the types of fear that made much of the world tremble, and the author's relevance to case studies that I will examine and come from different parts of the world. It was tempting to subtitle the book "From Thucydides to the End-Times?" but that would have given me away as a deep-seated pessimist. Moreover, I could be mistaken for subscribing to a set of religious beliefs predicating history's final events, that is, the eschatological fate of humanity. Let me be more of a realist, then, and accept that we are living through an unprecedented series of crises at this time that we seem to be at a loss to resolve, while embracing a hopeful vision of what is to come.

That said, global scorching, particularly in implausible regions such as the Arctic and Antarctic, is worsening with each passing year. Population growth, unenforced borders, ethnic and religious conflicts, and even outright wars in Europe and beyond—nowadays fought with modern weaponry such as artificial intelligence, hypersonic missiles, kinetic earth-to-space weapons, and now commonplace drones—have become the new normal. Economic and social inequalities are unprecedented: in its January 2023 annual report to the World Economic Forum in Davos, the trustworthy British charity Oxfam claimed that the world population's top one percent acquired about two-thirds of the $42 trillion in new wealth created since 2020. We also cannot overlook the global tragedy caused by the COVID pandemic either: by January 2023 up to 700 million cases were recorded of which nearly seven million died from its symptoms. A lengthy list of regional and local catastrophes, complementing headline-grabbing global events, is too extensive to detail.

At the Davos Forum in 2023, United Nations Secretary-General António Guterres remarked how the world is in a "sorry state." It is "looking into the eye of a Category 5 hurricane." Climate change, Big Oil, and Russia's invasion of Ukraine, in particular, had been "piling up like cars in a chain reaction crash."[1] Such facts do not augur well for progressing toward a plausible end-times.

Given the rapid expansion of institutions, governmental and nongovernmental, convening to meet on global crises that are fundamentally systemic and typically beyond their control, Swedish environmental activist Greta Thunberg summed up their efforts with a trenchant comment: "Blah, blah, blah…. There is no planet B. There is no planet Blah." Indeed, "Our hopes and dreams drown in their empty words and promises" which, she argued, cover a span of over thirty years.[2] We sometimes make reference to a proverb associated with what originally might have been a Chinese curse: "May you live in interesting times." In the 2020s there is reason to reinvent this curse to "living in perilous times."

Highlighting processes of decolonization has become a newfound catchphrase in the 2020s. Yet simultaneously we overlook practices of re-colonization, known by its aliases—economic globalization and neoliberalism—occurring throughout the world. These have produced armed conflicts and wars between the haves and the have-nots. Tragically, they have also caused wars between the world's have-nots. Most dangerously, conflicts threaten wars among the world's haves with their multiple and continuously-modernizing weapons of destruction. To be sure, human agency may not always be indirectly or directly associated with earthquakes, cyclones, tidal waves, desertification, pollution, the mass extinction of fauna, the erosion of flora, and other events linked primarily to mother nature. But human agency alone is responsible for the outbreak of wars.

All the cases researched in this book were identified with belligerents fighting in World War II. These same states continue to make up today's great powers. Australia may be the lone exception but even here the country is preparing to introduce nuclear-powered submarines from Britain. What is distinctive in my study is that it is not about war but about fears of the Stranger, the Outsider, and the Other. This preemptive aspect of fear can in time, nevertheless, lead to armed conflict and even acts of genocide.

The subject of fear has always represented an engrossing yet unwieldy topic. It is a reason why many publications include the term in their book titles. What constitutes fear has produced countless debates and discussions ranging across many disciplines. The notion of political fear narrows the topic considerably. Oddly, however, an obvious place to start the debate is often overlooked; it begins with Thucydides (c. 460–c. 400 BCE) and his timeless *The History of the Peloponnesian War.* He is readily acknowledged as the founder of the study of international relations but he is usually overlooked as a specialist on fear.

My first acknowledgment goes to my secondary school in Montréal where I was introduced to the Greek and Latin classics. For better or worse, the "A" class at this school was not required to learn chemistry or physics or much math. While pupils in the "B," "C," and "D" classes went on to achieve enviable careers as medical doctors, air force pilots, and business entrepreneurs, the "A" class seemed largely left behind. What jobs were we fit to do after learning two dead languages quite well? The one exception was a classmate in the "A" class who took advantage of his Latin vocabulary, felt determined not to be left behind, and late in life was elected a Cardinal in the Vatican.

For my part, Montréal in the 1960s was illuminating in figuring out which groups would be recognized and valued in Québec society undergoing a Quiet Revolution, and which might be left on the margins. French Canadians were finally becoming *maîtres chez nous* and the anglosphere—in Québec at least—was losing ground. Many anglophones emigrated to other Canadian provinces while *allophones*—those whose mother tongue was neither French nor English—faced obstacles in reaching for greater socioeconomic mobility. Passed in 1977, Bill 101—the Charter of the French Language that made French the sole official language in Québec—resolved the issue *tout court*. I remember in the late 1960s traveling to a protest rally in Ottawa chanting "Québec *oui*, Ottawa *non*." I do not remember what the controversy was about and why we supported *oui* and not *non*. But as a university student, I was about to follow the "protest generation" attentively.

The research project I embarked on resulting in this book was structured by random and not-so-random events. In addition, when COVID in 2020 interrupted well-planned field research, I had to improvise like much of the world's population. I benefited from study leaves and sabbaticals that allowed me to carry out empirical research and connect with well-informed "local" specialists in different countries. Ultimately my first choice (when in high school) and last choice (to fine-tune applied concepts and methods) reflect a sentiment to make use of ancient Greek philosophy and Thucydides' categories of fear.

Many individuals having diverse approaches and formulating distinctive puzzles to solve sharpened my ideas for this book. My shortlist to whom I express gratitude includes: in England, Martin Davis, John O'Toole, Brieda Vincent, and Eric Whittington; in Saxony, Ivan Kalmar, Barbara Thériault, Ljubjana Wüstehube, and Alexander Yendell; in Russia, Sergei Akopov, Andrei Korobkov, David Lane, and Olga Malinova; in Japan, Soichiro Fukutake, Emiko Hirano, Suzuki Michitaka Sawa, and Sachi Shimada; and in Australia, Geoff Levy, Nina Markovic, Andrew Markus, and Samina Yasmeen. In the United States where I have spent most of my academic career, I received valuable advice from colleagues across the country. I also learned much from undergraduate and graduate students whether at Tulane University in New Orleans or other institutions where I have taught.

Colleagues and friends have inspired me with innovative, often counterintuitive, and even implausible ideas. They include Mercedes de

Luis Andrés (University of Vienna), Jerzy Bartkowski (University of Warsaw), Marek Berka (London), Marjorie Castle (University of Utah), Cardinal Michael Czerny, S.J. (the Vatican), Wendy French (UCH Macmillan Cancer Centre Poet-in-Residence), Tanya Golash-Boza (University of California, Merced), Aleksandra Jasińska-Kania (University of Warsaw), Tudor Jones (Oxford University), Mark and Marty Kytola (Montréal), Christel Lane (Cambridge University), Molly O'Neal (US State Department), Bo Petersson (Malmö University), Jacek Raciborski (University of Warsaw), Donat Taddeo (Stanford PhD and Order of Canada luminary whose last name in high school came just before mine, determining seating arrangements for the next four years), Stephen White (University of Glasgow), Hakan Yavuz (University of Utah), and Jen Zieff (Fraser, Colorado). I also pay tribute to the late Mick Moran (University of Manchester), a pioneering politics scholar and generous friend who set me heading in the right direction when we shared the same PhD office at Essex University in the 1970s.

The Anthem Press editorial team served as a backbone for editorial and production professionalism culminating in its publication. Among its staff, Jebaslin Hephzibah was the editor that made it all come together. Editorial support was provided by Nathiya Thirumurugan who guided me through the thick and thin of the production process. Finally, as project manager Mathew Rohit made it all come together. A more professional hands-on overseer of the final product I could not have asked for. I am grateful as well to three anonymous reviewers who offered substantive and substantial critiques in a timely fashion. Their revisions and ideas that flowed out of Thucydides' magisterial work were an inspiration.

A special place is set aside for family. I extend profound appreciation to Mike, Kris, Gabriela, and Marc Taras for their boundless support, encouragement, and no-nonsense attitudes (though not always) touching different markers in my life. Y'all rock!

Notes

1 "Davos 2023: Special Address by António Guterres, Secretary-General of the United Nations" (January 18, 2023), https://www.weforum.org/agenda/2023/01/davos-2023-special-address-by-antonio-guterres-secretary-general-of-the-united-nations/.

2 Jennifer Hassan, "Greta Thunberg Says World Leaders' Talk on Climate Change is 'Blah Blah Blah,'" *Washington Post* (September 29, 2021), https://www.washingtonpost.com/climate-environment/2021/09/29/great-thunberg-leaders-blah-blah-blah/.

Chapter 1

MEDITATIONS ON FEAR: THE CONTINUING RELEVANCE OF THUCYDIDES

The Concept and Its Iterations

Fear is a pervasive term used to describe an individual's or group's perceived insecurity, threat, and angst. It can also denote a person's wariness, suspicion, and skepticism about events that may soon occur which affect and alter one's standing. Furthermore, it can evoke a future threat to the person. Fear can therefore be applied in many different ways and contexts. When parts of a whole nation sense fear, the relevance and significance may affect its international relations, whether immediately or belatedly.

For a nation, the causes, sources, and bases of fear differ. In his seminal volume on *Fear: The History of a Political Idea* (2004), Corey Robin understands political fear as entailing "a people's felt apprehension of some harm to their collective well-being." It has far-reaching repercussions: "It may dictate public policy, bring new groups to power and keep others out, create laws and overturn them."[1]

It is the politics of fear-making that Robin has called attention to, not fear *ipso facto*. He argues how "the politics of fear is far less dependent upon the actual psychic experience of the public than analysts would have us think. While many believe that the individual emotions of the citizenry propel the policies the government pursues, I see little evidence of this." On the contrary, the author inveighs, "Even if we assume that each and every member of the public is experiencing fear, that experience still doesn't explain the policies. A frightened population could just as easily inspire the government to pursue policies that would dampen rather than arouse fear." In the end "It is politics that produces policies, not fear."[2] Or, we can add, it is the gunman, not the gun, who kills.

Political fear's main protagonist today is a transformed Western liberalism departing from its nineteenth-century counterpart. It has metamorphosized into a rigid and doctrinaire, even quasi-authoritarian philosophy. Its prevailing status in Western thought has led to it becoming a victim of its own success. In Patrick Deneen's timely volume, liberty is redefined in such a way as to signify the opposite of its original meaning that was a prerequisite for self-governance. Instead, it now insists on maximizing the greatest possible freedom from external constraints while maintaining order among unfettered individuals.[3] The open society and its enemies, in Karl Popper's conceptualization, have merged into one.[4]

My argument, expanded in the book's final chapter, is that the junctures of fear and liberalism may have critical implications for our future. Judith Shklar pierced these interstices by claiming that "the liberalism of fear" can unite society against cruelty and injustice, thereby providing a normative framework combating the politics of fear and underscoring the moral basis for social solidarity. For her it was not the *summum bonum*—the highest good—but the *summum malum*—the highest evil—that provided the motivational power to mobilize the public.[5] There was an innate rivalry between the two conceptualizations that would prevent overlapping structures.

Taking his cue from Shklar's groundbreaking theoretical approach, Jacob Levy's book *The Multiculturalism of Fear* argues for a liberal account of multiculturalism concerned less with preserving cultural communities and their identities and instead centering on reducing evils and cruelties, such as interethnic civil wars and recourses to violence, whether carried out by the state or nonstate actors. Ethnic minorities would be the main targets. Contesting the sources of minorities' fears thus becomes of critical importance.

Granted, the value attached to people expressing their ethnic identities, particularly when migrating to other lands, must be recognized and accepted. For Levy, however, it should not necessarily produce a celebration of their cultural belonging; it may serve as a source of pride to them, but of fear and revulsion by adversarial groups. Liberal principles can easily come apart under the stresses imposed by diverse cultural demands.[6]

I turn to such critical sources of fear, and perhaps their undoing, in the chapters that follow. My analyses of nationalism, nationhood, migration, and belonging can be found in my earlier studies.[7] So the focus here is on different *types* of fear, their characteristics and scope, and the case studies that explain their evolution.

Thucydides' Ruminations

Thucydides is known for his paradigm-shifting book, *The History of the Peloponnesian War*, which appeared around 400 BCE. He was the first true historian offering a dispassionate account of war and fear in which the gods played no part whatsoever. He has been called the father of the school of political realism which views the outcomes of relations between states as constructed upon fear and self-interest; it was Napoleon who, more than twenty centuries later, reiterated that only these two forces can unite human beings. Thucydides as author has provoked a deluge of literature on such diverse aspects of his thought as the opposition of force and justice in Greek city-states and his less realist views of aspects of international relations.[8]

The Athenian historian, proud of his city-state, introduced a number of key concepts rarely used today that outlined his registry of fear and its causes.[9] Revisiting these ideas is essential if we want to deconstruct and disaggregate political fears for our times. Given that nearly all his Greek terms for fear are unfamiliar and even unwieldy, for reasons of style, I use them selectively and for the most part employ approximate English translations in their place. It is in their subtlety and nuance, whichever language we use, which stand out in Thucydides' insightful overview.

It is never a bad idea to turn to the classics for creativity and wisdom. Thucydides dominates the limelight among classical Greek scholars and his reach and influences are extensive. However, as part of my counterfactual inclinations, I refer to Oxford University classicist scholar Simon Hornblower to bring a modicum of skepticism into how his works were received in his own lifetime and shortly after. "Not always favorably" is what we conclude from Hornblower's review.[10]

As noted, Thucydides' status is important to historians since he was the forefather of the study of not just conflict but fear (Figure 1.1). Indeed his detailed analysis of the Peloponnesian war (431–404 BCE) has been described as "a meditation upon fear—its varieties, ubiquity, potency, and even rational necessity.[11] His focus on the role played by fear in politics highlighted how the notion posed a grave danger to democracy itself. This represents a major topic today when debating democratic backsliding and erosion across many countries. Fear's complexity offers insights into different versions extending from sudden panic to distant suspicion.

Another eminent classicist, Gregory Nagy, a Harvard University professor, asserts how "There is no single word in ancient Greek that matches the modern English word *fear* in all its comprehensiveness."[12] I interpret this as the need to write this book even if I am not a classical Greek scholar. It is intriguing that like Inuit nations who have many different words for snow, classical Greek has multiple terms for what we would describe as fear.

Greek terms have their use, then can be quietly forgotten, as I learned in secondary school. Thucydides' catalog setting out definitions of fear contains the noun *deos* (δέος), derived from the word "to doubt." In Homeric

Figure 1.1 Thucydides.

Greek, to doubt also signifies being afraid. In this sense, *deos* constitutes a form of cerebral fear—an anxiousness about a more distant, ill-defined threat bringing fear with it.

Classical scholars single out *phobos* (φόβος) as of particular importance—the word for fear that faithfully remains commonly used today. It corresponds to a stronger, more instinctive, less rational fear of an imminent threat. Rather than exclusively standing for fear, the English rendering of phobia has been transformed into a register of a wide gamut of human passions. These encompass feelings of animosity, antipathy, antagonism, and even disdain and hatred toward adversaries. On occasions, Thucydides used *deos* interchangeably with *phobos* and so notionally they should not be treated as mutually exclusive. But let us just say that they do exclude each other: *phobos* signals an instinctive fear of an imminent menace while *deos* entails a logical fear of a remote threat.

The other word Nagy extrapolates from Thucydides' notion of fear is *ekplēxis* (ἔκπληξις), which for Nagy means shock, astonishment, and even panic. He cites Thucydides: "In the narrative of Thucydides, we can see here a crescendo of panic. Each instance of great panic that defies the imagination leads to another instance of even greater panic that defies the imagination all the more. But the ultimate panic is yet to come." Thucydides made little use of the *ekplexis* and closely-related *kataplexis* (καταπληξία) word groups. But they denote stronger feelings that express fear, for instance, terror and trepidation.

So far we encounter three different terms that refer to fear: *phobos* and *deos* are notions evoking primal fear though the first involves greater urgency than the second. *Ekplexis* spells panic. The last two nouns Thucydides identified for fear have fallen out of use today: *orrodia* (ορρόδια) and *hypopsia* (υποψία). These two deserve to be revived today to enforce greater conciseness and explanatory power when fear is under discussion.

The welcome news is that *orrodia* appeared only five times in his *History of the Peloponnesian War*. What is more, it was found in quoted speeches and orations of a few classical Greek political leaders. The case study that I examine for employing *orrodia* is especially fitting and I will identify the speech maker in the next section.

When Thucydides wished to capture a fear evoked by a breakdown in confidence in the state of things, he invoked *hypopsia*. It should not be mistaken for a somewhat different but interrelated word *hupopsis* (hupopsis), specifying anxiety about perceived threats associated with a tyrannical or oligarchic upheaval. It is to *hypopsia* that I gravitate to since it offers a semantic alternative to the generic, imprecise, and overused term "phobia."

The literal meaning of *hypopsia* is "looking underneath the surface" evoked by a suspicion that what will be discovered beneath will be found to be threatening. It, therefore, represents the condition of being suspicious about the way things, or people, appear to be. It entails distrust, even deep distrust, which may capture the gist of fear. It is also an appropriate word to use in political science and psychology. Rather than a focus on the significance of trust that can build on social capital favoring a particular government— it was popularized by a Swedish political scientist who emphasized trust in authority—today it may be more valuable to examine citizens' distrust of politics and the way it can shape society.[13] Thucydides did not regard Athenian democracy as compatible with a surveillance system designed to protect a city-state or regime but he did believe in the resilience of democratic systems in managing fear. In the twenty-first century, some observers note that we are marked by a return of old fears, deep suspicions, ingrained criminality, and random chaos that hastens the weakening of democracy.[14]

The Greek historian's investigation of fear and the terminology he developed to understand it were semantically trailblazing. It displayed a prescient awareness of how the emergent system of Athenian democracy collided with human passions and could be destroyed by them. Now we see how a turnaround in the linkage between fear and democracy has emerged. Contemporary democracies are surveillance states fearful and suspicious of those threatening the democratic order, let alone an authoritarian one. In contrast to Thucydides' logic, then, it is suspicion, surveillance, and the liberal democratic system that mutually reinforce one another.

Thucydides paid special attention to the part played by fear in international relations too. Harvard professor Graham Allison coined the phrase "The Thucydides Trap" when recounting how the Spartan city-state felt threatened by the rise of Athenian power and launched a preemptive attack on it. Over the course of history, Allison's research team argued, emergent or rising powers, like China today, sparked a conflict with dominant powers, such as the United States, which resulted in war.[15]

As another example, Thucydides cited the emergence of fear as essential to raising the fleet that set out to attack Troy. What Brian Calabrese called "a 'panic benefit,' the advantage that a state receives following a sudden, unexpected fear," plays a significant role. It creates "the unity and resolve that develop after the panic and that enable the city to overcome the conditions that caused the panic, usually the threat of invasion."[16] Fear, then, whether arising from within society or outside of it, as in the case of Greek fear of Persian invasions, has proved functional for political leaders.

The presence in society of xenophobia, literally a fear of foreigners but used colloquially as animosity, dislike, and hostility toward them, characterized Greek city-states. It was characteristic of Spartan society, but of Athens too. The meanings of xenophobia make it an ambiguous and opaque term. Political scientist Marie Demker captured its multiple connotations: "xenophobia today is used as shortcut, describing the societal sentiment of distress, agony, antagonism, fear, alarm, and suspicion that has come to be a companion of migrant flows to Europe after the end of the cold war."[17]

Some parallels exist with the way that the concept of anti-Semitism and the rise of xenophobia have developed. From an early fear of Jews and Jewry, it was expanded to a pervasive dislike of them, then of an altogether systematic fear, and finally to their extermination demonstrated in the Shoah. Such semantic fluidity has led in many countries worldwide to the criminalization of anti-Semitic speech, in particular, Holocaust denial. Nevertheless xenophobia is harder to pin down.

Approaching fear using different tools of analysis throws greater light on the kinds of fear that threaten us. The first question to ask is how profound the public's fears are. Can these originate from the top down, manipulated by cynical politicians, or do they represent grassroots fears? Which perceptions of threats cause immediate fears and which have distant resonance?

We are not helped by social surveys that rarely probe whether respondents sense a near threat or a remote one. Narratives of fear are useful but difficult to code in a meaningful and concise way. The meaning of the term as used in Thucydides' catalog provides us with an advantage even when sometimes interchangeable words are used to convey fear. How convincing the evidence is in an empirical case study can serve as the *explanans*—that which can explain—indicating the weight given to immediate versus distant threats.

A useful hypothesis is that some case studies furnish more explanatory power than others about which type of fear is most significant. In a comparative study, an assumption can be that the doubting Thomas will question how ubiquitous and prevalent fear develops in contrasting societies. Examining six case studies can explain how fear affects countries differently.

Applying Theory to Cases

Thucydides' vocabulary is well poised for undertaking an analysis of multiple types of fear. To be sure, there can be no substitute for carrying out a multifactorial comparison of cases preferred by quantitative method specialists; a one-factor approach to as liminal a subject as political fear is bound to prove unreliable. On the other hand, zeroing in on just one factor, especially a malleable one like fear, has its advantages, especially when a *series* of case studies is under examination. In short, all of Thucydides' understandings of fear can apply to multiple countries, though not to the same degree. Concentrating on one factor so as to verify its impact on the dependent variable, that is, *explanandum*—what it is that is being explained, which type of fear is aroused—is the crux of the matter.

An alternative approach raising questions about the "infallibility" of using Thucydides to arrive at explanations involves casting the research design as a plausibility probe. This exercise tests a theoretical construct by focusing on one empirical instance of it. What it does not do is to then draw causal inferences or tell a causal story. Weighing the salience of "coefficients of variation" may be insignificant and even irrelevant when measuring the intensity of fear in a society. A plausibility probe, therefore, allows social scientists to go further, dig deeper, and choose their own cases.

A common factor that welds together the case studies I have selected is immigration and the societal attitudes toward it. These orientations—and not individual behavior—can be found in attitudinal surveys. Respondents are asked, for example, if immigration numbers can improve or worsen the quality of life in a society. When applied to migration policy, the "contact hypothesis," originally developed in the 1950s by Gordon Allport, is put to the test: Does contact between two particular groups promote tolerance and acceptance or does it not?

The assumption in this theory is that intergroup contact under appropriate conditions can reduce forms of prejudice between group members and reduce stereotyping, discrimination, and innate bias that may otherwise occur.[18] Survey research can discover whether contact improves or worsens intergroup relations. Pointed questions often ask, for example, how "locals" living many years in a society view asylum seekers, economic migrants, or those claiming to have a better life in a country that they are migrating to.

These are the issues to be probed in this book. Across six case studies, it represents a *comparative* analysis that identifies a range of factors structuring political fears. The cumulative effect of assaying these cases provides a panoply of explanations for why fears emerge across different societies. But is the study symmetrical or asymmetrical? It is not because each case study singles out a distinctive independent variable originating from Thucydides' categorization and estimates its "fear factor." When we look at England as our first case, for instance, a national fear caused by being left behind helped produced the Brexit outcome. When we turn to the United States, it is an identity quandary that appears critical in affecting America's weakening and perhaps decline.

One objective of this framework is to avoid conceptual stretching which is fraught in many comparative studies. For David Collier and James Mahon, conceptual stretching is the distortion that occurs when a well-traveled concept does not fit new case research.[19] Should two civil wars at opposite ends of the globe be compared when the one thing in common is that they are branded as civil wars? Generally, the outcome variable is not the way to frame comparative research since it is explanations that we are searching for. Conceptual stretching misleads and the goal here is to avoid it at all costs.

A final note on theory and case research is warranted. We have six country studies: England as part of the UK; Saxony in the German Federal Republic; then Russia; Japan; Australia; and the United States. All are acknowledged to be part of the Western world except for Russia, which for some observers never truly was a part of it and was forever the Other or at most an Apprentice. Some others conclude that Russia left the European sphere in February 2022 when it started a war against a fellow Slav state to the west. Still, other observers maintain that western parts of the former Soviet Union still form part of Europe, for example, Saint Petersburg.

The assumption in this study is, then, that the six "most similar cases" could be compared, thereby making it simpler to find out what differentiated them in terms of fear. Notionally, the "Western values" they shared would not have distinguished them. That may no longer be the case and revision of the globe's security architecture may need to reflect this.

The case of Japan at war with the United States from 1941 to 1945 also raises questions about whether it was never "Western" until it was defeated; Japan then gradually was integrated into the Western world. Some may argue that a similar process is being applied to Ukraine. Like conceptual stretching, civilizational borders are never as simplistic as politicians and pundits make out they are.

Which Are the Case Studies?

Let us make a quick return to classical Greek terms (Table 1.1). In Chapter 2, we start off by applying the idea of *deos* to the research. We recall that *deos* comprises a largely cerebral but nebulous and intangible fear of a distant, ill-defined threat. In the example of England, I argue that it constitutes a *national* fear. Was the arrival of millions of European citizens after 2004 who felt entitled to exercise their freedom of movement clause integral to the European Union, producing a reduction in England's sovereignty over the United Kingdom? As will be discussed below, English residents were not the culprit of xenophobia; on the contrary, England profited from having taught

Table 1.1 Charting Thucydides' theories

Greek Term	Literal Meaning	Case Study	Type of Fear	Operational Definition
deos (δέος)	to doubt, to be afraid of	England (Brexit)	national	concern about a more distant, ill-defined threat
phobos (φόβος)	to fear, to feel animosity, to hate	Germany (Saxony)	regional	less rational fear of an imminent threat
orrodia (ορρόδια)	a speech act	Russia (Putin)	ethnic	invoking policies
hypopsia (υποψία)	to harbor a deep distrust; trepidation	Australia (relations with China)	inter-state	suspicion of ambiguous threats
ekplēxis (ἔκπληξις)	shock, astonishment, stupification	United States	identity	tribal politics, moral panic
angst (Freud—not Thucydides)	insecurity, loathing	Japan (single artist)	individual	rejection and exclusion

the world the English language and making the anglosphere a privileged space. However, a perceived pernicious threat involved a whittling away of Englishness itself. This case study, therefore, examines the threat to White English identity exposed in the Brexit debates and after.

In the minds of many voters at the time of the June 2016 referendum, the goal of Brexit was to allow new member-states of the enlarged EU—overwhelmingly Central European countries—to exercise the free movement of people clause. But unlike Germany or France where movement and settlement were delayed for several years, free movement to the UK occurred immediately and in numbers few UK leaders had anticipated. In the process, English identity was viewed as being swamped by foreigners. Furthermore, those English people "left behind" included men, young and old but mainly those with a limited education, who felt that the country gave preference to women in hiring practices. Other arbitrary factors contributed to the Brexit vote being passed in the referendum, all linked to a national fear that England's hyper-multiculturalism was proceeding too fast.

Focusing on the example of a specific region of Germany provides us with a classic exemplification of the idea of *phobos*—a direr, more irrational fear of a present threat. This was associated with the migration crisis of 2015 that brought over a million third-world refugees to the country. But the groundwork for fear preceded this event. The main region affected was eastern Germany, which comprised the former German Democratic Republic (or GDR) and in particular one of its States (*Länder*), Saxony. The rise of the right-wing Alternative for Germany (AfD or *Alternative für Deutschland*) was critical to this process and encompassed the mobilization of widespread anti-immigrant sentiments in Saxony. Paradoxically, a kind of Saxon-bashing emerged in other parts of Germany, concerned that this region was unique: it was far right, reactionary, and violence prone.

Chapter 3, then, considers rage against the newcomer. Migration into Saxony was driven by a preexisting history of xenophobia. Confined mainly to a number of hot spots, it was sheltered from other parts of the country. A regional fear erupted that was regarded in other parts of the country as not a German value. Differences between the western and eastern parts of the Federal Republic have long drawn the attention of academics, journalists, social media, bloggers, and others. Questions they asked included how distinctive eastern German anti-Muslim attitudes were in Saxony. Were cities like Chemnitz and Cottbus—the most densely populated *Land* in eastern Germany—home to extremist radical-right movements? Or on the contrary, did pervasive *western* German influence have a xenophobic impact on eastern Germany's transition politics, including abetting Islamophobia?

In focusing on Saxony, an inverse question appears: was Saxony bashing becoming the core of Germany's self-righteousness and virtue seeking? Or, in spite of efforts to integrate eastern lands into the rest of the country, are eastern Germans still marked by their bitter, abhorrent experience inside the GDR? Can we even find *phobos* directed not just toward migrants from non-Western countries but to western Germans as well?

The case study in Chapter 4 is of the Russian Federation. Debates have emerged about how anti-American its citizens are and, conversely, how the spread of russophobia has spiked in many European countries, not just in the United States. The framework I adopt does not belong to the phobia group and instead I concentrate on speech acts that make up *orrodia*; let me remind readers that Thucydides' use of this term is limited to citations of speeches made by Greek political leaders that backed up Thucydides' own discursive anxieties.

For instance, in describing a sea battle, the Greek historian remarked that Phormio, the General in charge of the Athenian fleet, was "anxious because of his men's state of dread (*orrodia*)" due to the enemy's numerical advantage. For Thucydides, a direct quotation by a public official merited the introduction of a separate word for fear. Today the *Oxford English Dictionary* tells us that *orrodia* signifies apprehension and anxiety toward future events which lead to a tipping point.

Who is the speechmaker in Russia formulating the grounds for policymaking toward migrants? From about 2006 on, it was President Vladimir Putin who, as a result of existential questions relating to the country's demographics, adopted open-border policies with Central Asian states and even with neighbors to the West such as Ukraine. Before COVID, the scale of in-migration to Russia had been unique: it constituted the second-largest immigrant population size after the United States. Putin's discourses also took into account ethnic fears that Russians harbored and he included plans set out to manage migration. Questions we need to answer are whether its long-serving President slammed the door on foreigners, particularly Muslims from Central Asia, or not. Less plausibly, did he advocate establishing a form of multinationalism, multiethnicity, or even Western-style multiculturalism that would flatten the ethnic Russian presence to the status of a nation no more?

Migrants had been attracted to the Russian Federation for many disparate reasons: partly for economic and occupational reasons, partly because of longstanding cultural and historical connections with Russia, and partly because Russia was faced with a worsening labor shortage. What were the push-and-pull factors behind in-migration to Russia and what policies did Putin prefer? Was it on track to generate a xenophobic blowback among its citizens as had occurred in many EU countries when faced with migration waves? Would Russians welcome diversity in place of Orthodox ethnocracy? As mouthpiece-in-chief, would Putin declare an end to in-migration or, instead, liberalize immigration policy?[20]

Individual fear is an idea that Thucydides' historical study overlooked. To assess the case study in Chapter 5, a term that is out of keeping and asymmetrical to the ancient Athenian needs to be added to the schema of fear. Let me nevertheless include his general observations relating to individual fear even if they did not fit his classification.

Focusing on the Peloponnesian war, he underscored collective reactions to fear adversaries, not individual ones. Fear was viewed as a primal sensation that human beings experience. In the case of the Divine, fear plays a constructive role: *principium sapientiae timor Domini* or "the fear of God is the beginning of wisdom." In interpersonal relations, fear and its related sensations—anxiety, concern, loathing, and even paranoia—are regarded by psychologists as a natural reaction having both positive and dysfunctional consequences. We can infer that Thucydides skirted around individual-level fears. The result is that his catalog needs to be supplemented by introducing the concept of *angst*— an individual's sense of trepidation, foreboding, and disquiet.

At the individual level of analysis, the naturalness of human fear often originates in cultural and psychological sources. In the works of Japanese-born artist Yasuo Kuniyoshi, pictorial expressions of fear are evident in his early paintings and drawings; the most illustrative period is from the early 1920s to the end of World War II. His own status as ethnically Japanese living in the United States but as a recognized alien troubled him greatly. It reflected more general fears pervading Japanese society where he was born and raised.

Key themes in his art are the emergence of prejudice out of fearfulness and insecurity, and of loathing out of a perception of rejection and exclusion. These lend support to the descriptor of an artist overcome with angst. Demonization of Japan, America's mortal foe in World War II, through his depiction of enemy images of the Japanese that included racist features of them, was difficult to swallow for Kuniyoshi the artist. He faced a Hobbesian choice: acceptance of being an alien in the United States as opposed to being depicted as an emigrant in Japan.

Personal angst in this artist torn between two civilizations seems an apt replacement for the collective notion of fear that Thucydides referenced and it breaks with his otherwise meticulous typology. An early existentialist, Søren Kierkegaard, and the renowned twentieth-century psychoanalyst, Sigmund Freud, will this one time serve as substitute for Thucydides; they remark that neurotic angst is a state when fear exists as a permanent neurotic condition.[21]

Chapter 6 broadens Thucydides' framework and explores a case of interstate fear—Australia's manifold conflicts with China. He reserved a special, if rarely used, word for this phenomenon, *hypopsia*: looking beneath the surface of things and discovering a distant fear of a vague threat. This term applies also to fear emerging *between* countries far removed from each other, not just emigration from that country to the host state as in our other cases.

The trend line suggests that the remoteness of this threat has increased. In Australia's domestic politics, it reflects growing anti-foreigner, protectionist, nationalist sentiments originating in a slowly disappearing White Australia policy. Putting it differently, from Amy Chua's perspective (to be discussed later), it is a distanced fear but that of an expanding, economically dominant Chinese minority group that resides in Australia. This combined dyad has produced a purported Sinophobic backlash.

Racial makeup constitutes a factor that shapes fear of strangers. For decades, Australia was privileged by being linked to skin color: White people rarely experience systemic prejudice; at times it is responsible for causing it; and generally it enjoys the benefits of racial advantage. Admittedly, this does not apply to non-White populations in existence for over 50,000 years on the continent: Aboriginal Peoples who have not shaken off their subaltern postcolonial status.

As Chua observed, rich and powerful minorities attract resentment everywhere. When these minorities are ethnically distinguishable and highly visible, resentment increases and creates ethnic competition and, subsequently, ethnically rooted schisms and conflict. The Chinese presence stands out in Australia: Mandarin is now the second most common language spoken. Before COVID, some 250,000 Chinese students were at Australian institutions. Before the pandemic, 1.5 million Chinese short-term tourists spending over $12 billion contributed to the country's economy. Privileged economic elites include those managing direct foreign investments; a concession made by the Investment Facilitation Arrangement is to allow a project company registered in Australia but with 50 percent Chinese ownership to bring Chinese workers over for infrastructure development projects.

Hypopsia, a suspicion and even distrust of long-term Chinese motives—much of China's strategic thinking is viewed as long term—has resulted in worsening relations between China and Australia. Longstanding liberal values such as pluralism, tolerance, human rights, and multicultural coexistence have come under challenge in this interstate relationship. Deepening Chinese involvement in Australia's economics, politics, and international relations, exemplified by the creation of the 2021 Aukus security pact comprising the United States, the UK, and Australia, has fueled a "hypopsic" reaction on this continent.

The last case study is of the United States. Chapter 7 comprises a fundamental instance presented by Thucydides of *ekplexis*—consternation, moral panic, and terror evoked by a breakdown in the nature of things. It raises questions about the very identity of a society that allows moral panic to spread. It also has repercussions on the institutional crumbling of the country, and this is a world power regarded as too big to fail. The issue to be examined, then, is how the United States unmade its national identity.

The interconnected words *ekplexis* and *kataplexis* can be translated as "to confound, paralyze, render somebody beside themselves." It captures the idea of being not merely fearful but surprised, amazed, astonished, and causing moral panic. For Stanley Cohen, who introduced the term, panic in itself connotes a lack of control and irrationality.[22] Its irrational sources identify how some evil person, his or her behavior, or some inanimate object threatens the values, interests, or well-being of a social order. Moral panic can stem from the loss of national identity.

Today moral panic entrepreneurs and lawmakers, often using virtue signaling—for Cohen, "right-thinkers" and "holier than thou" thinking—have been joined by social media in carrying out policing and surveillance of society. In the 1970s, a British specialist on communications, Stuart Hall, inferred that moral panics following a rise in crime rates in England could serve as a fuse mobilizing public support in order to "police the crisis."[23]

We need to be cautious when applying the term moral panic. Even Frank Furedi, an expert on the culture of fear, seemed lost when trying to define it: "In everyday language the term moral panic tended to be attached to anxieties that were related to uncertainties about values."[24] Which is it, then—anxieties, uncertainties, or values?

In a convoluted way, Chapter 7 explains how the United States has undergone a process of unmaking its long-held national identity, which had been underscored by its appellation of being "the first new nation."[25] Have Americans become confounded and splintered as a society? Do both its major political parties engage in pandering to particular identities, whether related to ethnicity, gender, national origin, body type, disability, or medical condition, among others? Can identity politics replace ideological politics?[26] Applying Thucydides' *ekplesis* as a variant of fear, we can dig deeper and unravel the causes for the gradual disintegration of American national identity and hopes for a reimagined national one.

The final chapter asks whether our current version of liberal democracy has, unwittingly or intentionally, raised the notion of fear to a new plateau. Particularly in four "model" liberal democracies—England, Germany, Australia, and the United States—the signs of backsliding have been visible. Do semi- or fully authoritarian states exemplify ruthlessness either in encouraging fear of the all-powerful state or negating it by stamping fear out? Is tolerance, to be sure often equated with liberalism, the supreme value that can mitigate fear? Or is "intolerance of the tolerant" becoming increasingly acceptable? Thucydides' fondness for Athenian democracy is a starting point suggesting a hybrid acceptance of democracy combined with autocratic rule.

What Have I Left Out?

Fear is a word that is related to many things: the fear of God, of a Divine Being, or of a First Cause; to death; to a moral order; to the End Times. Given the expansiveness of the term, and this over the centuries, in multiple civilizations, and by a host of writers from different backgrounds and disciplines, it is prudent to lock our framework into that of an ancient historian who was rigorous in his use of the concept of fear. This is also a practical way to address the topic since we cannot do justice to the myriads of writings about fear already in existence.

Perhaps this is the most "fear-mongering" time ever in human history, as some observers are drawn to believe. Surveillance techniques are here to stay and rival well-known fictional accounts by such English authors as Aldous Huxley in *Brave New* World and George Orwell in *1984*. Six case studies will not fully answer the question about the scope of fear today. In today's era, a personal blog can remake our opinion of political issues, or a bot running according to a set of instructions without a human user needing manually to start them up. Social media megastars boasting millions of online hits are part of influencers worldwide. It seems impossible, therefore, to do justice to media coverage whether through the printed word or online. Relying on social media coverage evokes mistrust. The preference in this study is to use sources associated with established scholars, even when at times themselves contradictory.

Few better-steeped political authorities on social media issues can be found than Jacinda Ardern, former Prime Minister of New Zealand and media-skeptic analyst. In a 2022 address to the Harvard graduating class, she summed up the media frenzy in a nutshell:

> What we consider to be mainstream media outlets have proliferated but ownership structures have not. Mainstream media have layers of accountabilities and journalistic expectations that others, who also present information to us, don't.
>
> There is competition for advertising revenue with subscription services and paywalls, all to aid in the survival of the fittest – with fittest now defined by how easy it is to monetise your content. And in amongst all of that lies the fact that we're not just talking about how we access

information to inform debate, but whether you can call it information at all. There are those far more learned than I who will argue where the source of the scourge of disinformation lies.[27]

In looking at an array of political fears when employing Thucydides' framework, we have a first-rate chance of recognizing the types of fear that persist and the impacts they have on their target audience. Fearing the wrong things is an important factor that Thucydides noted. For example, the Athenian plague that he was able to survive ("plague survivor," if coined today) was the result of other citizens fleeing their homes and moving into cramped quarters which he did not. Overcrowding spread the disease and "the mortality among them was dreadful."[28] Furedi interjected: Thucydides was convinced that "people simply stopped fearing gods, and their behavior contributed to the diminishing of the authority of moral norms."[29]

What of other writers who have contributed extensively to the subject of fear? Sigmund Freud described "expectant fear" which could be equated with worst-case scenarios. But he applied this to individuals and not states; arguably Kuniyoshi was an example. Yet "Freud was far from rigorous in maintaining the distinction between fear and anxiety."[30]

Hannah Arendt's term explaining the nature of the Holocaust was of its banality.[31] Is there a banality to fear, then, by its perpetrators that undercut arguments raised by doomsday speakers about war crimes, crimes against humanity, and genocidal acts? A seminal work published by anthropologist Mary Douglas dealt with risk, not fear—a separate but interrelated aspect. In her view, "fearing the worst" could very much be a result of risk-taking.[32] The six cases examined reveal striking divergences and distinct narratives about the place fear fills.

Postscriptum

A tribute to Thucydides' analytic talents was revealed in a novel written by Peter Handke, an Austrian writer and playwright who won the Nobel Prize in Literature in 2019. He spoke of "micro-epics"—concentrating on the small things he observed, their "simple, unadorned validity."

When encountering an ash tree in the center of Munich in October 1989, he enthused:

> the excitement of the day before was restored, but now it narrowed the scope of my focus and made my casual, selfless observation willful and overzealous. I did see a larger world again within the small one, but to do so, I was more than just looking. That larger world did not arise as effortlessly as it had the day before.[33]

Notes

1 Corey Robin, *Fear: The History of a Political Idea* (New York: Oxford University Press, 2006).

2 Corey Robin, "The Politics of Fear," *Democracy: A Journal of Ideas*, no. 22 (Fall 2011), https://democracyjournal.org/magazine/22/the-politics-of-fear/.

3 Patrick J. Deneen, *Why Liberalism Failed* (New Haven: Yale University Press, 2018).

4 Karl Popper, *The Open Society and Its Enemies* (Princeton: Princeton University Press, 2013).

5 Judith Shklar, "The Liberalism of Fear," in *Liberalism and the Moral Life*, ed. Nancy L. Rosenblum (Cambridge: Harvard University Press, 1989). See also Frank Furedi, *How Fear Works: Culture of Fear in the 21st Century* (London: Bloomsbury Continuum, 2019), 170–71.

6 Jacob T. Levy, *The Multiculturalism of Fear* (New York: Oxford University Press, 2000).

7 Raymond Taras, *Nationhood, Migration and Global Politics* (Edinburgh: Edinburgh University Press, 2018), ch. 1.

8 Lowell Edmunds, "Thucydides' Ethics as Reflected in the Description of Stasis," *Harvard Studies in Classical Philology* 79 (1975), 73–92; Laurie M. Johnson Bagby, "The Use and Abuse of Thucydides in International Relations," *International Organization* 48, no. 1 (Winter 1994), 131–53.

9 Raymond Taras, *Fear and the Making of Foreign Policy: Europe and Beyond* (Edinburgh: Edinburgh University Press, 2015), 1–4. See also Richard Ned Lebow and Barry S. Strauss (eds.), *Hegemonic Rivalry: From Thucydides to the Nuclear Age* (Boulder: Westview Press, 1991).

10 Simon Hornblower, "The Fourth-Century and Hellenistic Reception of Thucydides," *The Journal of Hellenic Studies* 115 (1995), 47–68, https://www.jstor.org/stable/pdf/631643.pdf.

11 William Desmond, "Lessons of Fear: A Reading of Thucydides," *Classical Philology* 101 (2006), 359, http://eprints.nuim.ie/827/1/William_Desmond.pdf. Brian E. Calabrese, *Fear in Democracy: A Study of Thucydides' Political Thought* (Ann Arbor: ProQuest, UMI Dissertations Publishing, 2008), 17.

12 Gregory Nagy, "The Subjectivity of Fear as Reflected in Ancient Greek Wording," November 2, 2020; originally published in *Dialogues* 5 (2010), 29–45, https://chs.harvard.edu/curated-article/gregory-nagy-the-subjectivity-of-fear-as-reflected-in-ancient-greek-wording/.

13 For example, Francis Fukuyama, *Trust: The Social Virtues and the Creation of Prosperity* (New York: Free Press, 1996); Charles Tilly, *Trust and Rule* (Cambridge: Cambridge University Press, 2005). Bo Rothstein, *The Quality of Government: Corruption, Social Trust, and Inequality in International Perspective* (Chicago: University of Chicago Press, 2011).

14 Jacques Ranciere, *On the Shores of Politics* (London: Verso, 2007).

15 Graham Allison, "The Thucydides Trap: Are the US and China Headed for War?" *The Atlantic*, 24 September 2015.

16 Calabrese, *Fear in Democracy*, 17.

17 Marie Demker, "Attitudes toward immigrants and refugees: Swedish trends with some comparisons," Paper presented at the International Studies Association 48th Annual Convention, Chicago, February 28, 2007, 2.

18 Gordon Allport, *The Nature of Prejudice* (Cambridge: Perseus Books, 1954).

19 David Collier and James E. Mahon. "Conceptual 'Stretching' Revisited: Adapting Categories in Comparative Analysis," *American Political Science Review* 87, no. 4, (1993), 845–55.

20 Anthony Baiz, "The Silent Invasion of Russia and Its Imperial Transnational Migration Campaign, 2006–2020," Unpublished PhD Dissertation, Tulane University, 2023.

21 Sigmund Freud, *A General Introduction to Psychoanalysis* (New York: Boni and Liveright Press, 1920).

22 Stanley Cohen, *Folk Devils and Moral Panics: The Creation of the Mods and Rockers*, 3rd ed. (London: Routledge, 2011 [1973]).

23 Stuart Hall et al., *Policing the Crisis: Mugging, the State and Law and Order* (New York: Palgrave Macmillan, 2013 [1978]).

24 Furedi, *How Fear Works*, 107–8.

25 Seymour Martin Lipset, *The First New Nation: The United States in Historical and Comparative Perspective* (New York: W.W. Norton, 1979).

26 Daniel Bell, *The End of Ideology: On the Exhaustion of Political Ideas in the Fifties.* 2nd ed. (Cambridge: Harvard University Press, 2000).

27 Jacinda Ardern, "Democracy, Disinformation and Kindness," Harvard Commencement Speech, May 27, 2022, https://www.beehive.govt.nz/speech/harvard-commencement-speech-democracy-disinformation-and-kindness.

28 Thucydides, *History of the Peloponnesian War* (London: Penguin Classics, 1954), 138.

29 Furedi, *How Fear Works*, 119.

30 Furedi, *How Fear Works*, 24.

31 Hannah Arendt, *Eichmann in Jerusalem: A Report on the Banality of Evil* (New York: Viking Press, 1963).

32 See Mary Douglas, *Purity and Danger: An Analysis of Concepts of Pollution and Taboo* (London: Routledge, 2003).

33 Peter Handke, *Once Again for Thucydides* (New York: New Directions, 1995), 73–74.

Chapter 2

NATIONAL FEAR: BREXIT, FREE MOVEMENT, ENGLISHNESS

While other interpretations abound, one plausible explanation for the success of the Brexit movement, leading to the Conservative Party's sweep of the 2019 elections, may be the linkage to Thucydides' concept of *deos*. It entails a rational if ill-defined and intangible fear of a distant threat. Trained in the classics, the Prime Minister at the time, Boris Johnson, would have been one of few to recognize the association. Alas, though knowledgeable in the classics, his role as Tory Prime Minister lasted from 2019 and 2022 though some influential Conservatives said he would be back.

Virginia Woolf's Prescience

Similarities exist between a sense that England was at peril in the late 1930s and a fear that the country had come under threat in the 2010s. The comparison comes from the pen of a brilliant author—as English as English may be—Virginia Woolf. Living a very English life in a townhome in Bloomsbury near the British Museum, as well as in a modest cottage in a small insular and adorable village in east Sussex, she was pampered and praised by a host of English high society representatives, from renowned economist John Maynard Keynes to art critic Clive Bell, fellow writer Lytton Strachey, and socialite Vita Sackville-West. Add to this her husband Leonard Woolf and we are in the company of well-bred intellectuals with progressive if quaint ideas.

Virginia Woolf would have recognized a rational threat to the shakiness of Englishness some eighty years ahead of Brexit. It was certainly not like the immediate threat of bombs exploding over London and firestorms blazing in the East Sussex Downs between her Rodmell cottage and the English Channel. A weakening of Englishness in England needed more time.

Woolf's last work was a jumbled "pageant embedded in a play" titled *Between the Acts*. Despite herculean moral support from her husband, she did not live to see the day when her pageant saw the light of day. In late March 1941, she drowned herself near her cottage by the River Ouse. Her body was discovered three weeks later floating down the river, at the village of Southease, by several children.

Had she been cut off from the mainstream, as she had attributed to England in her play? How did fear of international politics that were spinning out of control in the later 1930s contribute to her suicidal state that year? Was the fear of another world war—World War II—what drove her to the brink—and over the brink—of madness?

Much earlier, in *A Room of One's Own*, she had mocked her own literary sensibilities, though her own political ones remained clear. She ironized: "This is an important book, the critic assumes, because it deals with war. This is an insignificant book because it deals with the feelings of women in a drawing-room."[1]

Repeatedly she had insisted how "War is not women's history." About a half-century later, in 1985, Belarusian Nobel Prize laureate Svetlana Alexievich wrote a book called *The Unwomanly Face of War* offering an oral history of women in the western Soviet Union during World War II.[2] As with Woolf, here too war was viewed as alien to a woman's faculties. Woolf wrote: "War is a man's game," furthermore "the killing machine has a gender and it is male." To the very end, according to biographer Nigel Nicolson, her conviction was based on "a passionate condemnation of war and men's responsibility for it." This view was illustrated in another of her works dating from her later years in 1938. *Three Guineas* depicted the ends to which men would go to make male and masculine values unassailable.

"An England in peril" was a motif found in a letter she wrote in April 1936. She accepted how "I am always being warned that the end of civilization is just about to come."[3] With the Munich Agreement signed that year, she felt, like England itself, that "we were so afraid and so ashamed."[4] German bombing of London in 1940 quickly followed.

In Rodmell, her village four miles from the county town of Lewes, she experienced war first hand. Nicolson, her close friend, remarked: "When the air battles reached over the Channel to embrace her own village and bombs fell close enough to Monk's House to break the windows, she was physically courageous and even, at times, emotionally elated."[5] Perhaps she felt the experience constituted a less unwomanly face of war. Or perhaps she was becoming deranged.

In one of her last letters the author, associated with the modernist movement in England, acknowledged that politics and war had finally triumphed over art and literature: "No: politics at the moment seem more pressing than autobiography. We have the drone of raiders every night, and the village is now fire spotting— chiefly incendiaries over the hill."[6] Tangible horrors had been brought to the open in 1940, imperceptible ones were buried in her subconscious.

What does Virginia Woolf's fear of men making war have to do with the seemingly moribund politics of Britain's Brexit from the EU that took place seventy-five years later? It was triggered because of Woolf's fear that England was in peril as the Sussex Downs burned. Perhaps she borrowed a metaphor used by Fyodor Dostoevsky in *The Brothers Karamazov*—"fire in the minds of men" (see Chapter 4 for an interpretation). His sense of inevitable, abysmal revolutionary conflagration was applied to her in the late 1930s. Far-removed threats were becoming immediate, putting England and Englishness in danger.

Which are the groups today who view England as in peril? Those who voted "Leave" in the 2016 referendum may have regarded a federalizing European Union as threatening. The EU was releasing migrating populations from Central and Eastern Europe (CEE) to England and, in the fearful eyes of "No" voters, would finally submerge it. The threat of English locals being left behind while multicultural London prospered was also of great concern outside the metropolis. Another reason, though less palpable, for supporting Brexit was what Nigel Farage—taking on a largely taboo subject—identified as the new authoritarianism of EU leaders in their handling of political opponents. For some time the EU was viewed as a mainstay of democracy though throughout European countries calls were made to plug its democratic deficit.

Europe's crisis of migration reached its apogee during the long summer of 2015. Residing in Germany with generous welfare programs became the goal of the vast majority of refugees and economic migrants; other countries they passed through, such as the Balkans, were disregarded. The migration process unfurled a different threat from the perspective of Remainers—they identified a clear and present danger (*phobos* rather than *deos*) as reactionary right-wing populism in several European countries swept across much of the continent; Hungary's Prime Minister was frequently named as the EU's nemesis but actors in other states were named. Its appendages also took place in the United States with Donald Trump becoming President in 2016, and other non-European states such as the Philippines and Brazil.

Widespread populist movements, frequently mistaken for extremist nationalism, were therefore viewed as a threat to English civility, its civil society, the rule of law, and other purportedly inherently English—at times mixed in with Scottish—values. Nigel Farage, leader of the UK Independence Party (UKIP) from 2006 to 2016 when Brexit triumphed, was regarded by Remain supporters as a nefarious populist and xenophobe.

There was also the matter of international terrorism striking in European states: jihadism, anti-Russian attitudes, reviving anti-Semitism, and other malignancies that challenged Englishness. The "Leave" and "Remain" camps were agreed that such pathologies were not English, did not represent fair play, and had to be resisted. The Church of England at the head of which stood the Queen urged far-reaching fairness as well.

Brexit revealed the centrality of affect in people's lives. For Angharad Closs Stephens, a human geography specialist at Swansea University, Brexit involved what Brexit "felt like" in the years following the UK referendum. She interrogated the feelings of shame, hostility, and resentment that accompanied the vote. The part played by affective feelings and the way they could be acted upon had found "space" following the Brexit decision and added to the Brexit conundrum.[7]

When viewing the Brexit vote through the lens of emotional politics, the outcome was easier to see: "The Remain campaign lost because it relied on the arguments of experts about the economy and made little attempt to engage with the emotional issues of immigration and sovereignty."[8] The role of emotions was even clearer to see in how voters were caught up in rhetoric while overlooking fundamental economic issues. This angle was important when discussing subsequent "regret voting:" A small-scale study revealed that if a referendum vote was held based on survey findings, Remain would have won with a strong 57.2 percent.[9] On the other hand, the fairness of the result was accepted by nearly all sides in the referendum campaign; a call for a "people's vote" by some "Remain" advocates never got off the ground.

The phenomenon of backlash politics can become significant since international status is a goal that states set for themselves. It serves as an "intrinsic interest" that operates in the background of political decision-making.[10] The Brexit vote made clear that status anxiety could become a rhetorical focal point for backlash movements mobilizing within the state. When combined with political accelerants—emotional appeals, social taboos, and institutional reshaping—backlash politics could become transformative and often enduring.[11] Was this indeed the case when the outcome was known?

In 2014, Prime Minister David Cameron broached the subject of the future of Scotland and took comfort from how it had been resolved by its referendum verdict. The Scottish independence option lost by a comfortable fifty-five to forty-five-percent margin. But he redirected his major speech so as to focus on a separate referendum in England: "I have long believed that a crucial part missing from this national discussion is England. We have heard the voice of Scotland—and now the millions of voices of England must also be heard."[12] Cameron was certain what the verdict in England would be: it would raise the status of an often-overlooked England and, in the mix, raise his own as well.

He and his Remain allies, therefore, "presented the EU as a status enhancer and thus, a Brexit as something that would predictably lead to status loss." It was regarded as a zero-sum game: "Leave campaigners reversed the relationship arguing that the EU was actually a cause of Britain's depleted status in the world." Leave actors were the main backlash entrepreneurs as they mobilized in order to "tap into the psychology of individuals through emotive appeals." Consequently, "what allows status to be a powerful driver of state behavior… also allows status anxiety, and narratives of status loss, to be manipulated and deployed by entrepreneurs of backlash movements."[13]

In sum, status anxiety was at play, at least partially, as Britons made the choice of protecting their international image. Brexit may have been "an exemplar episode of postcolonial melancholy" in the way it crafted a narrative "by, and for, those who have still not come to terms with the loss of Empire and the resulting decline in global prestige." This was the way that Brexit's success as a backlash movement was defined—regret over its imperial past.[14]

This constituted one possible motive and many others were raised in explaining the success of the Leave vote. "England in peril" developed into a more complex phenomenon than the one Virginia Woolf had identified as plausible from her perspective of the late 1930s.

National Reconfiguration

Migration from former British colonies was an early stage of Britain's diversification that led to its hyperdiversity recognized at the turn of the twenty-first century. The EU's doctrine of the free movement of people who were members of the "Club" was technically a matter of mobility, not migration. The United Kingdom may possibly have been so enthusiastic—or naïve—about the extent of mobility into the island state that it opened its doors to enlargement countries immediately. Large states like France and Germany took advantage of the option of deferring mobility from newly admitted Central European member-states and delayed the mobility process. In fact, all other EU member states with the exception of Ireland and Sweden applied delayed controls; notably, a five-year transition period was permitted prior to opening up labor markets to nationals from new member states. One calculation was that had Germany opened up its borders initially (as Britain had done), only one in three EU citizens would have chosen Britain and two-thirds opted for the Federal Republic.

The culprit for misjudging mobility numbers may have been Labour Prime Minister Tony Blair. In 2004, he agreed to give Central European enlargement states immediate access to British labor markets. It was especially ironic that, in hindsight, in 2017 his Institute for Global Change came up with ways of revising free movement rules that would not have jeopardized the UK's membership in the EU single market.

Under pre-Brexit rules, citizens of EU states could be removed from an EU state they had moved to if they had not found a job, had no realistic possibility of finding one, or needed social welfare. To be sure, well-networked EU migrants could find ways around these hurdles. Blair's 2017 reforms would have required EU nationals to have offers of work before arriving to the United Kingdom. Moreover, those who did not have promises of a UK job but who had received permission to stay in the United Kingdom would not have the right to claim benefits, open bank accounts, or even rent a flat. Just as restrictive was the proposal to offer free healthcare only to employed migrants. Blair's rethinking about no longer free EU movement of people went as far as requiring tertiary education to charge EU nationals tuition fees much higher than those for UK students.

In theory, then, Blair's overhauled free movement approach would serve as a core principle while imposing restrictive rules on access to benefits. It was rational to the core consistent with Thucydides' *deos* doctrine; these proposals appeared reasonable. But they were merely "pie in the sky" when they were announced—it was too late to reverse the Brexit consequences and were seen as developing into an obscure, distant threat. Nevertheless, if an offender had to be found who was responsible for enticing CEE citizens to come to the United Kingdom, it was the Blair government that ruled from 1997 to 2007.

Was the EU playing fair in exporting several million people in low-wage postcommunist countries to better-paying jobs in the United Kingdom? Could it be that Blair's leadership embraced "the race to the bottom" that effectively lowered wages and salaries because of a bloated labor market? A middle way may have been to address the problems of unemployment, under-employment, and black market employment found in CEE. In some respects, too, the EU was complicit in advancing its principle of the free movement of people by exploiting British guilelessness.

The social background of Central Europeans who chose economic mobility to Britain is noteworthy. Overwhelmingly, most were Catholic or belonged to other Christian denominations, and they were White. Europe's long history included racial preferences dating back at least to Frankish king Charlemagne (c. 742–814). Sometimes referred to as the father of Europe, when he died his empire encompassed many added parts of Western Europe. As a devout Catholic he proved a staunch promoter of the expansion of Christianity in the West.

It had been in the cards for some time, then: freedom of movement was the fulfillment of Robert Schuman's ideal of establishing a Christian Europe. EU Commission President Romano Prodi, who held the position from 1999 to 2004, was hardly comparable to the political and military stature held by Charlemagne. But Prodi too was instrumental in promoting Christian values in Europe, specifically, those of the Catholic Church. He put it bluntly: "Europe cannot be understood without its Christian roots." Influenced at the time by a Polish Pope in the Vatican, John Paul II, Prodi's goal was to "revive the Christian soul of Europe which is the basis of unity."[15]

It surprised no one that Prodi was not renewed as EU Commission President after 2004. As late as 2007 he heralded "Europe's Judeo-Christian roots and common cultural heritage." But by 2009 the Lisbon Treaty rejected such language, opposed expressions identifying the Christian roots of Europe, and even removed the Choral movement of Beethoven's Ninth Symphony as a European anthem. Some speculate that cancel culture began in the EU itself.

For England's part, the historically minded were reminded of the time of King Henry VIII (1491–1547) when he sought to expel the Papacy from his lands. His Reformation entailed an attack on Roman Catholicism as well as the Ottoman Empire which had emerged as a threat to Europe. Yet the logic of German historian Christian Meier may take pride of place: the EU shows no gratitude to its forebears and has become uncoupled from its history. Indeed, "the European Union is emerging as the first political entity of the modern era that has no need for its own history and for a historical orientation."[16]

Beyond Referendum Day

The referendum result of June 2016 is familiar to us all: a not-so-narrow percentage of voters in England, 53.4–46.6 percent, backed Britain leaving the EU. Wales was a close imitator of England supporting Brexit by 52.5 versus 47.5 percent. But Scottish voters strongly disagreed with this verdict and wished to remain in the EU by a margin of sixty-two to thirty-eight percent. These represented the halcyon days of First Minister Nicola Sturgeon and her Scottish National Party (SNP). Lastly, recalcitrant Northern Ireland did what its Irish Republic counterparts did and supported the Remain side, by 55.8–44.2 percent. The sizeable Catholic vote in the Six Counties was significant in this choice; while the 2011 census had Protestants ahead of Catholics by forty-eight to forty-five percent, by 2021 the numbers were being reversed.

The Brexit result may have had as much to do with a "stuff it, Brussels" mentality as it did with locals being left behind in disadvantaged English communities. As for the new settlers, the research found that Poles, Slovaks, Estonians, Romanians, and others from CEE were eager to integrate, possibly even assimilate into, British society. The enormous value-added of learning English, in particular having children learn it in English schools, was an irresistible force. The distinct status of Britain as being not Europe or America made it an attractive country to settle into. The iconic image of "Cool Britannia" prevails to this day. CEE citizens also seemed more "worthy" and "hardworking," and they earned points for "deservingness," compared to minorities from third world countries.[17] With few exceptions, surveys showed that ethnic minorities expressed high levels of identification with Britain and British identity.[18] Paradoxically, then, for many who voted Leave, so-called "welfare tourists" coming from CEE were deemed not worthy or deserving of a place in English society even though they were among the top group of arrivals who wished to integrate, learn English, and deserved to be in the country.

Bristol University multiculturalist theorist Tariq Modood's ideal-type British citizen is today more plausible than ever: "The Britishness that is being embraced is a Britishness capable of extension and hybridity, a country happy to accept as Britons those for whom hyphenated identities, such as Black-British, British-Muslim, British-Indian, and so on are sources of pride." Modood, unofficially heading a Bristol School of Multiculturalism whose clarion call was for "remaking the British national story and broadening what it means to be British," asserted "challenging racial or ethnic definitions of Britishness, including the immigrant experience in and contribution to Britain in national stories."[19]

In practical terms, successive elections have resulted in increasing numbers of minority group candidates elected to Parliament. "Deservingness" therefore signified a generation of citizens originating in mainly Commonwealth countries who now "belonged" in Britain. By contrast, after the Brexit result many CEE citizens were shocked by losing their entitlement to live and work in the United Kingdom. A few of them felt that the United Kingdom was guilty of excessive multiculturalism and not enough Europeanness.

The belief that CEE citizens were supplying a reserve army of labor was not lost on disadvantaged British citizens. Although many of the newcomers were skilled, not many were given skilled jobs: lower-paid professional salaries back home influenced their choice abroad of menial employment. However, the perception of locals that wages in Britain were being driven down by settlers was a critical factor sealing the Brexit result. Admittedly, multinational corporations, supply-chain-dependent enterprises, and large-scale companies, eager to hire cheap foreign labor, were among the biggest backers of the Remain campaign.

The referendum result could also be viewed in the context of the rise of anti-establishment parties, often described as populist, across Europe; the mercurial rise and fall of the UKIP is an example. Two theories explain the growth of radical anti-systemic parties: one is the electorate's disenchantment with traditional parties—Tory, Labour, and even Liberal Democrats from their years in coalition with the Conservatives. The second consists of economic and cultural grievances sparked by migration spikes from CEE and third country nationals (TCNs).[20] Sweeping demographic and social changes

Figure 2.1 Discerning skeptics viewed the European Union as having ignored repeated calls for the democratization of its political institutions including the selection process for its rulers.

affecting British residents, and correspondingly the British electorate, added up to disaffection with the government (Figure 2.1).

Both theories underlay the rise of UKIP and the vote to leave the EU.[21] One study found that Euroscepticism, not immigration waves, had already ranked highest among UKIP voters in the 2009 elections for the European Parliament.[22] Issues once framed as EU threats to English identity— the Virginia Woolf phobia—were reframed as grievances about the inability to control immigration.

According to a major research project spanning the years 2000–2013, public trust in the British political system had become volatile over the years.[23] Unpopular economic policies plus a sharp increase in European arrivals exacerbated feelings of a growing divide between traditional parties and the interests of British citizens.[24]

The rise of UKIP was explained by how it had benefited from taking away both Conservative and Labour voters.[25] Shifts in political attitudes and electoral behavior contributed to the rise of anti-systemic parties like UKIP based on social changes deeper than class; this was the divisive factor.[26] Political marginalization—the left behind—was of a piece with disillusionment about mainstream political parties.[27]

The increasing strength of far-right parties in Europe has been explained as cultural and economic blowback against immigration from Third Country Nationals (TCNs).[28] No far-right party in Europe, it is said, has achieved success "without mobilizing grievances over immigration."[29] Many studies inquire if cultural and/or economic grievances are weightier in explaining the successes of these far-right parties; overall there is little consensus.[30]

Both feelings and fear about immigration to Britain are especially strong because for centuries the country had constituted an empire. It was then transformed into a Commonwealth allowing in-migration, family unification, student influxes, and migration chains to flourish. Since it was renamed UKIP in 1993, this movement cultivated near-exclusive political ownership on the question of immigration;[31] that had also occurred in other countries, Denmark being the best example—the Danish People's Party was formed in 1995. Some writers claim that immigration decreases wages for native workers below the 20th percentile of the wage distribution scale.[32] Fear about immigration from afar, where cultural, ethnic, and religious identities make it seem difficult to arrive at swift integration outcomes, can spark growth in political parties. But Brexit is more complex than such often-repeated claims.

Anti-Establishment Politics

In the eleven years between mid-2005 and mid-2016, the UK population increased by over five million people. The previous increase of five million had taken thirty-five years to occur, from mid-1970 to mid-2005. The five million added before that appeared over a seventeen-year period between mid-1953 and mid-1970. The push-and-pull factors shaping migration patterns are not easy to predict but in the United Kingdom sizeable increases in population size have been a regularity since World War II; the baby boom was not solely responsible for a demographic spike.

Immigration to Britain hit record levels just before Brexit, a factor that played into the hands of UKIP supporters. About 650,000 immigrants from around the globe—the highest number ever—arrived before June 2016. It was spearheaded by a historically high number of 284,000 EU citizens. This was more than three times the government's target which was aimed at reducing annual net migration to below 100,000 a year.

Data after the Brexit result suggested that migration to the United Kingdom had decreased. Net migration—the difference between those entering and leaving the United Kingdom—fell significantly. For example, national insurance data confirmed that Poles and other CEE citizens registering to work in Britain dropped by seventeen percent in the twelve months to

September 2016, especially after the June result. Was Brexit succeeding in quashing migrants? Not really. There was an eleven percent growth in Romanians and Bulgarians registering for national insurance. The signs that post-Brexit Britain was becoming a less attractive place for EU migrants to live and work in seemed improbable.

An unusual explanation for why EU citizens felt unwelcome by "overstaying" their time in Britain was that hostility may have seeped into the better-off British social classes. One *Guardian* contributor depicted the end of free movement this way: "Call it the Brexodus: well-educated EU nationals with the global job market at their feet turning their back on a country they had thought of as a good and safe place to make their homes." Furthermore, "Most EU nationals have also become used—even immune—to the English superiority complex in Europe, and to the periodical insults by leading politicians and media figures. The hate crimes and subtle discrimination genuinely hurt."[33] The Thucydidean concept of *deos*—persistent doubt adding up to a rational fear about an intangible distant threat—may perhaps be directed by out groups at the smug, well-off English social classes for whom condescending and snotty attitudes toward outsiders seemed all too easily a natural reaction.

Summing up the referendum result, salient factors that determined the outcome of the UK referendum included the following:

- The Leave camp was manipulating popular concerns about public spending, the economy, and, above all, immigration.
- They promoted anti-establishment feelings frustrated with current political elites.
- Special hostility was directed toward key global institutions such as the IMF, the World Bank, and the Treasury in the United Kingdom.
- The role of experts was called into question and produced "more visceral politics in place of the evidence- or at least expertise-based approach."
- The recalibration of British politics blurred party lines within Labour and Conservative parties resulting in "defeat of the liberal *Remainia* elite that had governed the country since the late 1990s."[34]

Danish cultural theorist and semiotics specialist Ulf Hedetoft contended, however, there were caveats to the paradox of populism. Thus "the role of migration in the populist imagination is often exaggerated or misrepresented. First, it is exaggerated because migrants only represent the fundamental issues, they are not their core." Of greater significance, however, is that migrants

signify that the political regime has lost control, not merely of national sovereignty but of the last and most important part of national sovereignty that matters for political elites. The logic runs like this. First we lose control of our economy and our finances, then of our ultimate decision-making powers, then of our borders and finally of our popular base, which is or risks being polluted through immigration, diversity, intermarriage and multiple citizenships (read: identities). Thus, we lose control of the socialization of "our people" and, by implication, their undivided loyalty as well. This is both the view of populist ideologues and their ethnic base of supporters, who cherish popular sovereignty and their preferential position therein as much as do political leaders.[35]

A clearer elaboration of *deos*—a national crisis associated with a rational if intangible fear of a distant threat—would be difficult to find.

A special place must be set aside for the UK's relationship with the European Court of Justice (ECJ). The institution was of critical importance because British sovereignty and control over its borders were at issue. Innumerable questions were raised about the future of the ECJ-UK relationship: areas of jurisdiction; the legal rights of British citizens living outside the United Kingdom; and the extent to which precedents set by the ECJ would be incorporated into British courts.[36] Michel Barnier, the EU's chief Brexit negotiator, insisted that the United Kingdom had to remain under ECJ jurisdiction regardless which form Brexit took.[37] By contrast, Brexiteers drew a red line in the sand on this crucial issue and demanded that the supremacy of the ECJ over British courts must end.

The icing on the cake may have been the summit meeting between EU leaders and Prime Minister Theresa May in September 2019. It proved to be a fiasco, whether from her inept interventions *or* the EU's humiliating treatment of her. A photograph of May sitting alone at a long table, with only a bouquet of flowers to cheer her up, while waiting for EU chiefs (overwhelmingly men) to enter the room, spoke volumes. When back in London, she went to great pains to assert that the EU would never gain control of free movement into Britain again.

By this point, Jeremy Hunt, British foreign minister at the time, described the EU's approach to Brexit as an attempt to "keep the club together" by punishing "a member who leaves." But he hit hard at its botched negotiations: "The EU was set up to protect freedom. It was the Soviet Union that stopped people leaving." He added: "The lesson from history is clear: If you turn the EU club into a prison, the desire to get out won't diminish. It will grow and we won't be the only prisoner that will want to escape."[38]

Boris Johnson succeeded May as Prime Minister in July 2019 and his boundless enthusiasm for completing the Brexit deal was compelling to many.

Three years earlier he reported how "Napoleon, Hitler, various people tried this [unifying Europe], and it ends tragically. The EU is an attempt to do this by different methods." If this continued the United Kingdom would become a "vassal state" while Theresa May's Brexit proposals would result in a "political car crash."

Zeroing in on the free movement, Johnson fulminated that anything which allowed access or preferential treatment for EU citizens over other groups would be anathema. Giving in to Brussels' demands would have produced "the first foreign rule since the battle of Hastings in 1066" when the Normans conquered the Anglo-Saxons. Johnson knew his history and invented matchless Brexit analogies for it.

Short-Term Chief Engineer

In Greek tragedy, hubris (ὕβρις) means an excessive pride toward, and even a defiance of, the gods. Today it signifies someone who possesses excessive pride or self-confidence. Boris Johnson excelled in classical Greek and knew the term intimately. What can be said of a person, then, whose hubris exceeded his own best interests?[39]

When all is said and done in politics, Boris Johnson was exceptional. Queen Elizabeth presided over sixteen UK Prime Ministers (Elizabeth Truss was the last), equaling the numbers registered in both Australia and New Zealand. But it would be hard to match the exuberance of Johnson when he took over from Theresa May in "getting Brexit done." Taking up the Conservative Party leadership he led it to a staggering election victory in 2019 and broke through the Brexit deadlock. Writing in 2021 *Spectator* writer Tom McTague identified his unique character.

> Johnson is nothing like the other prime ministers I've covered. Tony Blair and David Cameron were polished and formidable. Gordon Brown and Theresa May were rigid, fearful, cautious. Johnson might as well be another species. He is lively and engaged, superficially disheveled but in fact focused and watchful. He is scruffy, impulsive, exuberant. He is the first British leader I've seen who genuinely appears to be having a good time.[40]

In the end, having a good time cost him his privileged job.

The question infrequently asked by academics and journalists who regard themselves as specialists on the subject is whether Johnson was truly a populist, or just *popular*? In discussing a reorganized super European football league that would have degraded lower-tier clubs that were playing in traditional

English stadiums with their rabid followers, he employed a peculiar turn of phrase: "To be deracinated is to be uprooted from your customs, your culture, your home—in this instance, from England."[41]

The one political role where Johnson's populism would most aptly have been greeted with fervor was, obviously, with Brexiteers. He shunned nativist rhetoric while still serving up a patriotic message for England. His pragmatism was often lost in the swirl of hubris and charisma. As examples, the UK government rejected a visa route for low-skilled migrants and temporary workers and substituted instead a new points-based immigration system in which the priority would go to those with the most valued skills such as scientists, engineers, and professors. A government policy paper had underscored the need to shift from an economy relying on cheap labor from Europe to a concentration on investment in technology and automation.[42] In this respect, the United Kingdom was following the example of other countries enacting a points system for entry focusing on qualifications and skills, such as Canada and Australia.

Johnson's politics posed a threat to Scotland's national ambitions and even to continued peace in Northern Ireland by overriding the Protocol that Britain had signed with the EU. In 2016, Scotland had voted by a large margin to remain in the EU, including by each and every council in the country. The SNP was making preparations to hold a second referendum on independence, while leading the campaign to "take back control" from the EU. Johnson inadvertently intensified calls for Scotland to wrest control from London.

Eliminating the free movement principle increased Johnson's appeal to other groups of people. He supported amnesty for undocumented immigrants, offered a path to British citizenship to millions of Hong Kongers, and reset Britain's immigration system so as to treat European and non-European migrants equitably. But he was unable to complete his work. In August 2022 he resigned from his office, principally due to a revolt by many of his Cabinet members. In his resignation speech, hubris had not vanished: "as we've seen at Westminster the herd instinct is powerful and when the herd moves, it moves."

Johnson took credit for the milestone that Brexit had marked, and of negotiating through COVID too. He declared:

> I'm immensely proud of the achievements of this government: from getting Brexit done to settling our relations with the continent for over half a century, reclaiming the power for this country to make its own laws in Parliament, getting us all through the pandemic, delivering the fastest vaccine rollout in Europe, the fastest exit from lockdown, and in the last few months, leading the West in standing up to Putin's aggression in Ukraine.[43]

A long-awaited biography of Shakespeare remains Johnson's unfinished business. But for purposes of this book, the question looms: How large a role did classical Greek play in creating Boris Johnson's hubris?

Race and Gender Twists and Turns

Let me zero in on three singularities of weighty importance to Brexit and its consequences: the issue of cultural racism; related to it, Black, Asian, and Minority Ethnic (BAME) politics; and gender issues.

Cultural Racism

Structural racism based on race, often gravitating on skin pigmentation, was alleged to have inclined some British voters to opt for the Leave choice. But it does not hold up well when contrasted with the charge of cultural racism that targeted White CEE citizens. Cultural racism is specific and anchored in cultural differences between groups rather than biological markers. In either case, such differentiation establishes the supposed superiority, or inferiority, of collectivities of people. Each can be real, imagined, or constructed.

For Arun Sivanandan, director of the Institute of Race Relations and founder of the acclaimed British journal *Race and Class*, one legacy of cultural racism is the continuing appeal of colonial culture with its visible signs of superior and inferior nations.[44] The term gained adherents in Europe when perceptions awoke that Central European "laggards" were moving to Western Europe and the United Kingdom where they were judged to have inferior qualities when compared to native populations there.

Besides the factor of cultural racism, a strong case could be made that "four decades of Euroscepticsm, coupled with the Eurozone crisis and the mass migration from the Middle East, were more important than what happened in the campaign in determining the result."[45] A reasoned explanation for the Brexit outcome was that Caucasian Europeans were taking advantage of the EU enlargement opportunity and heading for a better life in England. In their case, with the exception of Roma and certain other historic European peoples, skin color had nothing to do with it.

A general dislike of EU rules, at times its autocratic behavior, the perceived arrogance of its leaders, a persistent democratic deficit, and fickle European Court of Justice decisions filtered through to British policymakers and members of the affected public. To reiterate, a great deal more than migration policies figured in the Brexit vote and its effects.

The hard core of the Remain campaign was found in London; it was regularly branded as the country's only cosmopolitan conurbation, to the chagrin of other major cities and towns in the United Kingdom. The City had expanded beyond the reaches of the Bank of England, the Stock Exchange, and St Paul's Cathedral to London East postal codes, Canary Wharf, and the rebuilt Stratford expanse designed in the first instance to host the 2012 Summer Olympics. Already in the 2011 census, thirty-seven percent of London's population was foreign-born; that figure included twenty percent from outside of Europe. In 2015, over three million London residents had been born abroad and sixty-nine percent of babies born in London had at least one parent who was born overseas. Research forecast that close to three-quarters of students living in London entering university by 2030 would be from ethnic minorities.[46]

A smaller-than-anticipated voting block showed up at the polls for the referendum leaving younger Londoners believing the result would be a no-brainer. They were left in a state of shock and repugnance with those living in "the north"—in other words, those north of London's historic 32 boroughs. One observer put it this way: "Remainers are following a well-trodden path to polarized group think, dismissing their social 'inferiors' who voted for Brexit as stupid, racist and easily misled."[47] For Tom McTague, summarizing the research findings of two clinical psychologists, "For Britain's pro-European middle classes, Brexit is akin to a psychological trauma which has left many unable to behave rationally," yet "They are acting no differently to what psychologists would expect from those suffering from chronic anxiety caused by loss of control and insecurity."[48]

It is unlikely that well-off cosmopolitans enjoying London life were targeting their Brexit frustrations at arriving Estonians, Poles, Romanians, and others from CEE. What was the case of those feeling left behind, in particular, "people of color?"

Black, Asian, and Minority Ethnic Communities

The unfortunately named BAME collectivities are largely made up of disadvantaged people who live in London but also in such different regions as the industrial Midlands, the populated cities of Lancashire and Yorkshire, as well as rural East Anglia and the West Country. Were they the cause of not well-educated "locals" (sometimes called nativists) reacting to demographic patterns and supporting the Leave campaign?[49]

On the contrary, some Leave supporters from immigrant communities who were not all disadvantaged threw their weight behind Nigel Farage's UKIP movement. Some had become disenchanted with lifestyles in the United Kingdom, others even with arriving Central Europeans who felt ostracized by Britain's multicultural environment. Farage himself curried support from

Anglo-Pakistani shopkeepers in Birmingham and Muslim communities in Leicester.

Survey results can reveal a good part of the story. A longitudinal study found that "White British were the most pro-Leave, followed by those of Indian background who were almost twice as likely to support Leave as other minority groups." By contrast, "There were much higher levels of support for Remain amongst Pakistanis, Bangladeshis, Black Caribbean, and Black African groups—on average a quarter being more pro-Leave than Remain."[50] Indications of support from those of immigrant background for Brexit weaken the causal link between xenophobia and Leave.

Another factor has it that some ethnic minority Leavers were convinced other EU member states were more racist or Islamophobic than Britain. A corollary was that minority rights seemed better protected in Britain than on the continent. Some female Muslim Leave voters expressed concern about bans imposed on facial coverings such as burqas in EU states and were unconvinced that the EU was committed to gender equality.

The referendum revealed tensions between longer-settled BAME groups and newer CEE arrivals. Europe was perceived as becoming a "White Fortress" permitting White immigration to continue to expand while obstructing the entry of non-Whites; the EU's response to the refugee crisis underscored these differences with African groups feeling left out of the migration club. Even the EU's Common Agricultural Policy was regarded as disadvantaging developing countries in Africa and Asia.[51] In 2022, moves were afoot to remove the catch-all acronym BAME because, according to one report, this group is "held together by no more than what it is not."[52] Anomalies of this kind exist in other immigration-receiving states.

As noted earlier, turnout in the referendum was crucial. Those abstaining were more Remain supporters (nineteen percent) than Leave ones (eleven percent). Where there had been an influx of immigrants from CEE, disgruntled voters more often chose Leave.[53] This tendency further supported the cultural racism thesis than the anti-Black, anti-Brown, and anti-Muslim scenario.

In the 2016 referendum, two different worlds existed, then, exemplified in the town of Stoke-on-Trent. Proportionately, it had the largest number of Brexit supporters at nearly seventy percent. Its opposite, Lambeth in London south of the Thames, revealed seventy-nine percent voted for Remain; nine other inner London boroughs also voted Remain with figures above seventy percent.[54] Overall Brexit support would have increased dramatically had London inner boroughs not been counted.

A further predictable survey result was that White British respondents who considered their ethnic identity important to them strongly supported the

Leave camp. By contrast, prizing one's ethnic identity had no significant effect on other ethnically defined groups including ethnic non-Whites.[55] Was an acute sense of Englishness (discussed below) beginning to appear as a reason for wishing to leave the EU?

A counterintuitive observation by Protection Approaches, an academic team focusing on identity-based violence including hate crimes in the United Kingdom, is worth noting. It suggested that we may have been barking up the wrong tree when foisting blame on rebel-rousers hostile to minority groups:

> many of those who hold negative attitudes towards minorities cannot be described as coming from a socio-economic background commonly attributed to Britain's "left behind." A significant proportion of those who consider minorities to be a threat to Britain are both financially secure and educated beyond GCSE/O level; a majority feel satisfied with their lives, able to influence decisions that affect them and feel valued in their local communities.

Survey data claimed that one in four respondents held negative views of minorities. Nevertheless, according to the 2019 report *A Gathering Storm?* "many who consider Muslims, immigrants, Roma, Gypsy, or Travellers to be a 'threat to Britain's success and prosperity' could be described as the 'winners' of the past decades rather than Britain's 'left behind'."[56] If we are searching for xenophobic identities who backed Brexit, we may need to reconsider whether the left behind was of crucial importance. The left behind, the less well-educated, the unemployed, and the historic, now decimated working classes may not have a monopoly on discrimination against Others including migrants.

Gender Agenda

An innovative, perhaps startling approach to understanding the backlash behind Britain's vote to leave the EU is to consider gender-based backlash effects in the Brexit vote. Gender had never featured much in the campaign itself. The assumption was that women and men showed no average aggregate-level differences in voting Leave or Remain so the issue remained dormant. However, according to Jane Green and Rosalind Shorrocks, this overlooked an important point: gender-based resentment supported voting for Brexit through perceptions of unfair discrimination felt against men by men.[57]

In their view, perceiving discrimination against men increased voters' likelihood to vote Leave. In effect, it counted as weightily as attitudes related to racial discrimination. Of course, men were more likely to perceive discrimination against men than women were. It rang true for men of all ages but was particularly the case for young men without jobs. Such a grievance-based attitude was affected more by age and working status than levels of income and education. The Leave campaign had presented itself as a broad rejection of the status quo and supporting it offered an outlet for resentment and dissatisfaction with changes that were emerging throughout society. High-politics questions about the UK's sovereignty and its EU membership flaws were not trivial, but also not dominating.[58]

For the two authors, the backlash argument is rooted in the marginalization of social groups defined by their economic precariousness, their declining social status, and their waning features connected to traditional cultural values. The White working class was affected by less job security, rising socioeconomic inequality together with declining social mobility, and the reduction of traditional, decent working-class jobs in manufacturing. The result was that it faced "nostalgic deprivation"—social class used to have greater status but it had been transferred to different social groups that included women entering the work force.[59]

Men without a college education whose subjective social status had declined in post-industrial societies became more anti-elitist, anti-immigrant, and anti-globalization, in other words, they were treated as hallmarks of the Brexit profile.[60] Working-class men had been particularly affected by technological change, low pay, and precarious job security. In contrast, women had gained increased relative status as they entered the workforce in growing numbers.

In short, gender-based discrimination against men proved to be a significant predictor for Leave support in the referendum even though the referendum was never supposed to be about gender. Backlash was primarily based on resentment or grievances against women. The authors' results also led them to suggest that a significant minority of men may have learned to cast their vote in British elections on the basis of anger and resentment about their unfair treatment. This voting pattern was likely to continue in Parliamentary elections.

Focusing on a different time period provides a different stereotype going in the other direction—the macho character of Englishness. Alison Light's *Forever England: Femininity, Literature and Conservatism Between the Wars*, published in 1991, revealed a domesticated version of Englishness that highlighted hearth and home between the two wars. It had a positive side to it: a shift from "formerly heroic and officially masculine public rhetorics of national destiny and from a dynamic and missionary view of the Victorian and Edwardian middle classes in 'Great Britain' to an Englishness at once less imperial and more inward-looking, more domestic and more private—and in terms of pre-war standards, more 'feminine.'"[61]

For Wendy Webster writing in *Englishness and Empire: 1939–1965*, such a view of Englishness not only emphasized a female sphere of domesticity but also "the quiet, pipe-smoking Englishman, tending his garden." During the Second World War, "common people" were celebrated through their "quiet courage," a small sporting country battling "the Great Dictators."[62] Virginia Woolf might have agreed with this characterization, and was frightened by it.

By the 1960s, "much 'Angry Young Man' literature, as well as the films of the British 'New Wave' that were often based on novels, relocated a masculine nation in the North of England, removing their anti-heroes from associations with notions of the effete and effeminate South."[63] Admittedly, Webster was not sure how "English" these features were since, with few exceptions, her book conflates British and English, which is all too common as I consider below. Differences in British and English gender roles may have been the exception, spotlighting the perceived preoccupations of each.

Englishness and Brexit

In V. S. Naipaul's 1987 book *The Enigma of Arrival: A Novel in Five Sections*, he recounted his arrival from Trinidad and Tobago to London, then followed studying at Oxford, yet living in England proved that he was a stranger among strangers.

> That idea of ruin and dereliction, of out-of-placeness, was something I felt about myself, attached to myself: a man from another hemisphere, another background, coming to rest in middle life in the cottage of a half-neglected estate, an estate full of reminders of its Edwardian past, with few connections with the present. An oddity among the estates and big houses of the valley, and a further oddity in its grounds. I felt unanchored and strange.

After his move to a home in the country, the Nobel Prize literature laureate commented: "I felt that my presence in that old valley was part of something like an upheaval, a change in the course of the history of the country."[64]

Perhaps nineteenth-century novels by Charles Dickens were centered on different social classes but today Englishness is a term associated with the well-to-do, with a prospective and present aristocracy that is disappearing. Its past status and glamor are now being transferred into the hands of the National Trust which cares for its abandoned castles, manors, estates, stately homes, and even battlefields. But there is a more plebeian Englishness today connected to the debate on Britain leaving the EU.

For British authors Ailsa Henderson and Richard Wyn Jones, what is involved is "the remaking of British politics by focusing on what we regard as the motor force behind it—namely, Englishness." That is because "since 2016, the argument that English nationalism is somehow at the heart of the decision to leave the European Union has been heard relatively frequently." They add that in the past, "In England, choosing to describe oneself as British or English was generally regarded as being a matter of taste or, in particular, of context, rather than a matter of political consequence."[65] Monash University political scientist Ben Wellings believed that the neologism Brexit was a misnomer and its outcome had been decided in England, not Britain.[66]

In their data-packed volume, Henderson and Wyn Jones underscored the fact that until recently a major barrier to understanding English nationalism was scarce hard evidence of any kind. In 2011, the authors took part in the first "Future of England Survey" (FoES) which got off the mark with their publication of *The Dog that Finally Barked: England as an Emerging Political Community*.[67] Using various survey measures, they discovered that those who viewed themselves as strongly English remained deeply attached to Britishness. Hence in the referendum, "In England the more British you saw yourself the more you would vote Remain." With London being a partial exception, little regional variation occurred in patterns of national identity. However, socioeconomic and demographic differences were noteworthy: older people, Anglicans, less skilled manual workers, state pensioners, the unemployed, and those born in England were more likely to feel strongly or exclusively English. In contrast, younger voters, non-White British, and those born outside England tended to identify as British.

The authors explained the "English world view:"

English attitudes towards England's place in the union and Britain's place in the world are underpinned by a distinctive understanding of what constitutes legitimate government and that devolution and European integration offend, in part at least, because they offend against it. There is a clear sense among English identifiers that they no longer live in a state that is interested in them or acts on their behalves.[68]

For Wellings, however, Leave support was more a mix of disparate attitudes across the United Kingdom: "Instead of the Brexit vote being caused by a deepening parochialism, it was an awkward but decisive alliance between sections of the electorate disaffected by the effects of neo-liberal globalization and elites attempting to expose Britain to more of the same."[69]

In their summing up, Henderson and Wyn Jones focused on a methodological issue: "Even when scholars are relying on samples that are England dominated, very little if any consideration is given to the relationship between English identity and attitudes and behaviors." What is more, "Even in those cases where national identity is mentioned as a potential factor, the treatment lacks finesse."[70]

However, instances of a clash between English and Scottish identities have appeared regularly. For instance, in 2015 a measure to bring back fox hunting to England was abandoned when Scottish National Party members in the House of Commons threatened to oppose it; otherwise, the ruling Conservative Party had expected to win the vote. In 2023, Scotland's Parliament, referred to as Holyrood, passed a gender recognition reform bill that allowed transgender people aged sixteen and older to apply for legal recognition through a Gender Recognition Certificate. The British government blocked the legislation, using its veto power on Scottish legislation for the first time. The debate went beyond the subject of trans rights and set up a legal standoff over political autonomy between London and Edinburgh. Englishness can make a difference, therefore, on questions of law.

Lyrical England

Many poetic pieces about England are discoverable among a nation of poets. They are found in lyrical and popular versions including songwriting. "The Last Farewell" is a romantic folk song first performed in 1971 by a writer of English background who was born in Kenya. Roger Whittaker was an artist who traveled the world but it was this song that became a popular hit in England; it was recorded in his 1971 album "New World in the Morning."

> There's a ship lies rigged and ready in the harbor
> Tomorrow for old England she sails
> Far away from your land of endless sunshine
> To my land full of rainy skies and gales
> And I shall be aboard that ship tomorrow
> Though my heart is full of tears at this farewell
> For you are beautiful—I have loved you dearly
> More dearly than the spoken word can tell

The lyrics recount that "there's a wicked war a-blazing, and the taste of war I know so very well." They continue:

Though death and darkness gather all about me
My ship be torn apart upon the seas
I shall smell again the fragrance of these islands
And the heaving waves that brought me once to thee
And should I return home safe again to England
I shall watch the English mist roll through the dale
For you are beautiful—I have loved you dearly
More dearly than the spoken word can tell.[71]

Did this song commemorate an English sea battle in Napoleonic times? Was it the lament of a homesick sailor? Who was the mysterious "other"—a faraway island and tropical paradise or a specific place, like the Caribbean, the Philippines, Polynesia, or even a place off Kenya? Is the fervent reference—"I have loved you dearly"—to an exotic, alluring woman he had to leave behind? Or could it simply have signaled a deep nostalgia marking the last pages of the British empire?

To some listeners today, it is a song that deservedly merits being downgraded to an outdated decolonizing history of empire. It boasts of racially tinged lyrics along with decolonizing era it embraced, the vapid sentiments it enshrined, the abject colonial studies that require rejection, and even the syllabus and the publications that have no pedagogical place in our virtue-signaling society. However "The Last Farewell" is not a patriotic song. It praises foreign lands over the homeland. It is essentially an anti-war song. As important, aesthetically it is reflective and beautiful.

Enoch Powell was a famed Tory politician, linguist, poet, and classical scholar who attended Oxford but himself came from Birmingham, not from a country manor. In 1968, he delivered a speech in his home city that was both lyrical, invoking classical Latin vocabulary, and also distressing. He spoke about the "rivers of blood" which would flow should England follow through with unlimited immigration from the Commonwealth. The infamous speech by the UK's Minister of Health was intimidating and referenced the precariousness of Englishness and the drawn-out threat facing it. It emphasized Thucydides' *deos*, a logical fear of a still-distant threat— Powell was unquestionably a thinker—as a warning about its fading empire. His prognosis proved wrong and England has emerged today as a model of hyper-multiculturalism, whether considered an achievement or a failure. But in many respects, his words cast a long shadow on the future of Englishness.

Postscriptum

In *Between the Acts*, her very last book published in 1941, Virginia Woolf divulged this about England:

> Sprung from the sea
> Whose billows blown by mighty storm
> Cut off from France and Germany
> This isle.

Notes

1 Virginia Woolf, *A Room of One's Own* (London: Penguin Books, 2000 [1929]), ch. 4.
2 Svetlana Alexievich, *The Unwomanly Face of War: An Oral History of Women in World War II* (New York: Random House, 2018).
3 Virginia Woolf, "To Violet Dickinson," in *Leave the Letters Till We're Dead—The Letters of Virginia Woolf*, VI: 1936–1941, ed. Nigel Nicolson, 3120: April 21, 1936 (London: The Hogarth Press, 1980), 28.
4 Woolf, "To Jacques-Émile Blanche," 3451: October 5 1938, 282.
5 Nicolson, Introduction, *Leave the Letters*, xv.
6 Woolf, "To Ethel Smyth," 3699: March 10, 1941, 478.
7 Angharad Closs Stephens, "Feeling 'Brexit': National Affects and the Politics of Movement," unpublished paper (2018).
8 Jonathan Moss et al. "Brexit and the Everyday Politics of Emotion: Methodological Lessons from History," *Political Studies* 68, no. 4 (November 2020), 837–56, doi:10.1177/0032321720911915.
9 Alan Collins et al. "A Picture of Regret: An Empirical Investigation of Post-Brexit Referendum Survey Data," *Rationality and Society* (August 2021), doi:10.1177/10434631211035202.
10 Joshua Freedman, "Back of the Queue: Brexit, Status Loss, and the Politics of Backlash," *British Journal of Politics & International Relations* 22, no. 4 (November 2020), 631–43, doi:10.1177/1369148120949824.
11 Karen J. Alter and Michael Zürn, "Conceptualizing Backlash Politics: Introduction to a Special Issue on Backlash Politics in Comparison," *British Journal of Politics & International Relations* 22, no. 4 (November 2020), 563–84, doi:10.1177/1369148120947958.
12 David Cameron, "In Full: David Cameron Statement on the UK's Future," *BBC News* (September 19, 2014), https://www.bbc.com/news/uk-politics-29271765.
13 Freedman, "Back of the Queue."
14 Freedman, ibid.
15 Romano Prodi, *Europe as I See It* (Cambridge: Polity Press, 2000).
16 Christian Meier, *The Uses of History: From Athens to Auschwitz* (Cambridge: Harvard University Press, 2005).
17 Nazli Kibria, Megan O'Leary, and Cara Bowman, "The Good Immigrant Worker: 2013 US Senate Bill 744, Color-Blind Nativism and the Struggle for Comprehensive Immigration Reform," *International Migration and Integration* 19 (2018), 7.
18 Raymond Taras, *Nationhood, Migration and Global Politics* (Edinburgh: Edinburgh University Press, 2018).

19 Geoffrey Brahm Levey, "The Bristol School of Multiculturalism," *Ethnicities* 19, no. 1 (2019), 219, https://journals.sagepub.com/doi/pdf/10.1177/1468796818787413.

20 Harold D. Clarke, Matthew Goodwin, and Paul Whiteley, *Brexit: Why Britain Voted to Leave the European Union* (Cambridge: Cambridge University Press, 2017), ch. 6.

21 Eric Kaufman, "The Politics of Immigration: UKIP and Beyond," *The Political Quarterly* 85, no. 3 (2014), 247–50.

22 Richard Whitaker and Philip Lynch, "Explaining Support for the UK Independence Party at the 2009 European Parliament Elections," *Journal of Elections, Public Opinion and Parties* 21, no. 3 (2011), 359–79.

23 Paul Whiteley, Harold D. Clarke, David Sanders, and Marianne Stewart, "Why Do Voters Lose Trust in Governments? Public Perceptions of Government Honesty and Trustworthiness in Britain 2000–2013," *The British Journal of Politics & International Relations* 18, no. 1 (2016), 234–54.

24 Harold D. Clarke, Matthew Goodwin, and Paul Whiteley, "Why Britain Voted for Brexit: An Individual-Level Analysis of the 2016 Referendum Vote," *Parliamentary Affairs* 70, no. 3 (July 2017), 439–64. See also Robert Ford and Matthew J. Goodwin, *Revolt on the Right: Explaining Support for the Radical Right in Britain* (London: Routledge, 2014).

25 Matthew Goodwin and Caitlin Milazzo, *UKIP: Inside the Campaign to Redraw the Map of British Politics* (Oxford: Oxford University Press, 2015).

26 Matthew Goodwin and Robert Ford, "Britain after Brexit: A Nation Divided," *Journal of Democracy* 28, no. 1 (2017), 17–30.

27 Ford and Goodwin, *Revolt on the Right*.

28 See Matt Golder, "Far Right Parties in Europe," *Annual Review of Political Science* 19 (2016), 482–90.

29 Elisabeth Ivarsflaten, "What Unites Right-Wing Populists in Western Europe? Re-examining Grievance Mobilization Models in Seven Successful Cases," *Comparative Political Studies* 41 (2008), 3–23.

30 Daphne Halikiopoulou and Tim Vlandas, "When Economic and Cultural Interests Align: The Anti-Immigration Voter Coalitions Driving Far Right Party Success in Europe," *European Political Science Review* 12, no. 4 (2020), 427–48.

31 Matthew Goodwin and James Dennison, "Immigration, Issue Ownership and the Rise of UKIP," *Parliamentary Affairs* 68, no. 1 (2015), 168–87.

32 Christian Dustmann, Tommaso Frattini, and Ian P. Preston, "The Effect of Immigration Along the Distribution of Wages," *Review of Economic Studies* 80 (2013), 145–73.

33 Joris Luyendijk, "Brexodus Has Begun," *The Guardian* (June 29, 2017), https://www.theguardian.com/commentisfree/2017/jun/29/brexodus-eu-nationals-citizenship-uk-brexit.

34 Geoffrey Evans and Anand Menon, *Brexit and British Politics* (Cambridge: Polity, 2017), 68–69.

35 Ulf Hedetoft, *Paradoxes of Populism: Troubles of the West and Nationalism's Second Coming* (London: Anthem Press, 2020), 54.

36 James Crisp, "Brexit Cases are Already Piling Up Reveals European Court of Justice Boss," *The Telegraph* (April 19, 2018), https://www.telegraph.co.uk/politics/2018/04/19/brexit-cases-already-piling-reveals-european-court-justice-boss/.

37 Michel Barnier, *My Secret Brexit Diary: A Glorious Illusion* (Cambridge: Polity, 2021).

38 Charlie Cooper, "Jeremy Hunt to Brussels: Don't Turn EU into 'Prison,'" *Politico* (September 30, 2018), https://www.politico.eu/article/jeremy-hunt-to-brussels-dont-turn-eu-into-prison/.

39 See Matthew Flinders, "Boris Johnson: A Terminal Case of Hubris Syndome," *The Conversation* (July 7, 2022), https://theconversation.com/boris-johnson-a-terminal-case-of-hubris-syndrome-186495.

40 Tom McTague, "The Minister of Chaos: Boris Johnson Knows Exactly What He's Doing," *The Atlantic* (July-August 2021), https://www.theatlantic.com/magazine/archive/2021/07/boris-johnson-minister-of-chaos/619010/.

41 Tom McTague, "Who is the Real Boris Johnson? What I Learned on the Road with the PM," *The Times* (July 10, 2021), https://www.thetimes.co.uk/article/who-is-the-real-boris-johnson-what-i-learnt-on-the-road-with-the-pm-jv9swgljj.

42 Cristina Gallardo, "UK Shuts the Door to Unskilled Migrants," *Politico* (February 18, 2020), https://www.politico.eu/article/uk-shuts-door-unskilled-migrants/.

43 Heather Stewart, "Boris Johnson's Resignation Speech: What He Said, and What He Meant," *The Guardian* (July 7, 2022).

44 Arun Sivanandan, "New Circuits of Imperialism," *Race and Class* 30, no. 4 (1989), 1–19.

45 Tim Shipman, *All Out War: The Full Story of How Brexit Sank Britain's Political Class* (London: William Collins, 2016), xxv.

46 Eleanor Busby, "Three in Four Students from London will be from Ethnic Minorities in Hyper-Diversity Era," *Independent* (September 20, 2018), https://www.independent.co.uk/news/education/education-news/diversity-university-students-london-ethnic-minorities-access-he-bame-a8547141.html.

47 Tom McTague, "Britain's Middle-Class Brexit Anxiety Disorder," *Politico* (August 21, 2018), https://www.politico.eu/article/brexit-anxiety-disorder-britain-middle-class/.

48 McTague, quoting Philip Corr and Simon Stuart in *Politico* (August 17, 2018), https://www.politico.eu/article/brexit-anxiety-disorder-britain-middle-class/.

49 Aihua Zhang, "New Findings on Key Factors Influencing the UK's Referendum on Leaving the EU," *World Development* 102 (2018), 304–14.

50 "The UK Household Longitudinal Survey," https://www.understandingsociety.ac.uk/.

51 The UK in a Changing Europe, *Brexit and Public Opinion*, King's College, London, 2018, http://ukandeu.ac.uk/wp-content/uploads/2018/01/Public-Opinion.pdf.

52 Commission on Race and Ethnic Disparities, *The Report* (March 2021), https://assets.publishing.service.gov.uk/government/uploads/system/uploads/attachment_data/file/974507/20210331_-_CRED_Report_-_FINAL_-_Web_Accessible.pdf.

53 Evans and Menon, *Brexit and British Politics*, 68–69.

54 Andy Pike, Danny Mackinnon, Mike Coombes, Tony Champion, David Bradley, Andrew Cumbers, Liz Robson, and Colin Wymer, *Uneven Growth: Tackling City Decline*, Joseph Rowntree Foundation (2016).

55 Neema Begum, "Minority Ethnic Attitudes and the 2016 Referendum," *The UK in a Changing Europe Newsletter*, February 6, 2018, http://ukandeu.ac.uk/minority-ethnic-attitudes-and-the-2016-eu-referendum/.

56 Kate Ferguson and Andy Fearn, *A Gathering Storm? Assessing Risks of Identity-Based Violence in Britain* (Lambeth, London: Protection Approaches, 2019), 5, https://img1.wsimg.com/blobby/go/131c96cc-7e6f-4c06-ae37-6550dbd85dde/downloads/A%20Gathering%20Storm%20Assessing%20risks%20of%20identity-.pdf?ver=1587383841691.

57 Jane Green and Rosalind Shorrocks, "The Gender Backlash in the Vote for Brexit," *Political Behavior* (2021), https://doi.org/10.1007/s11109-021-09704-y.

58 Pippa Norris and Ronald F. Inglehart, *Cultural Backlash: Trump, Brexit, and Authoritarian Populism* (Cambridge: Cambridge University Press, 2019).

59 Justin Gest, Tyler Reny, and Jeremy Mayer, "Roots of the Radical Right: Nostalgic Deprivation in the United States and Britain," *Comparative Political Studies* (2017), https://journals.sagepub.com/doi/full/10.1177/0010414017720705?casa_token= VKwztmZyH8AAAAA%3Alfa1llFEdbjp8WZOwYeCgaFTECkMY18VGEB9Zh 9bX MinDtvGkGm6D5VuAZuHMJzkcnlnlbDDWtqP.

60 Noam Gidron and Peter A. Hall, "The Politics of Social Status: Economic and Cultural Roots of the Populist Right," *British Journal of Sociology* 68, no. S1 (2017), 57–84, https://onlinelibrary.wiley.com/doi/full/10.1111/1468-4446.12319.

61 Alison Light, *Forever England: Femininity, Literature and Conservatism Between the Wars* (London: Routledge, 1991), 28.

62 Wendy Webster, *Englishness and Empire: 1939–1965* (New York: Oxford University Press, 2005), 9.

63 Webster, *Englishness and Empire*, 185.

64 V. S. Naipaul, *The Enigma of Arrival: A Novel in Five Sections* (New York: Vintage, 1988).

65 Ailsa Henderson and Richard Wyn Jones, *Englishness: The Political Force Transforming Britain* (Oxford: Oxford University Press, 2021).

66 Ben Wellings, "Was Brexit a Misnomer? Exploring the politics of Englishness," *Australian Book Review*, 429 (2021), https://www.australianbookreview.com.au/abr-online/ archive/2021/960-march-2021-no-429/7478-ben-wellings-reviews-englishness-the- political-force-transforming-britain-by-ailsa-henderson-and-richard-wyn-jones.

67 Richard Wyn Jones, Guy Lodge, Ailsa Henderson, and Daniel Wincott, *The Dog that Finally Barked: England as an Emerging Political Community* (London: Progressive Policy Think Tank), January 23, 2012, https://www.ippr.org/publications/the-dog- that-finally-barked-england-as-an-emerging-political-community.

68 Henderson and Wyn Jones, *Englishness*, ch. 5.

69 Ben Wellings, *English Nationalism, Brexit and the Anglosphere: Wider Still and Wider* (Manchester: Manchester University Press, 2019).

70 Henderson and Wyn Jones, *Englishness*, 211–12.

71 For a video of this song featuring tall ships, see https://www.youtube.com/ watch?v=sGWs1HK8iDU. But for a more poignant, romantic cover of Roger Whittaker's song (there are tall ships too), see Marlon Brando and Tarita Teviipaia's clip from *Mutiny on the Bounty* at https://www.youtube.com/watch?v=VGugzvOQNGs.

Chapter 3

REGIONAL FEAR: SAXONY AND THE FAR RIGHT IN GERMANY

The Sources of *Phobos*

The classic understanding of *phobos*—an irrational fear of an immediate direct threat—can be applied to different cases of fear in the contemporary world. Using the previous case of Brexit, for example, the threat to people left behind by continuous in-migration from Central and Eastern Europe (CEE) or third countries *is* plausible and can be perceived as near, thereby invoking Thucydides' term *phobos*.

A helpful metaphor explaining this phenomenon can be found in the South Pacific. In rituals in some of the Pacific Islands as well as New Zealand, the war dance of the *haka* is given high priority before clashes with the adversary; some of the Islanders give it a different name. The performance displays the bravery—more, the ruthlessness and even murderous intent—of the assembled group carrying it out. In rugby, its purpose is utter intimidation of the opponent. The New Zealand All-Blacks rugby side is the best-known example. Creating fear in the adversary moments away from the start of a match surely conveys inescapable *phobos*.

The notion of an immediate threat to a way of life and culture can, in particular, be associated with particular regions of a country undergoing rapid demographic transformation. The example of Germany can be cited: in recent times a direct threat to a part of the country, Saxony, was transmitted by way of an "immigration wave" that brought Muslim groups from the Middle East and the southwestern Balkan states to what used to be east Germany. Some of the local population believed that the threat had been present even earlier with Germany's intake of guest workers (*Gastarbeiters*) in the late 1950s and throughout the 1960s.

Thucydides' example of *phobos* has been at play in the eastern region of Germany. It became manifest in what can be labeled as "rage against the newcomer"—in-migration into Saxony—where a history of xenophobia had been cultivated. Lying in the Soviet-created German Democratic

Republic (GDR), the fear of the foreigner, and even of western Germans, had become palpable when the Berlin Wall was erected in 1961. Confined mainly to one hotspot *Land* (or county), for nearly five decades Saxony was sheltered and isolated from the pro-Western Federal Republic of Germany (FRG).

The threat posed specifically by Muslim immigration to that region—up to the 1990s only "fraternal peoples" from the Soviet bloc were encouraged to visit the state—occurred when the unification of the two German states in 1992 opened the door to west Germans and also nationals of foreign countries. For different reasons which this study will list, the "nativist" population of Saxony began steadily to expound anti-migrant attitudes and behavior. It soon became stigmatized by its western counterpart as the hub of right-wing eastern German xenophobia.

Some have argued that in many of the Western countries where it arises, xenophobia (underscoring the *phobos* syndrome) reflects the desire on the part of affluent Western European societies to protect their islands of prosperity against an outside world that is troubled by inequality, poverty, environmental degradation, interethnic conflict, and widespread desperation because of deteriorating lifestyles and living standards. Absent these islands of prosperity, fearful states wished to guard against unskilled, illegal, or sham migration often associated with supposedly uncouth peoples.[1] In Germany's case, leaders who inspired such apparent demographic turmoil originated not in the east but in the Federal Republic.

Denmark's anti-immigration policies protecting a close-knit community of five million stand out in mobilizing constant fear of an immediate threat that would shake that society. Generally recognized as a liberal, tolerant, open society with considerable respect for human rights and a prosperous and generous welfare state to boot, since the 1990s under successive governments, whether led by conservative or social democratic parties, it veered toward illiberal asylum policies that resembled those of Austria or Hungary, not of Nordic states. Denmark had been the first state to sign the UN Refugee Convention in 1951 but in 2021 residence permits for Syrian refugees were revoked on the grounds that security around Damascus had improved allowing the removal from its territory of a hundred Syrian refugees.[2] Many other examples of immigrant-skeptic Danish policies abound.

It was Germany's immigration policy that may have served as the litmus test of tolerance and the liberal order. The migration crisis of 2015 challenged its welcoming approach to foreigners and what had been its largely successful integration policies for new arrivals. Many west Germans felt they were beyond reproach but survey results indicated that the average German was, in time, becoming more hostile to refugees arriving from faraway, poorly understood cultures; in the eyes of nativists they were branded as backward "faraway peoples."[3]

Since 1992 an annual study conducted by R+V, Germany's largest insurance firm, has asked Germans about their biggest fears. It represents an ideal way to carry out research into Thucydides' framework even if its methods can be less than scientific. For the first time in 2019, a majority of respondents reported that they were most afraid that the country would not be able to deal with the aftermath of the migrant influx of 2015. That issue took priority over other fears: economic downturns, terrorism, and President Donald Trump's influence on world politics.[4] In subsequent years such fears were replaced by the COVID pandemic in 2020, then the Russian invasion of Ukraine in 2022. Each had severe economic consequences for the Federal Republic. In former east Germany, the level of fear was calculated to be more than ten percent higher than in the west.

Support for the right-wing populist party *Alternative für Deutschland* (AfD) had been growing steadily. The direct cause of the party's *raison d'être* was the increasing presence of Muslim groups in Germany generally and in the eastern part in particular.[5] Viewed as an imminent threat sparking demographic upheaval, Saxony was transformed into a hotbed of protests, riots, and denunciations. Who would have thought? Johann Sebastian Bach had wanted to move to Dresden, its center, as a court composer—his repertoire had served to inspire harmony and peace for three centuries. How had this historical turnaround resulted from Bach to the far right? Could the legacy of the ex-communist state on fear-making contribute to *phobos* of the foreigner?

Eastern Europe as Purveyor of Fear

Of the many explanations for the rise of *phobos* and, accompanying it, of political intolerance and illiberalism, an unusual perspective was offered by scholars Ivan Krastev and Stephen Holmes:

> The region's illiberal turn cannot be grasped apart from the political expectation of "normality" created by the 1989 revolution and the politics of imitation that it legitimized. After the Berlin Wall fell, Europe was no longer divided between communists and democrats. It was instead divided between imitators and the imitated. East-West relations morphed from a Cold War standoff between two hostile systems into a moral hierarchy within a single liberal, Western system. While the mimics looked up to their models, the models looked down on their mimics. It is not entirely mysterious, therefore, why the "imitation of the West" voluntarily chosen by East Europeans three decades ago eventually resulted in a political backlash.[6]

The fact of a mainly agnostic region may have come into play as well. In 2016, statistics showed that four percent of the populace in Saxony was Catholic, nineteen percent Protestant, and seventy-five percent unaffiliated with any religion. Forty years of socialism had effectively driven religion out of the state.[7]

Although it was part of the former Soviet bloc for forty years and easily susceptible to processes of Sovietization and fear of the foreign, Krastev tied the GDR's legacy to German history rather than to mimicry of Slavic states to the east. The mimetic failure of all Eastern Europe in emulating the West had damaging consequences for the whole region, he claimed:

> What makes imitation so irksome is not only the implicit assumption that the mimic is somehow inferior to the model. It also entails the assumption that Central and Eastern Europe's copycat nations accept the West's right to evaluate their success or failure at living up to *Western* standards. In this sense, imitation comes to feel like a loss of sovereignty.[8]

Admittedly this intrinsic fault of mimicking the West held true not just for the GDR but for the majority of Central European states. The civilizational divide was drawn not on the Oder–Neisse border separating all-Germany from Poland but on the arbitrary line of demarcation created by the Soviet conquest of Berlin in 1945. Krastev and Holmes argued, further, that

> For two decades after 1989, the political philosophy of postcommunist Central and Eastern Europe could be summarized in a single imperative: Imitate the West! The process was called by different names—democratization, liberalization, enlargement, convergence, integration, Europeanization—but the goal pursued by postcommunist reformers was simple. They wished their countries to become "normal," which meant like the West. This involved importing liberal-democratic institutions, applying Western political and economic recipes, and publicly endorsing Western values. Imitation was widely understood to be the shortest pathway to freedom and prosperity.[9]

In sum, mimetic fallibility ensnared the EU enlargement states which were unable to match the West; this included the GDR. According to Dresden-based political scientist Hans Vorländer, the roots of a right-wing backlash movement extended from Pegida—"Patriotic Europeans Against the Islamization of the West" that originated in Dresden in 2014—to the AfD. It took pride in Saxon regionalism and even spoke of the existence of 'Saxon chauvinism:' the idea that Saxons know what's right and are thus entitled to more than others."[10] Was Saxony a region that was breaking from mimicry, then?

Oxford professor Jan Zielonka elaborated on this argument. For the past thirty years, liberalism has been the ideology of power and comprises "a set of values, a method of exercising government, a cultural ethos."[11] This trifecta marked the West's throttlehold over Europe which Russia's President had wished to break from through various tests of its solidarity in the twenty-first century. Zielonka realized that anti-liberal values in Europe had been increasing; indeed, his big tent of "Counterrevolutionary politics include neo-fascists, neo-communists, libertarians and conservatives, anti-austerity supporters, anti-Muslims, nationalists, and secessionists. The one quality shared in common was that they opposed the political order established after 1989."[12]

In my Introduction I listed many of the contemporary crises that the world has been facing; economic aspects included indebtedness, currency vulnerabilities, overall growth, widening inequality, productivity issues, and even the popular imagination undermining the status quo. Overwhelmed by this record, populist movements emerged and they became the favorite target of the liberal narrative: "Liberals are good at pointing to others' faults than at self-reflection. More time is spent on explaining the popularity of populists than on identifying the decline of liberalism."[13] For Zielonka, liberals no longer defended minorities against majorities.

Of particular frustration to CEE states was solidifying the position of Germany as *de facto* managing director of Europe. The author remarked how "Germany was not supposed to be running Europe. But Germany and several other countries with AAA ratings *are* in charge. There can be no talk of equality of member states."[14] The admittance into Germany of over one million refugees in 2015, in many ways shaming reticent enlargement states, was a blow to the illusion of EU equality.

At the time, Chancellor Angela Merkel insisted that CEE was not doing its share of sheltering refugees (economic migrants were regularly blended in with asylum seekers). The largest country in CEE, Poland, elected a conservative Catholic party in 2015 that accused the West of neo-colonialization in its policies on CEE migration intakes.[15] For some Polish academics, Germany had become the greatest beneficiary of postcommunist neocolonialism.[16] The liberal order came under attack from a variety of opponents before Putin hardened his line and undertook his special military operation against Ukraine in 2022.

Karl Popper's aptly-titled 1945 book, *The Open Society and Its Enemies*, did come with a catch. Liberal democracies' tolerance toward the intolerant cannot be infinite since, otherwise, the tolerant run the risk of eradication.[17] In such circumstances Popper viewed a fight back against the intolerant as necessary, thereby undermining the virtues—and tolerance in particular—of an open society.

Where did eastern Germany, in particular Saxony, stand in this shifting debate? Was Saxony's openness to expanding a populist anti-migrant movement becoming fused with concern about western German neocolonialism? Or was it primarily an Islamophobic backlash—an immediate threat to its demographic makeup?

Conditions Shaping Immediate Threats

Phobos is not a phenomenon affecting just the eastern part of Germany. However, specific and fertile conditions have aggravated its position. Among historic reasons for supporting anti-immigrant movements were, during World War II, "expellees" from their homes in the east. About fourteen million ethnic Germans fled from areas that had been Germany's eastern regions—Prussia, Pomerania, the Sudetenland, and Silesia—but were now an integral part of Poland and to a lesser degree Czechoslovakia. "Regained territories" (*ziemie odzyskane* in Polish) were how Poland branded its geographic shift to the west after World War II, leaving its vast eastern lands to be taken over by the USSR. Roughly twenty-five percent of Germans are descended from those expelled from the east after World War II. In Germany after the war, they had to re-settle in new areas and begin rebuilding their lives; the fine line between displaced persons and migrants is noteworthy. Some transplanted Germans decided to take out their grievances at being dislocated on others now moving into eastern German lands and Muslim groups became the obvious target.[18]

Older people were not the only ones relocated after the war to the east, some of whom were attracted to anti-immigrant movements; the conservative right-wing party AfD in Saxony became a magnet of migrant resistance. Was this region unique in embracing reactionary politics and, with it violence proneness? In the 2021 federal elections, AfD came first among voters under thirty. It "torpedoed the argument, repeated before the election by the government's commissioner for former East Germany, that some sections of the population there vote for the far-right because they grew up in a dictatorship." One-in-five voters born after 1991 cast ballots in favor of the AfD. In its election campaign, AfD emphasized that it cared for younger people and was aware of what had troubled "Saxony-Anhalt's youth in the past year: mainly, restrictions on freedom imposed for a virus that many young people don't believe can harm them."[19]

In Saxony, the party's anti-immigrant rhetoric was seen less as a political platform than as an expression of emotion—frustration: "after 30 years of reunified Germany, a distinct East German identity is being inherited by younger people—even those (or maybe especially those) who have moved west to study and work and then returned in their 20s and 30s." As for the elephant in the room—the AfD's growing right-wing radicalism—young people interpreted it to mean that "racism and right-wing extremism just aren't as much of a taboo in the east, and there's a different relationship to freedom of speech."[20] In other words, woke culture—displaying alertness to racial prejudice and discrimination, a meaning that originated in the African-American vernacular—had not penetrated in Saxony or much of eastern Germany.

Differences between western and eastern parts of Germany have long drawn the attention of academics, journalists, social media analysts, bloggers, and others. The question frequently posed is how distinctive eastern German Islamophobia is from that in other regions of the FRG. Are Saxon cities like Chemnitz and Cottbus—the most densely populated *Land* in eastern Germany—home to extremist radical-right movements? Or on the contrary, did the invasive western influence of western German influencers over Saxony produce a xenophobic impact on eastern Germany's transition politics including, intentionally or not, abetting Islamophobia?

In focusing on Saxony, a converse question emerges: does Saxony-bashing serve as the core of western Germany's sense of righteousness and virtue-seeking that takes pride of place in generating a European value? Islamophobic outbreaks in other regions of Germany may have been dismissed lightly, some Saxons hold, while the focus centers on the allegedly backward, reactionary, and pre-existing culture of Saxony. Above all, how have eastern Germans particularly in Saxony been marked by their bitter, abhorrent experience inside the GDR? That may help explain why regional *phobos* is directed not just toward Muslim migrants but transplants from western Germany.

From *Lumpen* to *Schleppers*

Stigmatizing immigrants—and "degenerates" too—is nothing new in the annals of Marxist thought. Karl Marx himself did it. He offered the following definition of the *Lumpenproletariat* (1852) which is both far-ranging and very specific:

> Alongside decayed degenerates with dubious means of subsistence and of dubious origin, alongside ruined and adventurous offshoots of the bourgeoisie, were vagabonds, discharged soldiers, discharged jailbirds, escaped galley slaves, swindlers, charlatans, idlers, pickpockets, tricksters, gamblers, pimps, brothel keepers, porters, literati, organ grinders, rag pickers, knife grinders, tinkers, beggars—in short, the whole indefinite, disintegrated mass, thrown hither and thither.[21]

After tackling the migration crisis through the admission of over one million refugees and economic migrants in 2015–2016, Chancellor Merkel was infamously tagged by outraged anti-immigrant groups as "queen of the *Schleppers*" and at other times "queen of the smugglers."[22]

Policy on asylum seekers has been a contentious subject in most European countries over recent decades. This seems unfair since they, alone among displaced people or economic migrants, express palpable fear of persecution and even death if sent back to their homelands. In a Bertelsmann report on this subject, the debate on admitting genuine refugees rather than economic migrants appeared to prioritize economic migrants for multiple reasons.[23]

EU policy on refugees took early steps toward coordinated action in the mid-1980s after the Schengen regime had taken shape but before the unification of Germany took place.[24] There was a "functional link between the opening of internal borders and the factual free movement of third-country nationals, including refugees and asylum seekers."[25] The Schengen agreement, signed in 1985, contributed to more liberal, generous policies on asylum. For example, in 1983, the European Communities had received just 71,000 asylum applications but after German unification in 1992 applications to Germany alone reached 438,000 out of total EU applications of 674,000. Numbers dropped after that and in 2006 asylum seekers applying to an enlarged EU fell to 180,000. All this dramatically changed during the long summer of migration in 2015.

The rising financial costs of, political backlash to, and security issues involved in accommodating asylum seekers forced policy changes in Germany even if it remained a unique migratory magnet. Already in the 1990s, a spate of racist attacks on hostels housing refugees, mainly in the former GDR, required more realistic asylum policy revisions. The 1997 Amsterdam Treaty, affirming the creation of a common EU pillar of freedom, security, and justice, resulted in refugee policy being treated as a matter of internal security.

Former German Foreign Minister Joschka Fischer outlined an EU Charter of Fundamental Freedoms which contained an explicit right-of-asylum clause. But fearing that such a generous policy would affect it most, federal Germany pressed for and won a veto on the policy. The 2007 Lisbon Treaty adopted qualified majority voting, thereby removing the unanimity principle, for decisions involving asylum policy and control of EU external borders. That gave Germany and its larger partners significantly greater leverage.

If in the 1990s horrific incidents of violence against migrants had brought criminal prosecution against the perpetrators, in the 2010s the focus tended to shift to the behavior of migrants themselves. Setting aside migrants' paperwork irregularities, among the reasons for higher immigrant crime rates was relative deprivation stemming from broad sectors of the immigrant population being denied access to the wealthy material culture of the host country.

With this argument, migrants were shaped less by the need to accept norms and shared values required by social integration, and more by their measurable materialistic gains. It became self-evident that the former GDR, which had experienced lower growth, higher unemployment, and feeble wage growth, became a less attractive place to migrate to than western Germany.

To what extent, then, were eastern German locals more phobic over the presence of migrants even if they arrived in smaller numbers in their region? Was violence against them instigated because migrants were more vulnerable and susceptible to casual, unpremeditated attacks? The response of the FRG was to apply strict limits on free speech and expression throughout the country aimed at reducing right-wing extremism. Thus it remains illegal to produce, distribute, or display symbols from the Nazi period. Holocaust denial has long been established as a criminal offense. Linked to this, the legal concept of *Volksverhetzung* ("rabble-rousing") forbids incitement to hatred: anyone who denigrates an individual or group based on ethnicity or religion or who incites hatred or promotes violence against it, can be sentenced to five years in prison. Furthermore, the Constitutional Court may ban political parties deemed intent on undermining the political order. Eastern Germany was a beneficiary of such anti-extremist policies.

Postwar generations of Germans have been taught to view their country's history and role in Europe critically. They have been socialized into a value system making skepticism a virtue and national pride a vice. This approach was summarized in Jürgen Habermas' *Verfassungspatriotismus*—loyalty to the 1949 FRG constitution. The assurance was that "United Germans are not necessarily nationalist Germans. Big Germany is not necessarily mighty Germany."[26]

Until 1990, east Germany missed out on applying de-nationalizing socialization measures of this kind. To be sure, an economically robust Germany emerged under the cover of Habermasian constitutional patriotism. Observer Wolfgang Streeck argued that German political leaders praise Europe while surreptitiously employing EU structures and institutions to advance German national interests.[27] Russia's war in Ukraine has further unsettled Germany's position in the EU and NATO.

The GDR had been restricted to labor market interactions with Comecon, the Soviet economic bloc established in 1949. This was at a time when, beginning in the late 1950s, the FRG began signing labor contracts with mainly Southern European states. By 1973, twelve percent (some 2.5 million) of the total FRG workforce comprised guest workers; by 1980 it had granted resident alien status (though not asylum) to an additional one million people.

In 1991, foreigners made up eight percent of the workforce in a now unified Germany; only one-quarter of these were European citizens.[28] For the most part, eastern Germany did not absorb its share of this migrant influx.

Unification weakened the status of minorities throughout the country because FRG policies gave economic priority to developing the east rather than continuing to invest in the FRG alone. To be sure, capital flows from western Germany may have unintentionally increased GDR aversion to foreigners since at this early stage of transition (as happens in many other countries) it produced a resentment of outsiders who ought not, it was believed, to have a share in the newfound wealth. As in the run-up to Brexit, they were not found worthy. Ironically, then, the rise of phobic eastern attitudes and a sense of relative deprivation were linked more to western German efforts to level the playing field.

When Syrian refugees turned above all to Germany for asylum in 2015, the country took in the largest number of any EU country though Sweden was not far behind. But simultaneously the FRG had one of Europe's lowest naturalization rates: only about three percent of resident aliens per annum became naturalized.[29] A reform-minded 1999 citizenship law corrected this incongruity and EU citizens now were viewed as co-nativists given similar rights to German citizenship. However, "Ossies"—former east Germans—complained that they were frequently treated as mere second-class denizens.

Stigma has been attached to where in Germany citizens were born. Prejudices against eastern Germans arose when the FRG was proclaimed in 1949. The GDR population was occasionally stigmatized as "Prussians," "advanced Communists," and "Stasi" (state security services). Little bridging capital or shared socialization occurred at that time between the two parts. It was an impeccable reason why the east felt estranged.

Bifurcated Attitudes

Most immigrants are attracted to and settle in urban areas of western Germany where magnets include strong local economies, plentiful jobs, and locals' experience with and acceptance of newcomers. In 2017, about twenty percent of the German population exhibited a migration background.[30] In the east the share was lower: less than 2.5 percent in most regions although in a large city such as Dresden, it reaches over seven percent.

After the 2015 migration emergency had receded, in excess of four million Muslims of different backgrounds were living in Germany. Islam was possibly changing the nature of the German state.[31] But according to the right-wing Gatestone Institute based in New York, the number of Muslims was much higher and Germany's open-door immigration policy created a surge that surpassed six million in 2016. For Gateshead, where former US

Ambassador to the United Nations John Bolton was chairman, Islamicization of Germany was well underway.[32]

A less panic-stricken approach is to claim that over the years a normative turn in the German population has increased immigration-skeptic attitudes. For some observers, "The attitude of Germans toward foreigners is characterized by considerable social distance, in particular in the eastern part of the country." At a time when violence against foreigners was peaking in 1993, greater numbers of both German and foreign respondents expressed a desire to reduce the social distance by living together in shared neighborhoods and supporting cross-cultural bonding.[33]

In the mid-1990s, Chancellor Helmut Kohl introduced the German Deutschmark currency in the east. However, local industries could not compete with those of the west. Unemployment soared from zero to twenty percent in 1996 where it was to remain for a decade. Two million eastern Germans moved to the west in search of jobs. As Paul Hockenos noted, "Rubbing salt in their wounds, many western Germans blamed the easterners for the debacle, implying that they were too dim to master the new system."[34]

Like other communist regimes, the authoritarian legacy of the GDR rewarded conformity and near-blind obedience to narrow-minded dogmatism. Groupthink was regarded as the standard behavior. In making the difficult transition to democracy and the free market, "The West's steamrolling of former East Germany aggravated the easterners' resentment, turning them away from the west's political system and liberal values."[35] If Central European populations largely embraced change and made efforts to integrate into European structures, polls suggested there was deep dissatisfaction in the former GDR with liberal democracy. *Nostalgie* had a specific quality not found elsewhere as the 2003 film *Good Bye, Lenin!* illustrated. Its main character was an older woman persuaded by family and friends that she was still living in her beloved east Germany.

When racist violence against foreigners peaked in eastern Germany in 1993, it was in the context of high unemployment that had reached thirty-five percent. Foreign nationals were warned to stay out of alleged "Nazi zones" in the east. In 2006, Germany's security branch *Bundesverfassungsschutz* reported that Saxony had become the capital of right-wing extremism in all Germany. It reported there were seventy-five right-wing extremists per 100,000 people while the overall Germany average was forty-seven. It was not clear how these calculations were arrived at.

Pro-market reforms of the 2000s launched by Social Democratic Chancellor Gerhard Schröder took forms similar to those adopted by President Bill Clinton and Prime Minister Tony Blair. Seemingly liberal politicians adopted neoliberal policies conflating ideological with economic prescriptions. Economic globalization had thus emerged triumphant from the receding communist abyss. Pro-business policies cut into the safety net offered by the social welfare state, hurting the jobless in the east hardest. Increasing numbers of Muslim immigrants in particular were blamed for both undermining Germany's security and bloating its welfare rolls.

Support for continued immigration weakened further when the EU enlarged its membership to Eastern Europe in 2004 (the island states of Cyprus and Malta were also added to this enlargement) and rebranded the countries as Central Europe. German fears of losing control over their homeland, even when newcomers came from fellow EU member states, were heightened. The stereotype of the disreputable foreigner living illegally in Germany exacerbated the feeling of *Auslanderfeindlichkeit*—animosity toward foreigners. At times Poles were viewed as the stereotypical most *louche* foreigners, not Muslim communities.

Measuring xenophobia was the job of the ALLBUS German public opinion survey. It was designed to uphold rigorous methodological standards, especially with respect to sampling. Based on repeated multi-thematic face-to-face surveys conducted every two years since 1980, and sampling a representative cross-section of the population, it provided an insightful peak into German societal attitudes. The number of respondents varied between 3,000 and 3,500 and were asked both repeated and variable questions. In 1996 and 2006, ALLBUS included a topical module focusing on attitudes toward ethnic minorities.

Since 1990, ALLBUS has asked respondents whether they believe the arrival of certain groups of immigrants in Germany should be unrestricted, limited, or stopped completely. Between 1990 and 2000 a larger number of respondents shifted their views on asylum seekers: they insisted that they should have just restricted entry. Among western German respondents, the proportion over the ten years climbed from fifty to seventy-three percent. Strikingly, for the year 2000, it was even slightly more phobic in the west than among the supposedly more fearful eastern Germans (sixty-nine percent).

By 2006, seventy-three percent in both west and east answered that "immigration should be restricted" for asylum seekers. Differences between the two were marginal: fourteen percent in the west and sixteen percent in the east agreed that "immigration should be stopped completely." Only thirteen percent in the west and eleven percent in the east still thought asylum seekers should enjoy unrestricted rights to settle in Germany.

In assessing how markedly the lifestyles of certain minority groups living in Germany differed from the German one, nearly half of ALLBUS respondents claimed that Turks somewhat or very much differed from

Germans; only the choice of "asylum seekers" was ranked more non-German in their lifestyles. Regarding the marriage of an ethnic German with a member of one of these groups, asylum seekers and Turks were neck-and-neck in terms of how unpleasant for a German respondent the prospect of such a marriage might be. To be sure, ten times more respondents in the west strongly disagreed that endogamous marriages were preferable; in the east, the ratio was closer to 3:1.[36]

The inescapable finding was that the average German showed more dislike of groups coming from far away, or who were Muslim, than those with cultural affinities: Italians, German speakers from Eastern Europe, and Jews. Germans appear therefore not to be exceptional or distinctive in the nature of their phobias when compared to France or other European receiving societies (Figure 3.1).

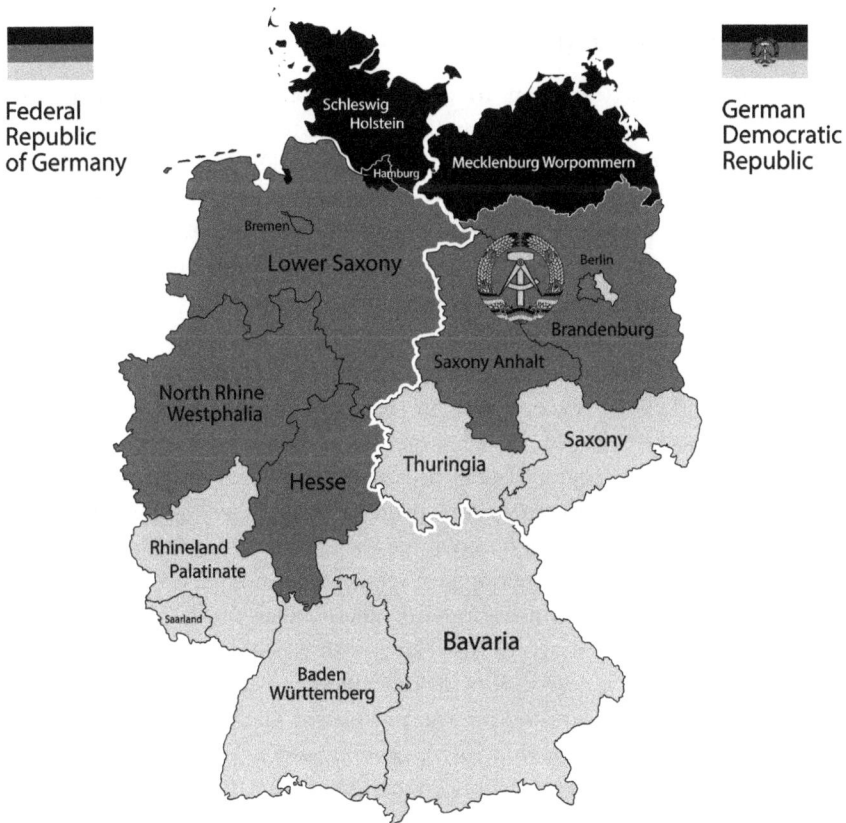

Figure 3.1 A map of divided Germany before the 3 October 1990 "Unification Treaty" came into force. Five eastern *Länder* had made up the GDR.

After the 2015 migration influx, Chancellor Merkel became an easy target for xenophobic attitudes. Widespread opposition to multicultural policies among nativists plus the lack of belonging felt by immigrant communities combined to lower public opinion support—the proverbial canary in the coalmine signaled xenophobic danger. Not only public opinion but electoral trends changed too, evidenced by German voters giving Merkel's party its worst drubbing in the 2017 elections since the founding of the FRG. Although she remained ahead of the field with thirty-three percent of the total vote, the swing against her was more than eight percent. The biggest winner was the AfD, going from 4.7 to 12.6 percent, and from no Bundestag seats to ninety-four.

The longstanding Chancellor did not contest the 2021 federal elections which offered a mixed result with the Greens being the party gaining an increased number of seats. The anti-immigrant AfD made relatively few gains.

Saxony's Exceptionalism

Eastern Germany's transition to a market economy has largely proved successful. Its median income per capita now approaches the EU27 average and Saxony is the most prosperous of the five new post-GDR federal *Länder*. But for one academic, "despite almost 30 years of unification, the income differentials between east and west Germany prevail and have solidified, working hours are longer in the east and many people have to leave their family and friends to find jobs in the west—all of which many consider to be humiliating."[37] Authoritarian tendencies have been shaping the region and civil society, political parties, and ministerial responsibility are regarded as less anchored there.

Saxony had been exceptional in serving as the setting for racist PEGIDA demonstrations in Dresden and other anti-refugee demonstrations in other cities of the region. Some politicians defended liberal democratic values but in media discourses the protests staged by right-wing groups indicated a blockage or erosion of democratic values. What were the reasons why Saxony has become exceptional in recurring phobias?

A direct cause of demonstrations in Saxony was the fatal knife attack in 2020 on a German citizen by a Syrian youth who had arrived during the migrant crisis of 2015; it was officially described as a jihadist terror act. The AfD expressed understanding for the protesters: an AfD parliamentarian and Dresden judge insisted that the AfD remained a "constitutional party" and recognized the state's monopoly on the use of force. But local anti-refugee networks staged a rally attended by some 6,000 people and among them were "many so-called ordinary citizens who expressed their anger about the killing and Germany's asylum policy."[38] On the back of these citizen protests, a right-wing extremist group called "Revolution Chemnitz" was charged with organizing a civil war-like rebellion in Berlin.[39]

Chancellor Merkel's spokesperson asserted that these events should not lead to vigilante justice. But the pro-Chemnitz movement unfurled a banner with a slogan from early twentieth-century poet Anton Günther which read: "German and free we aim to be."[40] The bold message could also mean "hands off eastern Germany." Merkel herself said that the protests that gripped Chemnitz following the fatal stabbing were a reason to do everything possible to make "the anti-migrant AfD as small as possible." She also called for greater compassion for the concerns of Germans living in the former east.[41]

A number of reports examined the nature of social conflicts in Saxony. In 2017, government-commissioned researchers concluded that cultural holdovers from communism—not just economic factors—encouraged right-wing radicalism. The Göttingen Institute for Democracy Studies (reporting at the request of the Ministry of Economy) also singled out western German influence on the region. Nevertheless, few challenged the consensus that people from the former GDR were more prone to holding far-right views and acting violently on them.[42]

The Göttingen Institute report highlighted how the east German population had been socialized in a way so as to exhibit an "exaggerated need for harmony, purity, and order," as well as to assert "collective, overwhelmingly positive, and ethnically pure identity"—in other words, *sangre puro*. It pinpointed a "selective culture of memory" in which "east Germans repress negative memories of the communist past, fail to come to terms with the legacy of Nazi anti-Semitism, and tend to blame foreigners for social and economic problems." In sum, the GDR was deemed to be a closed, ethnically homogeneous society that hosted relatively few migrants and had much less ethnic and cultural diversity than other parts of Germany.

Claims that the east has served as a cradle of xenophobia are regularly underscored in the west. Immediately after the migration crisis, in 2016 the AfD had surged into regional legislatures, initially in the east and then in the west. In places with small refugee numbers such as the eastern states of Mecklenburg, West Pomerania, and Saxony-Anhalt, the AfD had become the second strongest party.

The AfD position articulated by its deputy leader, Beatrix von Storch, also a member of the German Bundestag, was stereotypical: Muslims have been subjected to fundamentalist teaching through globalized infrastructures, for example, mosques financed and constructed by Saudi Arabia and Turkey. These mosques were designed to wage holy war on Christians and Jews and therefore posed a direct threat to the country. Von Storch added that Muslim associations in Germany needed to distance themselves from the radical parts of Sharia law. She did accept that a majority of Muslims represent "liberal Muslims."[43]

Ahead of the 2021 federal elections, AfD campaigned on the slogan "Germany—but Normal." Many voters still regarded its manifesto as too far right. In the federal elections, it saw a dip in the national vote share—10.3 percent, down from 12.6 percent in 2017. Nonetheless, the party recorded strong performances throughout eastern Germany and emerged as the largest party in the states of Saxony and Thuringia.

In addressing the Thucydidean notion of *phobos*, the Göttingen Institute study singled out immigrant-hostile attitudes in Saxony exemplified by the cities and towns that staged demonstrations and resorted to violence. A counterargument made by nativists was that reducing refugee numbers—perhaps even a total ban on them for a certain period of time—needed to be implemented across cities and towns in Saxony, Saxony-Anhalt, and Brandenburg, giving locals breathing space.[44]

Can we conclude that Saxony is now regarded as the core of Germany's *phobos*? We can. In 2018, Freiberg passed a resolution barring further refugees from arriving in the city for the following four years. The practical reasoning cited by its mayor extended from the city's inability to ensure incoming residents their legal rights, to enforcing mandatory school attendance in daycare facilities.[45]

Cottbus too was regarded as a source of anti-Muslim prejudice. Confrontations between neo-Nazis and mostly Syrian refugees occurred in 2018. Its mayor insisted he wished to keep Cottbus free of the radical right but refugees had continued to arrive in the town. The suggestion was made that a German city of 200,000 would have to be built each year to accommodate migrant numbers.

At one of the demonstrations, a retiree claimed that this was his first attendance at a protest meeting because he felt that Germans now needed to feel safe in their own country. He alluded to incidents of teenage refugees threatening German residents with knives. One sign at that demonstration labeled Islamification as a cancerous ulcer posing the greatest threat to humanity. The event resembled past PEGIDA demonstrations in Dresden.[46]

In Cottbus foreigners here made up 8.5 percent of its population of 100,000 residents (below the national average of 11.5 percent), but it became the home of radical-right movements in Germany. The city experienced severe unemployment after the fall of the Wall. Its mayor sought to increase employment for social workers in schools, as education guidance counselors, and for consultation services for immigrants. But ultimately Cottbus claimed that it could not accept any more refugees, especially when acts of violence between refugees and Germans, instigated by both parties, had grown. The exasperated mayor claimed: "we cannot handle this anymore."[47]

In turn, the AfD's state leader from Saxony-Anhalt condemned Turkish groups which he linked to the World War I Turkish genocide of Armenians in 1915. He alleged that "These spice traders are responsible for their own genocide of 1.5 million people and now want to tell us how to deal with history and nationalism." Adding insult to injury, the AfD head labeled Turks in Germany as "these camel riders." In response, the head of the German Turkish Association remarked: "This shows the level of the AfD which has no inhibitions about their discriminatory and racist messages they are promoting."[48]

An interested participant-observer in the debate about Islamophobia in Germany was Turkish President Recep Tayyip Erdoğan. He had long claimed that Islamophobia was an inherent evil in the West and was responsible for influencing negative German attitudes toward Turks. Erdoğan had made regular visits to Germany and canvased Turkish voters who generally supported him. In 2018, he renewed his attacks against Western Islamophobia: "There are efforts to degrade and defame Islam, which is the only religion that offers genuine solutions to the modern world's problems."[49]

Erdoğan reminded Europe that over twenty-five million Muslims were living on the continent. He urged Turkish citizens to learn the language of the place where they were living and to integrate so as to gain greater influence. But he added: "Never forget your mother tongue, your beliefs, and solidarity—your fatherland is always there for you."[50]

Turks have represented the primary target of xenophobia because they represent the largest Muslim minority in Germany. But other groups, particularly those who have claimed refugee status after 2015, have remained under public scrutiny. In August 2018, marchers stormed the streets of Chemnitz chanting "We are the people." A mantra originally used to protest against former communist east Germany, it had now been adopted by the radical right.

Whether in Dresden, Cottbus, or other municipalities in the east, some regional journalists in Saxony equate negative reporting about it with "Saxony bashing." One writer inveighed how "We shouldn't forget the transfer of ideas, elites, and money from western German neo-Nazi circles into the east after reunification in 1990." It was pointed out that AfD party leaders Alexander Gauland and Björn Höcke "are western German imports who found fertile soil in certain parts of eastern Germany."

The chicken-or-egg quandary comes into play when examining a regional phobia: what impact has extensive western German influence had on east Germany's transition politics including the spread of Islamophobia? Linked to this, how likely is it that east German residents sometimes feel they are being colonized by western Germany? The answers remain complicated over thirty years since German unification.

Are Russians Colluding?

No explanation for the rise of phobias in Europe is complete without invoking Russian meddling in various parts of the continent. Indications have shown that the kremlin supports anti-establishment parties and right-wing movements in various European states in order to destabilize the countries they are based in. Especially following its attack on Ukraine, this is seen as part of a hybrid war that Russia has locked into with Western states.

According to US newsmagazine *Time*, the AfD estimated that about a third of its support came from Russian-speaking voters who settled in Germany after the 1980s. They claim they now make up as much as five percent of the population. Even if this is exaggerated, core constituents of the AfD are themselves immigrants and at times in the Russian diaspora. They too "cannot believe what is happening to this country."[51] One study carried out in 2019 reported the following:

> Surveys show that the far-right Alternative for Germany (AfD) party performs notably better in areas that are densely populated by Russian-born Germans. This is no small advantage—there are currently 3,166,000 migrants from ex-Soviet states living in Germany, or some 3.8% of the country's population. The majority of them are so-called ethnic Germans who moved to Germany from Eastern Europe in the decades following World War II. This group, some 2.5 million people, were given German passports.[52]

Results from places like Bielefeld, Koblenz, Duisburg, and other German cities having significant Russian-speaking communities provide evidence of their distinct voting patterns.

In addition, according to Germany's official statistics office, between 2014 and 2016 "Russia annexed Crimea and pro-Russian rebels went to war in Ukraine's East, while millions of migrants triggered a crisis in Europe. Support for the AfD and far-right extremists, who urge tight migration control and removing the sanctions on Russia has gone up."[53]

Until the full-scale war began in February 2022, Russian state media in Germany confirmed that the kremlin had made use of its soft power toolkit to choose the instrument that best fits its target. Through social media and news outlets sponsored by the Russian state, viewers were provided with alternative views of German reality. Arguments were made that life under Chancellor Merkel had become dangerous, depraved, and undemocratic.

The AfD party's first success came in elections in Berlin in 2016 when it received fourteen percent of the vote, a mind-numbing result for a far-right movement in one of Germany's most liberal cities. Russia's hand was purportedly visible here: the party's share in Russian-speaking neighborhoods in the east of the capital, such as Marzahn-Hellersdorf, was twenty-three percent.

The Ukraine refugee crisis causing millions of emigrants to move to CEE and Western countries following the 2022 Russian "special military operation" yet again tested German welcoming attitudes toward arriving migrants. It has also tested attitudes toward Russia. Reports indicated that Saxony's support leaned toward the kremlin; one poll found that sixty-eight percent of Saxony respondents claimed that their opinion of Russia had not changed since the invasion and that close to forty percent asserted their perceptions that Putin had not changed. Those views were generally sympathetic to the Russian state.

Saxony's premier, Michael Kretschmer, from the Christian Democratic Union (Merkel's party), prided himself in having not joined the AfD. Still, "Many in Saxony, where Putin cut his teeth as an intelligence officer in the 1980s and returned in 2009 to accept the 'Order of Saxon Gratitude,' are reluctant to pick sides in a new version of the Cold War." From 1985 to 1990 the KGB stationed Putin in Dresden. The *Weltanschauung* of the time was sufficiently influential that the experience of authoritarian life in the GDR transferred over to east German understanding of the Russian model, not a fear of it. What is more, in this region "not all, but a large part, of the population took to the streets for prosperity and not for democratic values." This point can easily be dismissed but it needs further investigation.

Fondness even for a Soviet troop presence in the east became the "basis for an intense nostalgia or sentimentality." The 150,000-strong far-right Free Saxony movement, advocating independence from Berlin, insisted that the EU had provoked Russia into starting the war in Ukraine. The EU had also waged its own war on the "wallets of its citizens." The realism of taking a conciliatory approach to the kremlin was evidenced in 2021 when the Saxony-Anhalt *Land* imported eighty-four percent of oil and gas from Russia compared to a third nationally.[54]

In this chapter, I have argued that *phobos* gripped Saxony's regional identity when, in particular, it was threatened by the abrupt arrival of many Muslim migrants in 2015. The culmination of right-wing rallies, protests, and violence reached its height and then receded from view. At what point might *phobos*, then, be replaced by *hypopsia*—Thucydides' word for a mistrust of a longer-term process leading to the erosion, in this case, of regional identity? It is near impossible to say when a *caesura* occurred. "Feelings" polls based on citizens' sentiments are rarely administered and they may be highly inaccurate. The fact is that for a considerable time, *phobos* shaped Saxony's regional identity and inscribed in it a siege mentality.

Postscriptum

What explains the centuries-long passage from the spirit-lifting music of Johann Sebastian Bach in the eighteenth century to radical-right Saxon politics and extremism in the twenty-first century? For the Baroque composer,

"Harmony is next to Godliness"

Notes

1 Annette Jünemann, Nicolas Fromm, and Nikolas Scherer (eds.), *Fortress Europe? Challenges and Failures of Migration and Asylum Policies* (Wiesbaden: Springer VS, 2017).

2 Michala Clante Bendixen, "Denmark has Now become the First Country in Europe to Revoke Residence Permits for Syrian Refugees," *Politico.eu*, March 10, 2021. https://www.politico.eu/article/denmark-has-gone-far-right-on-refugees/.

3 German General Social Survey-GESIS (ALLBUS), https://www.cen.uni-hamburg.de/en/icdc/data/society/allbus.html.

4 R+V Insurance Fear Index, in Ralf Bosen, "What Do Germans Fear the Most?" *DW.com*, September 9, 2021, https://www.dw.com/en/what-do-germans-fear-the-most/a-59129913.

5 Aleksandra Lewicki and Yasemin Shooman, "Building a New Nation: Anti-Muslim Racism in Post-unification Germany," *Journal of Contemporary European Studies* (2019). See also Aleksandra Lewicki, "Race, Islamophobia and the Politics of Citizenship in Post-unification Germany," *Patterns of Prejudice* 52, no. 5 (2018), 496–512, https://doi.org/10.1080/0031322X.2018.1502236.

6 Ivan Krastev and Stephen Holmes, "Imitation and Its Discontents," *Journal of Democracy* 29, no. 3 (July 2018), 118, https://muse.jhu.edu/article/698922.

7 Maximilian Popp, Andreas Wassermann, and Steffen Winter, "What's Wrong with Saxony? A Search for the Roots of Fear and Racism," *Der Spiegel*, February 25, 2016, https://www.spiegel.de/international/germany/saxony-xenophobia-under-the-microscope-a-1079062.html.

8 Ivan Krastev, "The Big Question: What is the Root Cause of Rising Illiberalism in Central and Eastern Europe?" *National Endowment for Democracy*, July 16, 2018, https://www.ned.org/the-big-question-what-is-the-root-cause-of-rising-illiberalism-in-central-and-eastern-europe/.

9 Krastev and Holmes, "Imitation," 118.

10 Popp, Wassermann, and Winter, "What's Wrong with Saxony?"

11 Jan Zielonka, *Kontrrewolucja: liberalna Europa w odwrocie* ("Counterrevolution: liberal Europe backwards") (Warsaw: PWN, 2018), 46, 57. See also Roman Kuźniar, *Zmierzch liberalnego porządku międzynarodowego 2011–2021* ("The decline of the liberal international order") (Warsaw: Wydawnictwo Naukowe Scholar, 2022).

12 Zielonka, *Kontrrewolucja*, 33.

13 Zielonka, *Kontrrewolucja*, 11.

14 Zielonka, *Kontrrewolucja*, 203.

15 Witold Kieżun, *Patologia Transformacji* ("The pathology of transformation") (Warsaw: Poltext, 2013); see interview with Rafał Woś, "Przemiany gospodarcze w Polsce?" ("Economic changes in Poland?"), *Gazeta prawna*, November 8, 2013, http://biznes.gazetaprawna.pl/artykuly/744702,przemiany-gospodarcze-w-polsce-to-byla-neokolonizacja-jak-w-afryce-zostalismy-oszukani.html.

16 Bartłomiej Radziejewski, "III RP, czyli nowe kondominium Zachodu" ("The Third Republic, that is, the West's new condominium"), *Nowa Konfederacja*, October 10, 2013, https://nowakonfederacja.pl/iii-rp-czyli-nowe-kondominium-zachodu/.

17 Karl R. Popper, *The Open Society and Its Enemies* (Princeton, NJ: Princeton University Press, 2013).

18 James Jackson, "Germany's Far-right AfD Aims at a Forgotten Demographic," *DW.com*, October 27, 2019, https://www.dw.com/en/germanys-far-right-afd-aims-at-a-forgotten-demographic/a-50993725.

19 Ben Knight, "Why Young Eastern German Voters Support the Far-right AfD," *DW.com*, June 11. 2021, https://www.dw.com/en/why-young-eastern-german-voters-support-the-far-right-afd/a-57847028.

20 Knight, "Why Young Eastern German Voters."

21 Jean-Claude Bourdin, "Marx and the Lumpenproletariat," *Actuel Marx* 54, no. 2, (2013), 39–55.

22 Patricia Anne Simpson, "'Mama Merkel' and 'Mutti-Multikulti': The Perils of Governing While Female," in *Realities and Fantasies of German Female Leadership: From Maria Antonia of Saxony to Angela Merkel*, eds. Elisabeth Krimmer and Simpson (Rochester, NY: Camden House, 2019), 312.

23 Matthias M. Mayer (ed.), *Faire Fachkräftezuwanderung nach Deutschland: Grundlagen und Handlungsbedarf im Kontext eines Einwanderungsgesetzes* ("Fair immigration of skilled workers to Germany: Basics and need for action in the context of immigration law") (Gütersloh: Bertelsmann Stiftung, 2017).

24 Robert Miles and Dietrich Thränhardt (eds.), *Migration and European Integration: The Dynamics of Inclusion and Exclusion* (London: Pinter, 1995).

25 Monika Bösche, "Trapped Inside the European Fortress? Germany and European Union Asylum and Refugee Policy," in *Germany's EU Policy on Asylum and Defence: De-Europeanization by Default?*, ed. Gunther Hellmann (London: Palgrave, 2006), 42.

26 Niall Ferguson, "Uber the Hill: Why the New Germany's a Weakling," *New Republic* 204, no. 5 (February 4, 1991), 8.

27 Zachary Murphy King, "Germany's European Empire: An Interview with Wolfgang Streek," *Jacobin Magazine* (August 20, 2018), https://www.jacobinmag.com/2018/08/wolfgang-streeck-interview-germany-european-union.

28 Ray Rist, *Guestworkers in Germany: The Prospects for Pluralism* (New York: Praeger, 1978). See also, Ulrich Herbert, *A History of Foreign Labor in Germany, 1880–1980* (Ann Arbor: University of Michigan Press, 1990).

29 Gerhard de Rham, "Naturalization: the Politics of Citizenship Acquisition," in *The Political Rights of Migrant Workers in Western Europe*, ed. Zig Henry Layton (Newbury Park, CA: Sage, 1990), 182.

30 "Migration background" refers to: (a) those who immigrated to Germany since 1950; (b) those who were born in Germany as foreigners; and (c) those who have at least one parent who immigrated to Germany since 1950 or was born in Germany as foreigner.

31   Nina Haase and Sumi Somaskanda, "Is Islam Changing Germany?" *DW.com*, July 7, 2017, http://www.dw.com/en/is-islam-changing-germany/a-39076179.

32   On the Gatestone Institute, see Lee Fang, "Islamophobic U.S. Megadonor Fuels German Far-right Party with Viral Fake News," *The Intercept*, September 23, 2017.

33   Ferdinand Böltken, "Social Distance and Physical Proximity: Day-to-Day Attitudes and Experiences of Foreigners and Germans Living in the Same Residential Areas," in *Germans or Foreigners? Attitudes Toward Ethnic Minorities in Post-Reunification Germany*, eds. Richard Alba, Peter Schmidt, and Martina Wasmer (London: Palgrave, 2003), 252.

34   Paul Hockenos, "East Germans And the Far-right AfD," *Social Europe*, October 5, 2017, https://www.socialeurope.eu/east-germans-far-right-afd.

35   Hockenos, "East Germans."

36   German General Social Survey (ALLBUS), "Cumulated ALLBUS 1980–2004," V196–V199, V202, 172–175, 178.

37   Matthias Ecke, "What Does Chemnitz Tell us About the Growth of Right-wing Radicalism in Germany?" *Social Europe*, September 5, 2018, https://socialeurope.eu/what-does-chemnitz-tell-us-about-the-growth-of-right-wing-radicalism-in-germany.

38   Ecke, "Chemnitz."

39   Lena Kampf, Sebastian Pittelkow, Annette Ramelsberger, and Katja Riedel, " 'Revolution Chemnitz:' Terror-Anklage gegen Chemnitzer Rechtsextreme" ("Terror Charges against Right-wing Extremists in Chemnitz") *Süddeutsche Zeitung*, June 25, 2019, https://www.sueddeutsche.de/politik/revolution-chemnitz-anklage-1.4493938.

40   Charlotte Chelson-Pill, "Fresh Dueling Protests Break out in Chemnitz," *DW.com*, August 27, 2018, https://www.dw.com/en/fresh-dueling-protests-break-out-in-chemnitz/a-45242473.

41   "Merkel Urges Understanding for Eastern Germans," *DW.com*, August 29, 2018, https://www.dw.com/en/merkel-urges-understanding-for-eastern-germans/a-45684750.

42   "Study Links Far-right Extremism and Eastern German Mentality," *DW.com*, May 18, 2017; the Saxony defender is Michael Lühmann; http://www.dw.com/en/study-links-far-right-extremism-and-eastern-german-mentality/a-38892657.

43   "Beatrix von Storch and the Muslims," *Zeit Online*, http://www.zeit.de/politik/deutschland/2018-04/beatrix-von-storch-afd-islamdebatte-muslime-5vor8.

44   "Wir haben Städte, die sagen: Das geht einfach nicht mehr" ("We have Cities that are Saying: 'This is Not Okay Anymore'"), *Die Welt*, February 1, 2018, https://www.welt.de/politik/deutschland/article173100354/Fluechtlinge-Wir-haben-jetzt-Staedte-die-sagen-Das-geht-einfach-nicht-mehr.html.

45   " 'Wir saufen ab': Freiberg stoppt Zuzug von Flüchtlingen" ("We're drowning: Freiberg stops the influx of refugees"), *Junge Freiheit*, February 2, 2018, https://jungefreiheit.de/politik/deutschland/2018/wir-saufen-ab-freiberg-stoppt-zuzug-von-fluechtlingen/.

46   "Entsteht in Cottbus ein zweites Dresden?" ("Is Cottbus Becoming a Second Dresden?") *Märkische Allgemeine*, February 4, 2018, http://www.maz-online.de/Brandenburg/Tag-der-Gegensaetze-Demos-fuer-und-gegen-Fluechtlinge-in-Cottbus.

47   "Cottbus: Hier wohnt der Fremdenhass" ("Cottbus: Home of Xenophobia"), *Abendzeitung-Muenchen*, February 2, 2018, http://www.abendzeitung-muenchen.de/inhalt.az-vor-ort-cottbus-hier-wohnt-der-fremdenhass.04e3a3b6-c506-40d8-b752-d20a000a362f.html.

48 "Poggenburg beschimpft über Türken" ("Poggenburg Complains about the Turkish"), *Bild*, February 2, 2018, https://www.bild.de/regional/dresden/alternative-fuer-deutschland/poggenburg-beschimpft-tuerken-54814100.bild.html.

49 "Erdoğan Blasts West over Islamophobia," *Hürriyet*, April 16, 2018, http://www.hurriyetdailynews.com/erdogan-urges-new-foundation-for-world-peace-130384.

50 "Erdoğan Implores Turkish in Germany to Gain Political Influence," *Faz.net* (*Frankurter Algemeine*), October 4, 2018, http://www.faz.net/aktuell/politik/ausland/erdogan-fordert-von-den-tuerken-in-deutschland-mehr-einfluss-zu-nehmen-15536007.html.

51 Simon Shuster, "How Russian Voters Fueled the Rise of Germany's Far-right," *Time Magazine*, September 25, 2017, http://time.com/4955503/germany-elections-2017-far-right-russia-angela-merkel/.

52 Nikita Jolkver, "Are Russian Germans the Backbone of the Populist AfD?" *DW.com*, April 14, 2019, https://www.dw.com/en/are-russian-germans-the-backbone-of-the-populist-afd/a-48321687.

53 Jolkver, "Are Russian Germans."

54 Isaac Stanley-Becker and Vanessa Guinan-Bank, "Russia Finds Sympathy in Germany's East, Putin's Old Stomping Ground," *Washington Post*, April 15, 2022, https://www.washingtonpost.com/world/2022/04/15/germany-ukraine-communist-east-russia/. See Tobias Winzer, "So hat sich das Russland-Bild der Sachsen verändert" ("This is How the Saxons' Image of Russia has Changed"), *Sachsische.de*, April 7, 2022, https://www.saechsische.de/ukraine-konflikt/so-hat-sich-das-russland-bild-der-sachsen-veraendert-5661688-plus.html.

Chapter 4

ETHNIC FEAR: RUSSIA'S MANAGEMENT OF MIGRATION

Orrodia as *Explanans*

The claim in this chapter is that the Russian state has experienced Thucydides' notion of *orrodia* reflected in the speeches of supreme political leader Vladimir Putin. As noted in Chapter 1, *orrodia* was used by the Greek historian only five times in his writing of *History of the Peloponnesian War*. They subsumed quoted speeches by Greek political leaders concerning a looming state of dread, apprehension, and anxiety. This fear was connected to becoming outnumbered by an opposing side—and therefore descending into the status of a minority group—a fair translation of *orrodia*'s connotation. So although it is very rarely used today, the term can be interchangeable with fear. Most importantly for this book, it is a way to explain policymaking in the kremlin.

We can take this notion a few steps further and suggest other interpretations: "The Greek *orrodeo* (to fear) and *orrodia* (fear, anxiety) lead us through the initial Ionian *arr* to *arretos*, which is translated as 'dangerous' or 'terrifying' as well as 'unsaid,' 'undescribed,' 'immeasurable,' or 'mysterious.'"[1] Like using an advanced thesaurus, *orrodia* can subsume other closely related concepts.

Of the globe's many political leaders, Putin stands out and invites us to deconstruct his discursive practices. The kremlin ruler's place on the world stage has been unique, highly contentious, and even abominable. His speeches and reference points capture the attention of Russia's political class and much of the rest of the world; it held its breath to hear what other statements came from Russia's calculating ruler. Like scholars, journalists, pundits, bloggers, bots, and average citizens looking for the deeper significance of his insinuations, world leaders took notice of Putin as a self-appointed orator-in-chief.

This chapter singles out one policy area where *orrodia*—Putin's cited remarks that may elicit dread—is examined: migration. As in many other states, migration policies may provoke resentment by their skeptics and encouragement for diehard liberals. Under Putin, the hypothesis put to the test inquires how his counterintuitive policies on migration, for a short period of time at least, pointed to the kremlin's embrace of a liberal approach. In effect, it sought to welcome migrants not just those from neighboring states who were typically Orthodox but those having Muslim beliefs. The majority of migrants originated in former Soviet space, principally from Central Asia, and marked a contrast to attitudes in Western states where such groups evoked anxiety and suspicion.

Did long-serving President Putin acquiesce in, if at times not clearly advocating for, forms of multinationalism, multi-ethnicity, multi-confessionalism, and even perhaps Western-style multiculturalism? Without question its features border on different interpretations and explanations. Putin's fantastical imaginary—or was it stark Realism?—pictures a Russian world as fraternal, interconnected yet aggressive. For Russian literature specialist Elif Batuman,

> The Russian World imagines a transnational Russian civilization, one extending even beyond the "triune Russian nation" of "Great Russia" (Russia), "Little Russia" (Ukraine), and "White Russia" (Belarus); it is united by Eastern Orthodoxy, by the Russian language, by the "culture" of Alexander Pushkin, Leo Tolstoy, and Fyodor Dostoyevsky—and, when necessary, by air strikes.[2]

The irony is that if these policy initiatives backed by the President were the case, did it promise to put an end to Russia as an exclusively ethnic nation and lead to its diversification?

Or have Putin's discourses recognized just the opposite phenomenon—that Russia's empire by its very nature was always diverse, made up of different nations and nationalities, ethnicities, and religions? If that were the case, then we are led to the conclusion that Russia, at least for particular eras in its history, was not an imperium or exclusive ethnic state or ethnocracy but a fairly open society. That would confound many of our impressions of the country's past.

Orrodia, understood in my Russian case as assertions of fear that Russia is threatened with being downgraded to one of many ethnic communities embedded in a multinational society, may have occurred when it confronted a demographic threat, as in the last years of the Soviet Union and in the recent period. Russians were about to fall below fifty percent of the USSR's total population. This evolving threat came about when in 1991 Russia was on the brink of becoming a minority nation faced with a majority of non-Russian populations. This aroused dread among many Russians. Even its then President, Boris Yeltsin, successfully overthrew the Soviet leadership headed by Communist Party Secretary Mikhail Gorbachev and proclaimed a country where "Russia for the Russians" became the mantra.

Putin's public statements on migration are counterbalanced by an examination of the other side of the equation: how did average Russians react to his policies and shifts? Were citizens filled with trepidation when more liberal migration policies might produce "a nation no more"—the loss of an empire no longer controlled by ethnic Russians?

Migration experts often identify the pushes and pulls of migration politics including citizens' reactions to changing approaches. I follow their research and suggest a feedback loop that can explain where Putin was taking migration policy and if it could eventually produce a backlash. Migration slipped to becoming a less important subject with the outbreak of the COVID pandemic in 2020 placing the country in uncertain times. Then the full-scale war on Ukraine in 2022 was launched, creating new reasons to be fearful, whether opposing Putin's war, worrying about conscription and the country's economic isolation, or the unclear future of the international order. Migration policy itself became infected with multiple ambiguities.

Emergent Immigrant Society

The Soviet Union crumbled in December 1991 when the presidents of three republics—the Russian Federation, Ukraine, and Belorussia—signed the Belovezha agreement in a primeval forest remote from their capital cities marking an end to its existence. Russia had been on the brink of becoming a non-ethnically Russian country in the USSR, a fear that many Russians had become conscious of. According to two specialists on Soviet demography who analyzed the 1989 Soviet census, "Ethnic Russians composed 50.8 percent of the population in 1989 and they will fall below 50 percent of the Soviet population before the middle of the 1990s."[3] The once mono-national mono-ethnic state was about to vanish.

The psychological impact of the Soviet Union reverting to a country with ethnic Russians as minority may have contributed to its disintegration. No doubt many other reasons explain the Soviet demise. The resultant Russian Federation bore the same wedding-cake structure as its predecessor. According to the amended Russian Constitution approved in March 2014, there are eighty-five federal subjects of which twenty-two are largely ethnically defined republics and the remainder are made up of krais, oblasts, three cities of federal importance, and autonomous oblasts and okrugs. After the Soviet collapse, ethnic Russians made up eighty-seven percent of the population but according to census figures and other data that proportion began to dwindle: it dropped to eighty-one percent in 2010 and seventy-seven percent in 2017.

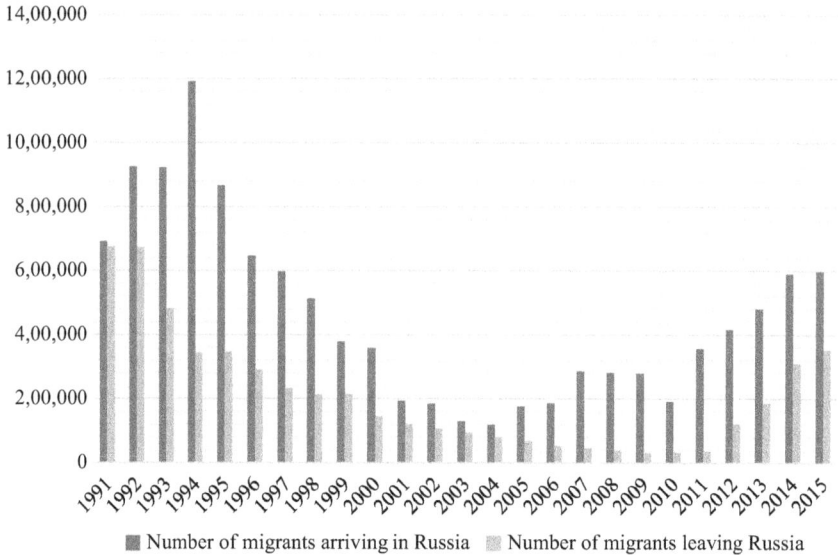

Figure 4.1 Migration to and from the Russian Federation, 1991–2015.

Source: Data from the Federal State Statistics Service (Russian Federation), www.gks.ru/wps/wcm/connect/rosstat_main/rosstat/ru/statistics/population/demography/#.

Immigration numbers, not Russia's birth rates, became the crucial reason for securing population size in the Russian Federation (Figure 4.1). For a time, depopulation was stemmed as in-migration increased. It included labor and construction workers brought in from former Soviet republics to prepare for sporting mega-events such as the Sochi Winter Games in 2016 and the FIFA World Cup in 2018.

Putin was behind helping transform Russia's shifting demographics. But in doing so he faced risks in weakening the hold of the ethnic majority and undermining the fragile political stability in place since he assumed power in 2020. The question arises: Did a latently authoritarian, nationalist leader help liberalize immigration policy?

A look back at the Soviet experience provided answers. Russian migration specialist Caress Schenk introduced an otherwise overlooked observation; she argued that "while the Soviet Union was famed for closed borders, Russia has some of the most open borders in the world." Much in-migration to Russia was visa-free and road-and-rail networks made migration easier to carry out. Nevertheless, for Schenk, "Like other major countries of immigration, Russia struggles to balance the economic advantages of migration with public anxieties."[4]

Among other explanations for keeping migration across state borders simple was the claim that "What is different about Russia is the degree of flexibility that is present in adapting to changes in the migration system." Furthermore, "In Russia, migrants have agency not least because of the opportunities provided by corruption." In sum, the exceptional aspect of twenty-first-century in-migration was the "centrality of informal strategies in migration management practices."[5] Even if Putin's policies were liberal on migration, then, other more important factors were at work. Ancillary factors could also slow down or halt migration. COVID effectively put an end to the in-migration wave. The war against Ukraine and the demographic chaos it created skewed in-migration. How many Russian speakers who were Ukrainian citizens were prepared to leave for Russia? How many others were forced to leave?

The war forced over four million Ukrainian citizens, mostly women and children, to flee to Western countries including, at its height, approximately half to neighboring Poland. Others transited through Poland to Germany— taxi services for this purpose were waiting on the border. Human smuggling led to more and more incidences of trafficking of women and girls.

Which were the push-and-pull factors behind in-migration to Russia and did Putin contribute to them? As background, in her book simply titled *Russia*, British specialist Vera Tolz outlined key features of the country and its multi-ethnic character that made it exceptional:

Russia differed from France, England and Germany in several ways. In addition to the persistence of autocracy, the lateness of industrialization and the delay with the emancipation of the serfs, which set Russia apart from its West European models, it was also a land-based empire, in which the political and geographical boundaries between the metropolis and the colonies were far from clear.[6]

Tolz offered the realistic assessment that "Within the empire, some non-Russian areas became more closely embedded in Russian national mythology than the others." Of great importance was that "Russia's multi-ethnic nature was proclaimed to be a sign of Russia's uniqueness and superiority." Intellectuals viewed Russia as "preserving a unique multi-ethnic state, profoundly different from the West European empires." Indeed, "the empire was the same as the Russian nation-state, by arguing that in the era of modern nationalism, Russians continued to think in pre-national terms and by referring to their alleged fear of reliving the troubles of the medieval period."[7] This was a reference to the Time of Troubles in the sixteenth century when no ethnic Russian ruler was able to take power in the country until the first of the Romanov Dynasty, Mikhail, did in 1613.

Peculiarities were noteworthy in comprehending Russianness even as the country was transformed into an empire: "Definitions of Russianness, from religious to linguistic, stressed the idea of Russian uniqueness rather than popular sovereignty and in effect, denied that membership of a nation could be voluntary."[8] As a corollary, Russianness was hereditary. This approach lingers today on the premise that national identity is ascribed to ethnic Russians. It creates "confusion over what constitutes the 'just borders' of the post-communist Russian state."[9] Not only "just borders" but peoples' ethnicities remain murky and labile, especially with migration transcending Soviet space.

It has been argued that Russian dominance in the Soviet Union was whittled away while a policy of *ukorenizatsia* (rootedness, in other words, affirmative action) for non-Russian minorities was implemented. A number of scholars pointed to the kremlin appointment of leaders of minority nations, including in Central Asian republics, to top positions in Moscow. By the 1980s, it was said, Russia's powers in managing ethnic relations were eroding.[10] The saying switched from "Ethnic in form, Russian in content" to its opposite: "Russian in form, ethnic in content."[11]

After the Soviet collapse, Stanford University political scientist David Laitin described the twenty-five million ethnic Russians who were living in other post-Soviet states as "beached diasporas." Their presence, moreover, was not always welcomed in the newly independent states.[12] Some moved back to Russia, others benefited from passportization policies giving them permanent access to Russia (such as in pre-war Ukraine, Transnistria, Abkhazia, and South Ossetia). Others still carved out special status while living abroad (such as obtaining residence and work permits). The *russkii* versus *rossiiskii* dyad has often been employed to distinguish between ethnic Russians and those descending from pre-revolutionary members of the Russian empire (*rossiiskaia imperiia*).[13] The distinction raises more questions than answers.

Data on Russian migration, at times contradictory, have come from many different sources: the Federal Migration Service, the Federal State Statistics Service (Rosstat), the Border Guard Service of the Federal Security Service (FSS), the Main Directorate for Migration of the Ministry of Internal Affairs, and the Central Bank of the Russian Federation. FSS figures indicated that in 2016 there were twenty-eight million immigrants in Russia. In that year alone, 575,000 arrived in the country of which nearly three-quarters purportedly worked illegally.[14] But others sought employment under the official work permit regime.[15] The most common jobs were in construction, industrial enterprises, small businesses, home care, agriculture and forestry, public transport, and housing and communal services.[16]

Mary Buckley, a British migration specialist on Russia, noted that twentieth-century migrations and movements into and out of Russia were commonplace. She believed that migrants came to Russia because it formed an intrinsic part of their identity. Mantras such as *priezzhii* ("those who arrive") and *druzhba narodov* ("friendship of peoples") explained why transnational cultures became more intertwined over time. She observed that many migrants came for work because it was advertised on television and radio in source countries. In addition, migration advocacy NGOs in Russia endorsed in-migration: "The CIS is 'so big' and migrants come as though this is their homeland." One NGO director spotlighted how even though the USSR had disintegrated, "mentally we live in one country." For Buckley, this belief was passed on from older to younger cohorts.[17]

Early changes affecting the status of migrants in the Russian Federation were implemented in 1999 when Putin's' liberalization turn first began. Any foreigner with "spiritual and cultural ties" to Russia became eligible for citizenship. Expedited applications were processed starting in 2002. In 2008, Putin defended passportization policies covering applicants from Georgia where a short war had been fought and Georgia was overwhelmed. Revised in 2015, rules established migrants' legal status but residence permits were offered only if they had first passed a Russian language test (introduced in 2012) and tests in Russian history and law.[18] This did not apply to Ukrainians who were presumed to speak Russian. Ultimately, Putin's liberalization was motivated by the need to increase the labor pool in the country.

In a world dominated by migration trends to Europe and North America, an overlooked fact was that in 2015 Russia was ranked third on the global list of both receiving and sending countries. Out-migration from Russia was massive between 2000 and 2015 when 10.5 million citizens left to live abroad.[19] Curiously, a Russian dissident newspaper claimed that far fewer—five million—left the country in Putin's first two decades in power.[20] Neither set of figures suggested where they ended up residing though many departed for France, Germany, the United States, Israel, and Cyprus. Much clearer were their qualifications: many emigrés "were under forty and almost all had university degrees (92 per cent) and a significant proportion had PhDs (14 per cent). Since February [the takeover of Crimea in 2014], hundreds of thousands more have bolted."[21]

In the late 2010s, Russia had struck an equilibrium as a sending and receiving state. Migration data often reveal one flaw, however: little or no information is available about returnees to their countries of origin.

Push and Pull Factors

Schenk wrote that "migration flows follow colonial links, are aided by a common language and cultural practices, and are reinforced by the networks created between migrants in the receiving and sending countries."[22] Generally, immigrants from countries making up the Commonwealth of Independent

States (CIS) have an easier time coming to Russia because the majority speaks at least passable Russian and can read Cyrillic. Most also claim to value Russian culture, its traditions and values, and even share religious beliefs as a result of their interconnected histories.

Pull factors draw migrants whose lands formed part of the tsarist empire and then of the USSR. Their imaginaries have roots in changes of habitus, cultural values, and norms.[23] Many migrants had families living in Russia, often boasting Russian citizenship. They created ethnic diasporas that served as national communities, public organizations, self-help bodies, and cultural centers helping migrants to integrate. The largest diasporas in Russia are Tajiks, Uzbeks, Kazakhs, Armenians, and Georgians. By contrast, sizeable Russian diasporas exist in many parts of the world. In 2019, a "Putin exodus" was identified resulting in a rising brain drain in the country.[24] It included an academic diaspora.[25]

Education, culture, and language have all been pull factors crucial to the surge of in-migration up to 2020. The Russian language in particular provided a bonding mechanism and has been exploited by Putin's nationalist regime to build solidarity with *russki mir*, the Russian nation living at home and abroad.

US-based academic Marlene Laruelle noted how the absorption of Crimea in 2014 contributed to an embellished sense of unification of Russia in place of ethnic divisiveness. For instance, the political movement *Rodina* ("Kinfolk") had been a nationalist grouping in the State Duma but it merged with the one-party-dominant United Russia party to deepen Russia's national movement.[26]

Collective remembrance of the Great Patriotic War (World War II) holds special pride of place, as Nobel Literature Laureate Svetlana Alexievich has underscored in her books.[27] Another pull factor consists of institutions that leave behind a cultural legacy in which political attitudes and behavior persist for an unexpectedly long time. Imagining past histories and sharing myths about them become factors that convince migrants to return to their "homeland," particularly in a country as vast and multinational as Russia (Table 4.1).

What are the principal push factors spurring populations to move to more prosperous, more secure, and culturally appealing countries? Endemic poverty clearly acts as the bottom line motivating migration. But ecological causes are increasingly important: drought, famine, floods, climate change, and pandemic. Conflicts within a sending society over the governance of lands and regions also occur.

Research on the religiosity of Central Asian migrants moving to Russia is illuminating and the question arises how religious beliefs may be affected by migration. A fascinating survey conducted in 2015–2016 by Sherzod Eraliev indicated that the religiosity of groups of migrants was not dramatically affected

Table 4.1 Out-migration into Russia by post-Soviet states (2017)

Armenia: 535,266 (18.2% of population is in Russia)

Azerbaijan: 936,852 (9.5% of population is in Russia)

Belarus: 809,353 (8.4% of population is in Russia)

Georgia: 656,888 (17.7% of population is in Russia)

*Germany: 144,895 (former GDR population)

Estonia: 62,441 (4.7% of population is in Russia)

Kazakhstan: 2,349,697 (13.2% of population is in Russia)

Kyrgyzstan: 433,625 (7.1% of population is in Russia)

Latvia: 95,730 (4.8% of population is in Russia)

Lithuania: 82, 889 (2.8% of population is in Russia)

Moldova: 292,807 (8.2% of population is in Russia)

Tajikistan: 424,727 (4.8% of population is in Russia)

Turkmenistan: 165,923 (2.9% of population is in Russia)

Ukraine: 3,301,922 (7.3% of population is in Russia)

Uzbekistan: 586,089 (4.9% of population is in Russia)

---

*Germany was included due to the holdover of Russian speakers who had lived in the GDR.

Source: United Nations, *International Migration Report 2017*, http://www.un.org/en/development/desa/population/migration/publications/migrationreport/docs/MigrationReport2017.pdf.

by their move to Russia. Some even became less religious after migration. But the reverse was true as well. A significant part of Central Asian migrants interviewed by Eraliev reported turning back to religion when immigrating to Russia. Religion offered them respect, resources, and refuge in a society that they found to be xenophobic, that culturally marginalizes Central Asian migrants, and that pushes them away from the public into private space.[28]

Out-migration can become the choice of migrants through campaigns of misinformation, public relations, and propaganda. Russia has utilized cyberspace, for instance, to influence citizens of near abroad countries to come to work for it.[29] The right to remain at home may be set aside when fellow ethnic kin living in the destination country convince them to migrate. Individuals regularly do what others in the culture around them have done. A culture of migration develops when migrants feel "that is what one does in our society."

The World Migration Report on Russia concluded that *not* migrating is usually not on the cards.[30] Even where unimpeded pathways such as visa-free travel, inexpensive transportation, and aggressive recruitment are in the mix, pressures on families and even entire communities to migrate are ratcheted up.[31] In short, cultures of migration are discernable when "non-migrants observe migrants to whom they are socially connected and seek to emulate their migratory behavior."[32]

Putin's Own *Orrodia*

Valery Grossman, a novelist and in-person chronicler of World War II, wrote these stirring words in 1942: "The hour of war came—and they gave this land their blood and their lives. May this land, then, be famed for labor, reason, honor, and freedom. May there be no words more sacred and majestic than 'the people'! This nation, like no other nation in the world, knows how to die sternly and simply." The novel, based loosely on real-life events, described the fate of a Red Army unit encircled by German forces in Ukrainian territory.[33]

Millions of Russians were killed in the Great Patriotic War. The Soviet Union defeated Nazi Germany in 1945 but the toll on human life was horrendous. No degree of birth rate increases or in-migration numbers from other countries could make up for the massive losses.

Writing nearly seventy years later in 2014, Moscow academician Vladimir Malakhov coined the phrase "Russia as a new immigration country" to outline how the country's policymakers had passed through successive stages of confusion, indifference, restrictiveness, and liberalization in manipulating migration policy. After 2006, however, a liberal trend became perceptible, to a certain degree encouraged by Russia's President.

Malakhov pinpointed the inconsistency of migration policy debated in the State Duma that pitted various ideological camps against each other.[34] Conservative members were keen to highlight the Russian language and culture as benchmarks for new immigrants. For them, language proficiency was crucial and Russia needed to exploit the pool of Russophone speakers in neighboring countries regardless of what their ethnic or religious origins were.

Putin initially endorsed the policy that appealed to Russian nationalists and conservatives who prized language and culture. He saw migration as a pragmatic way to invigorate the economy. During his third term, he emphasized the "pivot to culture" amplified in his policy document, "Foundations of State Cultural Policy" which furthered in-migration.

How assertive was Putin in making the case for a liberal migration policy while keeping conservatives on his side? Two Russian authors contended that

> If we were to summarize the speeches of Vladimir Putin on culture, the following key aspects of the "conservative position" could be distilled: first, culture and Russian language are seen as integrating

elements of the multinational nation of Russia; second, the cultural diversity of the world is understood to be one of the factors favoring the national sovereignty and self-sufficiency of Russia; third, "traditional" cultural values include, above all, support for multi-child traditional (heterosexual) families... and commitment to Christian values.[35]

For other authors, the "liberalization turn" in 2006 credited to Putin reformed migration policy. Residence registration requirements (*propiska*) authorizing people to live in other towns were abolished and work permits were made easier to obtain. New legislation was designed to penalize illegal labor practices.[36] Putin's language suggesting antipathy toward immigrants became less inflammatory than that of lower-level elites, according to Schenk; she found that often non-democratic governments are insulated from xenophobic impulses."[37]

After 2008 liberal pragmatists in Putin's administration became more influential than conservative statists over migration policy. The pragmatists discouraged grassroots anti-immigration movements. But the catch was that migration officials themselves "take on functions which are undertaken by far-right parties under democratic rule." They generate "an awkward situation for the Russian government: it implements liberal immigration policy and uses anti-immigration rhetoric at the same time."[38] A breach developed, therefore, between policy decisions and public rhetoric. Malakhov keenly observed how "Over the course of the last ten years we have witnessed a gap between the anti-immigrant rhetoric of the Russian authorities and their (neo)liberal approach toward immigration."[39]

Putin appeared to be more open-minded on migration policy, therefore, than migration officials were. He framed his approach in terms of threats to the country's social cohesion and to traditional cultural values. At the same time, he insisted that some 300,000 labor migrants were needed each year to push economic development further.[40] One writer was convinced that the kremlin leader eschewed a populist policy that had become the rage in Western European political circles and instead opted for a discourse that supported in-migration benefitting the state.[41] At the Valdai Club open principally to Russian and foreign sympathizers, Putin made clear in 2013 that

economic growth, prosperity, and geopolitical influence are all derived from societal conditions. They depend on whether the citizens of a given country consider themselves a nation, to what extent they identify with their own history, values, and traditions, and whether they are united by common goals and responsibilities.[42]

Putin rhetorically asked international Russia experts at the Valdai meet-the-press event: "Who are we? Who do we want to be?" He underscored how ethnic Russians, the Russian language, and Russian culture had become the focus of state-centered identity and urged "shared values, a patriotic consciousness, civic responsibility and solidarity, respect for the law, communion with the fate of the fatherland without losing touch with ethnic or religious roots."[43]

In an earlier essay in 2012 on "Russia: The National Question," he offered a robust critique of the system of multiculturalism, that is, what Russian society would not become. Published in *Nezavisimaya Gazeta*, its subtitle reconciled seemingly contradictory forces—"Self-Determination of the Russian People: A Multiethnic Civilization Sealed with a Russian Core." For the kremlin leader, the "failure of the multicultural project is caused by the crisis of the 'nation state,' namely, the state that has historically been built exclusively on the basis of ethnic identity: it is a challenge to be faced not only by Europe but many other regions in the world."[44] Putin accepted that a multiethnic society was gaining ground but, predictably, he understood it as belonging to a Russia-centric core.

The kremlin also recast itself as a defender of traditional values. Russia was a beacon of traditional virtues and family values, an effusive case of authentic Europe, in contrast to a Europe in the grip of moral decay. At this juncture, Putin's primary objective was to consolidate Russia's national identity rather than to favor particular multicultural elements within it. His discourse was less about fear of the stranger and more about the legitimacy of minorities living in the country.

Russia's President drew a fine line between thwarting Russian nationalism *and* stemming anti-Russian nationalism: "Attempts to expound on the idea of building a Russian 'national' mono-ethnic state is contrary to the whole of our thousand-year history." Indeed, "it is the shortest path to the destruction of the Russian people and Russian statehood and any viable, sovereign state on our land."[45] This was a strong affirmation of Russia but also of its diverse identities.

Simultaneously, monocultural identity was a thing of the past; immigration-driven Russian *multinationalism*—not multiculturalism—was, in Putin's view, destined to become the master signifier. The official kremlin view was, in sum, that multiculturalism leads to *particularistic ethnonationalisms* that produce a diffusion of sovereignty and identity. It may have been an early allusion to Ukraine's ethnonationalist resurgence that developed as its sovereignty became more cemented.

Some rethinking by Russian analysts had taken place over Putin's critique of Western multiculturalism. Political actors, particularly in regions in close proximity to EU member states (above all, St.-Petersburg), saw the value of framing Russia in multicultural terms. Analyst Sergei Akopov suggested that a *transnational* approach to identities and rights transcending multiculturalism could offer Russia the surest path to follow.[46]

None of these debates had relevance following Russia's attack on Ukraine. Putin once heralded Russia as a "civilizational model of state organization" in the wake of influential philosopher Alexander Dugin's thought.[47] The thinking was to flexibly accommodate the ethnic and religious specificity of particular territories, thereby ensuring diversity in unity. Put differently, Russian multiculturalism could be conceptualized as an integral part of Russia's DNA: it was ingrained and authentic, not fabricated and synthetic as in the case of much of the EU.

Or of Eurasianism as its DNA, we may ask? A writer closely associated with the kremlin argued that Eurasianism had become a trap for ethnic Russians and a tool in the hands of their enemies. Aleksey Kochetkov claimed how "initially, Eurasianism was considered by its founders as an extremely specific continuation of the Russian civilizational project." But this eventually "degenerated into an attempt to substitute for the ideas and meaning of Russian civilization" and substituting instead "alien Asiatic notions, the ideologies of Eurasianism.... They are prepared to recognize Russia as Turanian, Mongol, Yakut, Turkic, or whatever else but only not as Russian."[48] The shift to Asia-centric values would, in theory, have become the heart of Eurasianism but not all Russians were enthusiastic about this shift.

The question comes to this: Had a socially cohesive Russia emerged from the combination of state nationalism and in-migration? Successful social cohesion suggests that, when applied to migration, outcomes are positive: educated, productive, and vibrant communities are constructed. But today's Russia is not that and stands as the polar opposite of social cohesion; among its pathologies have been crime, lawlessness, xenophobia, marginalization, poor health, weak labor market integration, youth recidivism, mediocre educational results, violence, oppression, discrimination, increased social tensions, housing segregation, recruitment to criminal or terrorist groups, radicalization, ethnic discrimination, and contempt for liberal norms such as gender equality and a secular state.

In an opinion piece published in 2017, provocatively titled "Trump and Le Pen Would be the Opposition in Russia," *Nezavisimaya Gazeta* argued how Russia's news coverage "blasts Europe for multiculturalism, for receiving refugees from the Middle East and Africa, for tolerance to migrants." Yet at home anti-immigrant attitudes are officially treated as "an unacceptable form of nationalism."[49] The presumption was that Putin was ahead of the game in the "cancel culture" sweepstakes and had woken up to the threats posed by woke culture already in the mid-2010s.

If Trump and Le Pen represented the political opposition because they harbored hostile attitudes toward multiculturalism, the inference was that Putin supported liberal immigration policy. A more likely possibility, however, was that Trump, Le Pen, and Putin saw eye-to-eye on most migration issues.

Blowback Politics

If Putin's discourses on migration largely avoided arousing a sense of fear and dread among arrivals, this was not the case for citizens and their societal attitudes. No less a figure than Russia's Defense Minister noted in 2021 that Russia's opponents "would like us to be mired in internal discord so that we will eventually start feuding on ethnic, religious and class grounds." If Russia did not put an end to such provocations now, "then what happened in Syria, Libya, Yugoslavia, and many other countries will happen" to Russia as well.[50]

For Russian migration sociologist Vladimir Mukomel, "xenophobia pervades all layers of Russian society." It constructs social segmentation based on ethnicity. It permits the emergence of subcultural marginalized enclaves of migrants. Finally, it displays little concern for the pathologies of racism and ethnic discrimination. Mukonel underscored the identity marker that distinguishes *svoi-chuzhoi*, that is, one's own—not ours. For this writer, new imperialist thinking complicates migrant attempts to integrate.[51] In turn, Sergei Medvedev, an economics professor at Moscow State University, sketched how "The archaic forces of imperial revanchism have been brought back to life, shaking Russian society and threatening the outside world."[52]

Public opinion polls suggest that Russians, like other groups in Europe, had mixed views about migrants. A wave of xenophobia triggered by a particular event often leads to anti-immigration behavior and spotlights the issue. Moscow's Mayor, Sergei Sobyanin, stated in 2020, after the pandemic had gained ground in the city, that the number of migrants in the capital had decreased by forty percent. In December of that year, the Ministry of Internal Affairs estimated that almost half of all migrants living in Russia had left during the COVID-19 pandemic.[53] Russia, like other countries, was weakened economically by the rapidly spreading virus; over a million excess deaths were recorded in the first two years of the COVID-19 pandemic.

It was not just COVID that caused a decrease in the number of arriving migrants. According to a sociologist who headed the Migration and Ethnicity Research Group, attitudes toward migrants had already changed at the beginning of the 2010s, mainly because police and security forces effectively disbanded right-wing radical groups. For instance, the Movement Against Illegal Migration was banned in 2011 and was left on the margins.[54]

Attitudes about intermarriage are another barometer of a fear of foreigners. A 2010 VCIOM survey on Russians' attitudes toward international marriages revealed that the most preferred marriages were between ethnic Russian couples (seventy percent). Middle-of-the-road attitudes were expressed about marriages between Russians, Ukrainians, and Belarusians (forty-five percent); Slavs and Europeans (forty-four percent); citizens of the Baltic states (forty-three percent); and Americans (forty-one percent). Outright hostility, on the other hand, was expressed about marriages between Russians and Chechens (sixty-five percent); Arabs (sixty-three percent); Central Asians (sixty percent); those from the Caucasus (fifty-four percent); and Jews (forty-six percent).[55]

A different survey question asked Russians to identify nations and peoples that cause resentment. Respondents singled out nations from the Caucasus (twenty-nine percent) followed by Central Asia (six percent). Those who were averse to them expressed concerns about terrorism (thirteen percent) as well as the reluctance of newcomers to adapt to Russian norms and practices (eleven percent).[56] Ukrainians were not seen as a factor in these results.

In 2018, Levada survey researchers used an adapted version of the social distance scale in use among sociologists across many societies since 1924. It had been developed by Emory Bogardus and is still commonly used to measure prejudice.[57] The Russian survey found that in answer to the affirmation "I would not let them into Russia," prejudice increased progressively from fifteen percent directed at Jews to twenty-two percent at Ukrainians, twenty-seven percent at both Chinese and Chechens, thirty percent at those originating in Central Asia, thirty-three percent at Africans, and forty-three percent at Gypsies. Between 2004 and 2018 twice as many respondents had ethnophobic attitudes toward Roma as were ethnophobic to all other peoples combined. Once again Ukrainians were peripheral to these findings.

When asked about labor migration into Russia at the time that the first survey was administered in 2002, there was negligible difference between those who were in favor and those against such migration (forty-four versus forty-five percent). But the gap widened and in 2018 only fourteen percent were in favor, and sixty-seven percent were against labor migrants. The rise in the numbers of arriving migrants appeared to have the effect of raising prejudice to new heights.[58]

Let me consider the attitudes of young people. Of Russia's 146 million citizens (if we include those in Crimea), sixty-three million (forty-three percent) were under the age of thirty-four. Of these, thirty million belonged to Generation Y (Millennials in their 20s and early 30s); fifteen million to Gen Z (teenagers); while eighteen million are part of the youngest generation (under 10). Generation Y was born in the late 1980s and 1990s, Gen Z in the 2000s, and the youngest in the 2010s. Did any of these generations support or oppose the Putin regime?

For Laruelle, the irony was that different generations were simultaneously for and against the kremlin leader.[59] On core immigration issues, young people were more tolerant toward migrants and North Caucasians than their elders: thirty-nine percent believed it did not matter where they were from but forty-four percent did have negative views and only twelve percent were positive ones.

Finally, the Berlin-based Centre for East European and International Studies (ZOiS) conducted a survey on values related to national identity. Russian youth opted for a liberal understanding of nationalism defined as the right of foreigners to integrate into society while following established rules. Yet a conservative, more nationalist understanding was also discernable: everyone should follow Russian traditions. Of identity values, Western-style multicultural citizenship—recognizing and promoting differences—was the least popular option among Russian youth.

Three days before his country's invasion of Ukraine, Putin explicitly commented on undesirable migrants in Russia. He agreed that non-citizens who respect the country's values, culture, and laws are still welcome. But a hardnosed approach followed: "Any demonstrations of extremism, violations of law and order, and illegal labor operations [should] serve as grounds for prompt decisions for their deportation from Russia and have them banned from entering our country in the future."[60]

Following the pandemic and Russia's invasion of Ukraine, research on migration politics that analyses ethnic fear has taken a back seat. Many surveys have been suspended and others reveal fear in respondents expressing their views. Fewer migrants are around anyway to survey. Generally, in times of crisis citizens typically back incumbent leaders. In this respect, Russia is not exceptional and the self-appointed mouthpiece-in-chief holds sway.

Ukraine as Exceptional

Migrants from Central Asia and the Caucasus—both in North and South Caucasus where ethnic and religious relations were increasing—were often juxtaposed with the *kul'turnye* Baltic peoples which prospered (relatively speaking) in both Soviet and more recent times:[61] The World Bank categorized all three republics as high-income economies which rank highly on the Human Development Index. They have become members of the EU and NATO and have developed into Western-style liberal democracies. In 2020, the combined population of the Baltics hovered around six million. When given a chance to move to greener pastures such as the EU, however, up to one-quarter of their populations took it and migrated to wealthier states. These countries were also those which expressed considerable hostility to Russia when the full-scale war in Ukraine began and mutual enmity became the result.

Since 2014 it was Ukraine that has served as Russia's chief nemesis and, incongruously, as a primary migration-sending country to Russia. The 2010 Russian census identified the Ukrainian diaspora in Russia as just under two million, about one-quarter of Russia's total foreign-born population. Because large Russian- and Ukrainian-speaking communities live in Ukraine, these figures really depend on which country is doing the counting; both states inflate the numbers of their citizens who speak the native tongue.[62]

When Russia's osmotic absorption wrenched Crimea from Ukraine in 2014 followed by the conflicts in the breakaway Donbas regions, about a half million refugees living in eastern Ukraine made their way to their eastern neighbor between 2014 and 2017. Uncounted numbers also arrived in the displacement of that period.[63] According to Russia's Federal Migration Service, as of January 2015, the number of refugees living in Russia who came from Ukraine totaled about 2.4 million. That amounted to 5.6 percent of Ukraine's total population. In 2017, a different estimate suggested that about three million irregular migrants from Ukraine now lived in Russia; other experts claimed the figure was closer to five million.[64] It was in Russia's interest to magnify these figures. To further augment these numbers, in 2022 in the midst of the war in Ukraine Putin announced a policy of giving Russian passports to Ukraine citizens, confounding totals in both states.

Migration data, then, became part of the political struggle between the adjoining states. In 2017, one estimate suggested that Ukraine's diaspora in Russia had reached 3,301,922 and the figure had inched up to 7.3 percent of Ukraine's total population. In 2018, Ukraine still represented the principal source of people moving to Russia but numbers began to decline, from 150,100 in 2017 to 137,700 in 2018. The pool of prospective migrants from Ukraine's conflict-ridden southeastern region seemed close to being exhausted. We may never know with any accuracy how great the movement of people was in this period.

The 2022 war produced further spikes in migration to Russia, whether voluntary or forced. Putin signed an executive order simplifying how people living in the self-declared Donetsk and Luhansk People's Republics could obtain Russian citizenship. His conviction was that the Kyiv government had abandoned these regions' residents and ignored the plight of Russophone speakers in Crimea as well. For example, Ukrainian President Volodymyr Zelenskyy's administration lowered the salaries of Russophone civil servants and created uncertainty about their receiving pension payments.

According to one survey conducted in 2019, eighty-six percent of the population living in Ukraine's separatist-controlled Donbas region preferred Russian citizenship.[65] After Putin decreed that any Ukrainian citizen who wanted a Russian passport could now get one, over 800,000 Donbas residents made good on his offer. For one wartime correspondent in Ukraine, "It is an offer that may be hard to refuse. Russian citizenship is now required in many parts of occupied Ukraine to hold down a job and access services. Declining it can get you noticed, in a bad way."[66]

Although the overwhelming preference among Ukrainians was to migrate to the EU, many Russian-speaking Ukrainians left for Russia whether for family connections, safety and security reasons, jobs, pensions, Russian passports, ease of travel, or other cultural and historical links.[67] In 2017, the EU offered a visa-free scheme allowing those with biometric passports to enter the Schengen area for a period of up to ninety days. Both the United Kingdom (triggered by Brexit) and Ireland (as an EU member state) did not take part in the program. The largest recipient of Ukrainians whether refugees or migrants was its western neighbor Poland. According to the 2011 Polish census, the Ukrainian minority had been tiny, comprising about 51,000, but after the conflict in Donbas broke out the number reached upward of 1.3 million.

When the full-scale Russian attack was launched in February 2022 the total number of Ukrainians seeking refuge in Poland was up to 1.6 million. Paradoxically, according to the American think tank Council on Foreign Relations, that number was exceeded only by Russia: 2.9 million, that is, thirty-five percent of Ukrainian refugees departing for all of Europe including Russia, crossed into the Russian Federation.[68] To be sure, it was unclear what proportion was a result of forced migration. In March 2023, Putin was charged by the International Criminal Court with forcibly evacuating Ukrainian children; a migration criminal act finally snared the kremlin leader. The precise number of international refugees as well as of Ukrainians displaced by the war and moving to other places in the country are likely to be disputed for years to come.

The introduction of a Ukrainian language law requiring the use of Ukrainian in most areas of public life affected its Russian-speaking population and prompted the desire to migrate to Russia. The decision taken by the *Verkhovna Rada* (Ukraine Parliament) to strengthen its national identity was controversial and critics contended that its real aim was to disenfranchise Russophone speakers. The law was passed by a 278-38 majority and requires all citizens of Ukraine to know and use the state language when performing official duties.[69] It was one of the many contentious points that, for the kremlin, justified the February 2022 invasion.

Setting aside a barbaric war fought in the geographical heart of Europe, the high point of in-migration to Russia may have been in 2018, before the pandemic broke out. After that, Rosstat reported that nearly every CIS country including those in Central Asia was sending fewer migrants to Russia. The decrease in Russia's net migration marked its first decline in ten years and "The flow of migrants into Russia has fallen to 2005 levels. Ukraine is no longer the main source country."[70] It must be noted that it was not only from Ukraine but also from Russia itself that populations were departing for better shores.[71]

A Civilizational State

American sociologist Myron Weiner believed that "If there is a single 'law' in migration, it is that a migration flow, once begun, induces its own flows." Chain migration ensues: "The longer migration continues, the more difficult politically it is to stop it." With a spike in migrants, "sustained high-level immigration retards and can even obstruct assimilation."[72] The inference is, then, that in-migration, once introduced, will be hard to stop and will complicate efforts at social integration.

Writing before the 2022 war, migration specialist Malakhov held that "The current unwillingness of Russian society to recognize the fact that Russia is becoming an immigration country would seemingly indicate a relatively high level of xenophobia." Few political actors in the country, he claimed, supported a pro-immigration policy. A portentous collision course had been triggered, then, between large-scale immigration and entrenched xenophobia. At the same time, any type of migration was becoming a moot point when two neighboring countries were in a full-scale war.

In-migration was a gamble risking a xenophobic backlash. Russia which may have been an ethnocratic state appeared vulnerable. The multicultural reality shaping its large cities was becoming inescapable. Herein lay the ambiguity of Putin's claim—the premise was that Russia was a civilizational state but war illuminated a different dimension altogether.

The COVID-19 pandemic had already derailed most of Putin's carefully laid plans on migration. States were compelled to protect national borders and prevent the admission of infected COVID bearers whether migrants, refugees, tourists, or their own citizens stranded in other parts of the world. Many global processes were either put on hold or deteriorated in scope: globalization, climate change, oil prices, migration, and xenophobia. Clear evidence of this was that in 2021 Russia's population plummeted more than at any time since the USSR's demise. London's *The Economist* cautioned: "Don't be fooled that the diminished movement of people, goods and capital will make the world more humane or safer. With globalization in reverse, it will become harder to deal with planet-wide problems, including finding a vaccine and securing an economic recovery."[73] The pandemic and war took a heavy toll on Russia and Ukraine.[74]

A cautionary tale is not to trust Russian data and opinion polls. After all, it was Joseph Stalin who observed: "If only one man dies of hunger, that is a tragedy. If millions die, that's only statistics."[75] Instead of surveys *orrodia*—faith in the speech act particularly when it is the leader of the kremlin who is in charge of making it—may serve as a more dependable feelings thermometer of Russia. But a major caveat is in order: writer Salmon Rushdie remarked that politicians seldom use words to tell the truth; novelists invariably do.[76]

In 2020, the International Organization for Migration reported on migration to and from Russia. It cautioned:

Remittance flows—the lifeblood of several regional economies—has slowed to a trickle. Hundreds of thousands of jobs also have been lost abroad, with millions of families in danger of slipping rapidly into extreme poverty. Those migrants who do make it home, are returning to joblessness, stigma, and potentially, social unrest.[77]

Russia as a civilizational state rings hollow when the country, and its many neighbors dependent on it, are reduced to unparalleled health risks, impoverization, homelessness, and unemployment. As Vyacheslav Postavnin, head of the Center for Analytical and Practical Research on Migration Processes, asserted in 2022 after the war had begun, "For those millions of foreigners who work in Russia today, there are no jobs where they came from. Returning home in such conditions, they are doomed to unemployment and the question of physical survival will be an acute issue for them and their families."[78] For such migrants, finding work in Russia is a Hobbesian choice: they must compete with local labor to get a job—not a simple task at a time of war.

For Russia, migration patterns may be secondary to issues of status. Political scientist Andrei Tsygankov elaborated:

Russia's deep emotional connection to the West as well as Russia's own concept of national honor are the two factors that drive the nation's leaders' complex actions, feelings, and rhetoric. Russia displays emotions of hope each time it feels that its honor is being respected and those of frustration, fear and anger when in the eyes of Kremlin its identity/ honor as not recognized.[79]

Addressing Russia's anger points may explain how status issues can result in conflict.[80] No better a source for approaching anger points can be found than in the discourses of Russia's President.

Postscriptum

In *The Possessed*, also titled *The Devils* or *The Demons*, Fyodor Dostoyevsky depicted life in a quiet provincial town that was suddenly infected by a virus. After a tempestuous literary evening ended, the virus was transformed into a mysterious fire in a distant village. When the guests retreated from the estate "another bomb exploded exactly as in the afternoon."

"Fire! All the riverside quarter is on fire!"
"I don't remember where this terrible cry rose first, whether it was first raised in the hall, or whether some one ran upstairs, from the entry, but it was followed by such alarm that I can't attempt to describe it. More than half the guests at the ball came from the quarter beyond the river, and were owners or occupiers of wooden houses in that district. They rushed to the windows, pulled back the curtains in a flash, and tore down the blinds. The riverside was in flames. The fire, it is true, was only beginning, but it was in flames in three separate places—and that was what was alarming."
"Arson! The Shpigulin men!" roared the crowd."
...
"[His Excellency observed] It's all incendiarism! It's nihilism! If anything is burning, it's nihilism!"
"[He] suddenly noticed a fireman at the top of the burning lodge, under whom the roof had almost burned away and round whom the flares were beginning to flare up. 'Pull him down! Pull him down! He will fall, he will catch fire, put him out!...What is he doing there?'"
"He is putting the fire out, your Excellency."
"Not likely. The fire is in the minds of men and not in the roofs of houses. Pull him down and give it up! Better give it up, much better! Let it put itself out."

Fyodor Dostoyevsky, *The Possessed*, trans. Constance Garnett (New York: Macmillan Company, 1948) [1872], 520–24.

Notes

1 Janusz Dobieszewski, "On the Consolation Offered by Leszek Kołakowski's 'Metaphysical Horror,'" *Dialogue and Universalism* nos. 7–8 (2010).
2 Elif Batuman, "Rereading Russian Classics in the Shadow of the Ukraine War," *New Yorker*, January 23, 2023, https://www.newyorker.com/magazine/2023/01/30/rereading-russian-classics-in-the-shadow-of-the-ukraine-war?utm_source=nl&utm_brand=tny&utm_mailing=TNY_Daily_012623&utm_campaign=aud-dev&utm_medium=email&utm_term=tny_daily_digest&bxid=5ed68ef2dcb9eb

4857382d0c&cndid=61296158&hasha=228efac631f7ff85219b49eb145fbded&ha
shb=0fa2bd301921a18440c4886c9ea6a588f9efd649&hashc=200b23d5947f1a3
dce95d2c85620e4ecd7f0eebdf55cfece9c4384b8708d7f2b&esrc=bouncexmulti_
first&mbid=CRMNYR012019.

3 Barbara A. Anderson and Brian D. Silver, "Growth and Diversity of the Population
of the Soviet Union," *Annals of the American Academy of Political and Social Science* 510
(1990), 156, www.jstor.org/stable/1046801.

4 Caress Schenk, *Why Control Immigration? Strategic Uses of Migration Management in Russia*
(Toronto: University of Toronto Press, 2018), 1–2.

5 Schenk, *Why Control Immigration?* 219, 214, 33.

6 Vera Tolz, *Russia* (London: Hodder Education, 2001), 1–2.

7 Tolz, *Russia*, 189.

8 Tolz, *Russia*, 273.

9 Tolz, *Russia*, 236.

10 Terry Martin, *The Affirmative Action Empire: Nations and Nationalism in the Soviet Union,
1923–1939* (Ithaca: Cornell University Press, 2001); Francine Hirsch, "Toward an
Empire of Nations: Border-Making and the Formation of Soviet National Identities,"
Russian Review, 59 (April 2000), 201–26; Gregory Gleason, *Federalism and Nationalism:
The Struggle for Republican Rights in the USSR* (Boulder: Westview Press, 1990); Charles
King, "The Benefits of Ethnic War: Understanding Eurasia's Unrecognized States,"
World Politics 53, no. 4 (July 2001), 524–52.

11 Ray Taras, "From Matrioshka Nationalism to National Interests," in *New States,
New Politics: Building the Post-Soviet Nations*, eds. Ian Bremmer and Taras (Cambridge:
Cambridge University Press, 1997), 685–706.

12 David D. Laitin, *Beached Diasporas. Identity in Formation: The Russian-Speaking Populations
in the Near Abroad* (Ithaca: Cornell University Press, 1998).

13 Helge Blakkisrud and Pål Kolstø, *"Russkii* as the New *Rossiiskii?* Nation-building
in Russia after 1991," in *Nationalities Papers*, eds. Peter Rutland and Raymond Taras
(Cambridge: Cambridge University Press, 2022).

14 V. Eduardovna Matveenko, N. Mikhailovna Rumyantseva, and D.
Nikolaevna Rubtsova, "Migration in the Russian Federation Today," *Teorija i praksa*
54, no. 6 (2017), 974.

15 Marya S. Rozanova, *Migration Processes and Challenges in Contemporary Russia: St. Petersburg
Case Study* (Princeton: Woodrow Wilson International Center for Scholars & Kennan
Institute, 2012), 163.

16 Zh. Zaionchkovskaya, N. Mkrtchiyan, and E. Tyuryukanova, "Rossiya pered
vyzovami immigratsii," in *Postsovetskie transformatsii: otrazhenie v migratsiyakh*, eds.
Zaionchkovskaya and G. Vitkovskaya (Moscow: Tsentr migratsionnyk issledovanii,
Institut narodokhazaistvennogo prognozirovaniya Rossiiskoi akademii nauk, 2009), 34.

17 Mary Buckley, *The Politics of Unfree Labour in Russia: Human Trafficking and Labour
Migration* (Cambridge: Cambridge University Press, 2018), 246.

18 Buckley, *The Politics*, 229.

19 Migration Policy Institute Tabulation of Data from the United Nations, Department
of Economic and Social Affairs, Trends in International Migrant Stock: Migrants
by Destination and Origin (United Nations 2015 Database, POP/DB/MIG/Stock/
Rev.2015), http://www.un.org/en/development/desa/population/migration/data/
estimates2/estimates15.shtml.

20 Uliana Pavlova, "5 Million Russian Citizens Left Russia Under Putin," *The Moscow Times*, October 13, 2021, https://www.themoscowtimes.com/2021/10/13/5-million-russian-citizens-left-russia-under-putin-a75246.

21 Sadakat Kadri, "Passportisation," in *London Review of Books*, August 3, 2022, https://www.lrb.co.uk/blog/2022/august/passportisation?utm_medium=email&utm_campaign=20220803blog&utm_content=20220803blog+CID_dc3d5ac355cacfedc062 4ee8c34eefb4&utm_source=LRB%20email&utm_term=New%20on%20the%20blog.

22 Schenk, *Why Control Immigration?* 11.

23 Marlene Laruelle, *Russian Nationalism: Imaginaries, Doctrines and Political Battlefields* (London: Routledge, 2018), 9.

24 Bryan MacDonald, "Atlantic Council Claims Russian 'Brain Drain' but Emigration Rate is about Four Times Lower than UK," *Russia Today*, February 24, 2019.

25 Andrei V. Korobkov, "Russian Academic Diaspora: Its Scale, Dynamics, Structural Characteristics, and Ties to the RF," in *Migration from the Newly Independent States: 25 Years After the Collapse of the USSR*, eds. Mikhail Denisenko, Salvatore Strozza, and Matthew Light (Cham, Switzerland: Springer, 2020), 299–322.

26 Marlene Laruelle, "Russia as a 'Divided Nation' from Compatriots to Crimea: A Contribution to the Discussion on Nationalism and Foreign Policy Problems of Post-Communism," *Problems of Post-Communism* 62, no. 2 (2015), 88.

27 Svetlana Alexievich, *Secondhand Time: The Last of the Soviets* (New York: Random House, 2016).

28 Sherzod Eraliev, "Russian Readings," Oxford University, June 22–24, 2019, https://russian-readings.org/member/sherzod-eraliev/.

29 Todd C. Helmus, Elizabeth Bodine-Baron, Andrew Radin, Madeline Magnuson, Joshua Mendelsohn, William Marcellino, Andriy Bega, and Zev Winkelman, *Russian Social Media Influence: Understanding Russian Propaganda in Eastern Europe* (Santa Monica, CA: Rand Corporation, 2018), 1.

30 World Migration Report, "Understanding Migration Journeys from Migrants' Perspectives," *International Organization for Migration (IOM)*, ch. 7 (2018), https://www.iom.int/countries/russian-federation.

31 World Migration Report, 49.

32 World Migration Report, 50.

33 Vasily Grossman, *The People Immortal* (London: MacLehose Press, 2022), 151.

34 Vladimir S. Malakhov, "The Phenomenon of New Immigration Countries: Russia's Case in the European Context," *Europe-Asia Studies* 66, no. 7 (2014), 1062–79.

35 V. Kurennoy and R. Khestanov, "Culture-Between Pragmatism and Neotraditional Rhetoric," in *Russia: Strategy, Policy and Administration*, ed. Irvin Studin (London: Palgrave Macmillan, 2017), 308.

36 A. V. Korobkov, "Migration Trends in Central Eurasia: Politics versus Economics," *Communist and Post-Communist Studies* 40, no. 2 (2007), 169–89.

37 Schenk, *Why Control Immigration?* 27. Breunig, Cao, Luedtke, 2012.

38 Malakhov, "The Phenomenon," 1074.

39 Malakhov, "The Phenomenon," Ibid.

40 V. Putin, "Nam nuzhna novaya ekonomika," *Vedomosti*, January 30, 2012.

41 Caress Schenk, "Anti-Migrant, but not Nationalist: Pursuing Statist Legitimacy through Immigration Discourse and Policy," *Russia Before and After Crimea*, eds. Pål Kolstø and Helge Blakkisrud (Edinburgh: Edinburgh University Press, 2018).

42 Prezident Rossii, "Meeting of the Valdai International Discussion Club," Official Website, September 19, 2013, http://en.kremlin.ru/events/president/news/19243.

43 Prezident Rossii "Meeting."

44 V. Putin, "Rossiya: Natsional'nii vopros," *Nezavisimaya Gazeta*, January 23, 2012, 1.

45 Putin, "Rossiya," 1.

46 Sergei Akopov, "Multinationalism, Mononationalism, or Transnationalism in Russia?" in *Challenging Multiculturalism: European Models of Diversity*, ed. Raymond Taras, (Edinburgh: Edinburgh University Press, 2013), 279–96.

47 Aleksandr Dugin, *The Foundations of Geopolitics: The Geopolitical Future of Russia*. Kindle edn. (2020). See also Tara Isabella Burton, "The Far-right Mystical Writer Who Helped Shape Putin's View of Russia," *Washington Post*, May 12, 2022, https://www.washingtonpost.com/outlook/2022/05/12/dugin-russia-ukraine-putin/.

48 Paul Goble, "Moscow Must 'Unleash' Powers of Ethnic Russian Nation rather than be led by Eurasianist Fantasies, Kochetkov Says," *Window on Eurasia*, January 31, 2022, https://windowoneurasia2.blogspot.com/2022/01/moscow-must-unleash-powers-of-ethnic.html.

49 L. Ragozin, "Russia Wants Immigrants the World Doesn't," *Bloomberg*, March 14, 2017, https://www.bloomberg.com/news/features/2017-03-14/russia-s-alternative-universe-immigrants-welcome. See "Трамп и Ле Пен в России были бы оппозиционерами," January 31, 2017, http://www.ng.ru/editorial/2017-01-31/2_6916_red.html.

50 Paul Goble, "Shoygu Warns Russia Threatened Within by Ethnic, Religious and Class Discord," *Window on Eurasia*, August 15, 2021, tass.ru/obschestvo/12099913.

51 Buckley, *The Politics*, 264.

52 Sergei Medvedev, *The Return of the Russian Leviathan* (Cambridge: Polity, 2019).

53 Akash Maurya, "Deport 'Extremist' Migrants Immediately—Putin," *The Press United*, February 21, 2022, https://thepressunited.com/updates/deport-extremist-migrants-immediately-putin/.

54 Anton Novoderezhkin, "How has the Attitude towards Migrants Changed in Russia, Why They are Paid More and What is Publicly said about Them?" *Meduza*, October 24, 2020, https://meduza.io/feature/2020/10/24/kak-izmenilos-otnoshenie-k-migrantam-v-rossii-pochemu-im-stali-bolshe-platit-i-chto-o-nih-publichno-govoryat?utm_source=email&utm_medium=briefly&utm_campaign=2020-10-27.

55 VCIOM Survey, July 3–4, 2010, http://wciom.ru/index.php?id=268&uid=13774.

56 VCIOM Survey, May 1–2, 2010, http://wciom.ru/index.php?id=268&uid=13515.

57 Colin Wark and John F. Galliher, "Emory Bogardus and the Origins of the Social Distance Scale," *American Sociology* 38 (2007), 383–95.

58 Levada Survey, "Monitoring Xenophobic Attitudes," August 27, 2018, Tables 1, 5, http://www.levada.ru/2018/08/27/monitoring-ksenofobskih-nastroenij/.

59 Marlene Laruelle, "Beyond Putin: Russia's Generations Y and Z," *PONARS Eurasia*, Policy Memo 579, March 2019, http://www.ponarseurasia.org/memo/beyond-putin-russia-generations-y-andz?fbclid=IwAR10sNypwRSMMoewVuoobMPFUYfr26-bkpj71cTqq3mek2IcjOlPbTxRriY.

60 Maurya, "Deport 'Extremist' Migrants."

61 Buckley, *Politics*, 192.

62 Dominique Arel, "Interpreting 'Nationality' and 'Language' in the 2001 Ukrainian Census," *Post-Soviet Affairs* 18, no. 3, (2002), 213–49.

63 "Russian Census Population Data," *The Embassy of the Russian Federation to the United Kingdom of Great Britain and Northern Ireland Diplomacy*, Online website (2018), https://www.rusemb.org.uk/russianpopulation/.

64 Buckley, *Politics*, 193, 198.

65 K. Alizinov, "86 Percent of the People Living in Ukraine's Separatist-controlled Region Reportedly Want Russian Citizenship," *Meduza*, April 30, 2019, https://meduza.io/en/news/2019/04/30/86-percent-of-the-people-living-in-ukraine-s-separatist-controlled-region-reportedly-want-russiancitizenship?utm_source=email&utm_medium=briefly&utm_campaign=2019-05-01.

66 Kadri, "Passportisation."

67 Antonio Santino Baiz, "The Silent Invasion into Russia: An Imperial Transnational Campaign, 2006–2020," PhD diss. (Tulane University, New Orleans, May 2023).

68 Diana Roy, "How Bad is Ukraine's Humanitarian Crisis a Year Later," *Council on Foreign Relations*, February 22, 2023, https://www.cfr.org/europe-and-eurasia/ukraine.

69 Andrew Roth, "Ukraine Adopts Language Law Opposed by Kremlin," *The Guardian*, April 25, 2019, https://www.theguardian.com/world/2019/apr/25/ukraine-adopts-law-enforcing-use-of-ukrainian-in-public-life.

70 Fontanka.ru, Поток мигрантов в Россию упал до уровня 2005 года. Украина перестала быть главной страной-донором ("The Flow of Migrants to Russia Fell to the 2005 Level. Ukraine has Ceased to be the Main Donor Country"), *Fontanka.ru*, February 23, 2019, https://fontanka.ru/2019/02/23/028/.

71 Nikhil Kumar and Beril Eski, "'A Fascistic Regime': Putin's Ukraine War Triggers an Exodus—from Russia," *Grid News*, March 29, 2022, https://www.grid.news/story/global/2022/03/29/a-fascistic-regime-putins-ukraine-war-triggers-an-exodus-from-russia/.

72 Myron Weiner, *The Global Migration Crisis: Challenge to States and to Human Rights* (New York: HarperCollins, 1995), 21.

73 Zanny Minton Beddoes, "A Special Edition on the Coronavirus Pandemic," *The Economist*, May 23, 2020, https://view.e.economist.com/?qs=f44a6cb01147b04c6542344b411edca4544b848d22341a756d5ea8e2864cfc2ec9d8076cc2c388ee41b09777974fc23f9eaf7334d4bf0b17664a836780d38860d86c27ddf19f598fc6347db8701d4a1f.

74 Johns Hopkins University and Medicine, "Mortality Analyses," May 23, 2020, https://coronavirus.jhu.edu/data/mortality.

75 *Washington Post*, January 20, 1947, attributed to Joseph Stalin.

76 Salman Rushdie, Author's Interview, April 7, 2008.

77 UN News, "Millions of Migrants across Russia, Central Asia, 'Teetering on the Brink', as UN Launches Urgent Appeal," May 15, 2020, https://news.un.org/en/story/2020/05/1064182.

78 Javokhir Kabilov, "Digitization is 20 Years Late," MEDIA-MIG, March 21, 2022.

79 Andrei Tsygankov, "The Frustrating Partnership: Honor, Status, and Emotions in Russia's Discourses of the West," *Communist and Post-Communist Studies* 47, nos. 3–4 (Sept-Dec 2014).

80 Tuomas Forsberg, Regina Heller, and Reinhard Wolf, "Status and Emotions in Russian Foreign Policy," *Communist and Post-Communist Studies* 47, nos. 3–4 (Sept-Dec 2014).

Chapter 5

INDIVIDUAL ANGST: JAPAN'S AMERICANIZED ARTIST

Thucydides was convinced that the study of the Peloponnesian War constituted a phenomenon having extraordinary significance. But in his focus on collective fears experienced by the populations of Athens, Sparta, and other ancillary towns taking part in military conflicts, he may have overlooked, or at least undervalued, a simple behavioral reaction—fear of the individual. Wars typically evoke concepts of balance of power and bandwagoning versus balancing behavior and submission of the weak to the strongest. The contemporary focus is on structural levels of analysis. It comes as no surprise, then, that the individual level of analysis is frequently left out.

Regardless of international relations theories, fear is a primal sensation experienced by individual human beings. In the case of divine intervention, fear can play a constructive role: *principium sapientiae timor Domini*, the fear of God, is often regarded as the beginning of wisdom. But in interpersonal relations, fear and its related sensations—anxiety, concern, dread, loathing, prejudice, and other reactions leading even to paranoia—appear natural and have both functional and dysfunctional consequences. This study supplements Thucydides' classification with an asymmetrical addition comprising individual fear.

Understanding Angst

Arguably, the appropriate word to capture individual fear is angst, introduced into English from the Danish, Norwegian, Dutch, and German languages. In the nineteenth century, it was used in translating the works of Søren Kierkegaard and, later, Sigmund Freud, among others. Absent Thucydides' guidance, let me focus first on these two existential and psychoanalytic approaches.

For Danish philosopher Kierkegaard, Angst (with a capital "A") is a desire for what one fears. It is also relevant to his conception of original sin. *The Concept of Anxiety: A Simple Psychologically Orienting Deliberation on the Dogmatic Issue of Hereditary Sin*, written in 1844, was originally rendered in translation as *The Concept of Dread*.[1]

This is how he approached the concept. Kierkegaard used the example of a man who was standing on the edge of a cliff. When he looked over the edge, he realized there was a chance of falling over it and even felt a terrifying impulse to throw himself over the precipice. This psychological experience signified anxiety or dread because of the freedom to choose whether to throw oneself off or to stay put. The fact of such a terrifying possibility triggered dread, what Kierkegaard called the "dizziness of freedom."

However, he also recognized that anxiety was a way for humanity to be saved. It brought to mind our choices, self-awareness, and personal responsibility. It transposed a state of "un-self-conscious" immediacy to self-conscious reflection. Thus an individual, for Kierkegaard, became aware of her potential through experiencing angst. He also affirmed that anxiety served as the presupposition for inheriting hereditary sin; Saint Augustine had first called it *peccatum originale*, or original sin. The recognition or realization of a person's true identity and freedom emerged in the experience of angst.

By contrast, in his *Beyond the Pleasure Principle*, Austrian psychoanalyst Freud regarded pleasure as the driving force of the *id* which seeks immediate gratification of all needs, wants, and urges. But subsequently reversing his views on it, Freud highlighted how the term angst encompassed a state where danger, whether known or not, is imminent and perhaps prepared for.[2] Translators of his work chose different terms for how angst should be rendered. For example, French translators mostly chose *angoisse* or even *angst*. Spanish-language translators selected *angustia*, but also sometimes *miedo*, or fear. English-language translators preferred to translate angst as *anxiety*, using fear, alarm, and afraid when the context fitted it.

Freud himself, in *The Problem of Anxiety*, emphasized that he had abandoned his previous theory of "anxiety as the transformation of inadequately discharged sexual libido in favor of a reaction to a traumatic situation"; that is, it represented a signal of potential future traumas or losses and cited the trauma of World War I as an example.[3] In summary, then, angst describes an intense feeling of apprehension, anxiety, and inner turmoil. These words can be interchangeable with angst.

The Etiology of Fear

The sources, intensity, and character of any fear, regardless of whether people profess another religion, possess a different ethnicity, or belong to a specific civilization, are complex, occasionally obscure and ephemeral, and not usually concrete or tangible. In the study of politics and international relations, studies of fear do not always begin with an examination of the sources of an individual's predispositions, partialities, phobias, biases, anxieties, or antipathies.

Part of the reason may be that breakthroughs in the scientific study of our psychological and behavioral predispositions have largely taken place in the field of medicine. Arts, the humanities, and the social sciences have produced some important findings too, for example, in anthropology and psychology, or cultural studies and historiography.

The literature on the etiology of fear, prejudice, and discrimination is vast and growing. Here I review a cross-section of it. My focus is on individual fear as experienced by Yasuo Kuniyoshi (1889–1953), a Japanese-born artist who in World War II was caught up in the politics of fear-mongering when working for the United States government. He was even expected to create racist images of Japanese enemies. His attempts to transcend this double bind have been the subject of considerable research by psychologists, historians, and fellow artists.

It comes as no surprise that, as two American psychologists have argued, "Many of our political attitudes, particularly those we feel strongly about, have their source in childhood. What's wrong with that? Well, the primary problem with acting out or expressing childhood anger, pain, and fear in a contemporary political context is that it frequently results in very bad public policy."[4] Along the way, it represents a transgressive behavior pattern that can be injurious to others. Kuniyoshi was a likely victim of such a pattern.

For some psychoanalysts, stranger anxiety is an early manifestation of our rejection of others. While seemingly a negative personality trait—how many of us would willingly admit to being apprehensive about unfamiliar people when we are adults?—it stems from a positive quality: the assertion in infancy of a relationship of love, typically with a parent. We can perhaps speculate about the influence of Kuniyoshi's relationship in infancy to his mother and contrast it with the subsequent uncertainty and instability of his life, and the coping mechanisms he adopted. Such speculative observations may produce convincing tangible findings reflected in his art. Then again, it may not.

A more promising avenue for research is to invoke attachment theory, pioneered by psychiatrist John Bowlby and elaborated upon by developmental psychologist Mary Ainsworth. It underscores the importance of infant behavior that seeks proximity to an attachment figure by cultivating an affectional bond and establishing a "secure base."[5] Adaptive behavior prioritizing attachment may extend from infancy through adolescence. Where adaptive efforts fail, a reactive attachment disorder—a widely accepted diagnosis in psychiatry—may set in and reflect an individual's inappropriate social relatedness. Such adaptive strategies and struggles are perceptible in Kuniyoshi's personal search for identity and reflected in many of his *oeuvres*.

Psychiatric theories do not directly explain the appearance of phobias in an individual and it would be a mistake to assign them an overdetermined role in their emergence. Nonetheless, infant stranger anxiety does play a key role in the predisposition to prejudice.[6] In some cases, it can even produce pathological behavior later in life. Thus, attempts to cope with anxiety may "consist in distrust of others, projection of one's own hatred onto strangers, narcissistic rage, self-destructive tendencies, and belligerent differentiation from what is outside. Often the anxiety is linked with the narcissistic fear of a loss of self-esteem."[7]

The repertoire of emotions about the unfamiliar stranger who we perceive as alien and Other can range from anxiety to antipathy to hatred.[8] To be sure, a few cultures construct the stranger as being God in disguise or as being sent by God. Japanese folk religion sometimes regarded the outsider, imputed with an animal spirit, as a god. Within Christianity, Marcion of Sinope (living around the second century and identified as an early Gnostic) distinguished between the Creator God who made the world and the more significant if unknowable Stranger God who sent Christ to earth. Such differing constructions and valuations of the stranger suggest that fear and anxiety need not be the only primal response; it can be ritualized and tempered into an accepting romanticism.

Most often, however, the outsider is likely to be demonized. Polish psychiatrist Antoni Kępiński emphasized that an unfamiliar world evokes fear, aggression, and the need to escape from or destroy it. Cultures produce diverse symbols and languages of fear as ways of coping with it.[9] An initial step in managing fear is the recognition that it is a pervasive predisposition and no particular individual, or group of individuals, has a monopoly on fearfulness. When it is suggested that such a group does exist, it is typically to arouse prejudice against it because of their own paranoid nature.

Tracking the Artist as a Young Man

The naturalness of human fear and life-changing cultural and political upheavals go hand-in-hand. Pictorial expressions of fear are identifiable in many artistic works; one of the most memorable is Edvard Munch's expressionistic construction *The Scream* painted in 1893. But it dominates the artwork of Japanese-born painter and photographer Kuniyoshi. In launching a 2015 exhibition of his work, the Smithsonian American Art Museum published a short biography of his artistic evolution. The biography reads:

> Kuniyoshi emigrated to America from Japan as a teenager, rising to prominence in the New York art world during the 1920s to become one of the most esteemed artists in America between the two world wars. He drew on American folk art, Japanese design and iconography and European modernism to create a distinctive visual style. Kuniyoshi defined himself as an American artist while at the same time remaining very aware that his Japanese origins played an important role in his identity and artistic practices.

Figure 5.1 Yasuo Kuniyoshi, *Child* (1923).

Whitney Museum of American Art. Estate of Yasuo Kuniyoshi. Licensed by VAGA at Artists Rights Society (ARS), New York, NY.

An illustration of the "metissage" he instinctively invoked in his early works is found in his oil painting of *Child* (1923) (Figure 5.1). The Whitney Museum of American Art that exhibits this painting observes:

> this portrait draws inspiration from Western modernism and the artist's Japanese heritage, as well as from the folk art of both cultures. With its pared-down language of flattened planes and angular lines, *Child* brings together elements of these various traditions, especially evoking eighteenth- and nineteenth-century American folk art portraits of children. Here, Kuniyoshi's individualistic blend of modernist sophistication and folk art primitivism finds its corollary in his subject—a sitter who appears at once mature and naïve.[10]

The angst that he suffered from over the years while living in the United States came from his bifurcated status in the art world as well as in his interpersonal relations. While at first he successfully fit into its artistic milieu, trouble lay ahead:

> Kuniyoshi was thoroughly integrated into American life and the art world, but immigration law prevented him from becoming an American citizen.

Classified an "enemy alien" after the bombing of Pearl Harbor, he remained steadfastly on the side of his adopted country during the painful war years, working with the Office of War Information to create artworks indicting Japanese atrocities.[11]

A focus on some of his paintings and drawings from the early 1920s exposes his thought processes. From the time he served in the US Office of War Information after the Pearl Harbor attack in 1941, his status as an alien in the country became more apparent in his works. His general angst and fears pervading the society in which he lived began to scream out in paintings that he completed at that time. Key themes were the emergence of prejudice out of his fearfulness and insecurity, and loathing as a result of being shunned, rejected, and excluded.

Kuniyoshi's early works from the first half of the 1920s, just over a decade after his arrival in America but before his visits to Europe, point to a diffident form of fear. They stand in contrast to his art during World War II, above all, his series of propaganda posters targeting Japanese militarists and German racists. It was not the way that Kuniyoshi self-identified but his anxieties often mirrored those typical of the estranged immigrant making his way in an unfamiliar receiving society. They were typical of the fantasies and phobias of a man leaving his youth behind and entering his thirties.

While their paths took them in different directions, an intriguing comparison resting on strategies of coping with the unfamiliar was between Kuniyoshi, the artist from Japan, and Joel Hägglund, better known as Joe Hill, a recent Swedish immigrant to the western United States. Both worked in part-time jobs along the West Coast, from Seattle to southern California and, in theory, they may have crossed paths. Hill was born in 1879 and arrived in America in 1902, Kuniyoshi was older, born in 1893, and he arrived in the United States in 1906. They were both among a generation of immigrants arriving in the first part of the twentieth century. Hill drifted from New York to San Francisco, Seattle, and Salt Lake City, Kuniyoshi worked his way from Seattle to Los Angeles, then to New York in 1910. If Joe Hill could not find a comfortable space for himself in American society, he coped with it by engaging in labor organizing and song writing, typically embracing radical socialist ideals. Kuniyoshi, too, for a time adopted leftist ideas but after leaving the West Coast art became his profession and preoccupation.

Acquainting themselves with America, their paths were to divulge. In 1915, Joe Hill was killed by a firing squad on a bogus murder charge in Salt Lake City. Kuniyoshi's career was launched not many years after with a New York City art exhibit held in 1922. Hill never disassociated himself from Sweden nor did he have a chance to become fully Americanized. Instead, though, he was to become a veritable American icon. Kuniyoshi was following an unfaltering linear path to Americanization yet, ironically, he suffered from the criticism that he would never be an American artist, let alone an American icon.

Documentary evidence and personal testimonials revealed Joe Hill to be fearless even as he waited in prison on death row. His bravado was dramatized by the last word he shouted out to the firing squad in the prison yard: "Fire." Possessing an artistic temperament and the skills to express it, Kuniyoshi veered between different emotions extending from humor to fearfulness, and from seeking to embrace Americana to loathing his artistic production as the expanding militaristic Japanese empire threatened. His portrait of dairy cows in a pastoral setting, which appeared as early as 1923, represented for him a signature iconographic emblem and also an ideologically committed motif depicting America's peaceable rural past.[12]

Assaying Kuniyoshi's Art

Art critic Gail Levin highlighted how the rage for folk culture made its appearance in the 1920s. She cited Aaron Copland's remark that "The desire to be 'American' was symptomatic of the period."[13] But it had a downside: racial nativism emerged which led to policies of exclusion, evidenced in Congressional legislation restricting immigration. Laws were enacted like the 1924 Japanese Exclusion Act which both kept prospective Japanese immigrants out of America and made those already here, like Kuniyoshi, ineligible for American citizenship. Joe Hill was murdered but labor unrest and radical political activity—his legacy—was alive. Levin contended that widespread immigrant fear further contributed to rising collective xenophobia in the United States.

All the while Kuniyoshi single-mindedly pursued his dream of becoming an American. That is, until the Japanese attack on Pearl Harbor occurred when his official status changed: "He was legally an enemy alien and he was very hurt by that….He was still persecuted and he felt prejudice. And in that period he made the shocking series of violent drawings for the [US] government as propaganda to protest wartime atrocities, mostly by the Japanese."[14]

Anxiety deepened in him, not only by the well-documented identitarian crisis that beset Kuniyoshi but also by the receding possibility of acquiring US citizenship. Levin put it this way: "Kuniyoshi's 'desire to be American' may have resulted from fear of persecution by those eager to combat the Yellow Peril, as Asian immigration was then called by growing numbers of Americans who feared being inundated from the East."[15] The phenomenon extended beyond the United States, underscored by Australia's rising xenophobia recounted in the next chapter.

Other factors were at work in the artistic expressionism he conveyed in the 1920s, exhibiting an embryonic emergence of angst. Thus "Kuniyoshi must also have had Japanese folklore in mind when he conceived of the paintings *Boy Frightened by Snake* of 1921 and *Dream* of 1922, as well as the drawing *The Bad Dream* of 1924." The first painting[16] was flagged by art critic Tom Wolf as reflecting Kuniyoshi's "strange psychology:" "it is very unusual for an artist to make the emotion of fear a work's primary subject" yet "Kuniyoshi did so repeatedly." This happened in the 1920s at a time when his "un-American" persona came into play and before his recruitment to a crusading American cause was broached.

Referring to *The Bad Dream*, Wolf observed that the "passive face lends an unexpected mood to the emotion of fear, which is communicated primarily by the title."[17] If there was also a hint of despair in the subject, it was because of Kuniyoshi's own indeterminate and prolonged status as an assigned alien in America. Awareness of the bottlenecks that lay ahead of him in order to be fully accepted into American society was inscribed in his 1930 lithograph capturing the precariousness inherent in his life and projected to a *Circus Performer Balanced on a Ball* (1930) (Figure 5.2).

It would be inaccurate to attribute the cycle of paintings from the 1920s conveying angst and fear solely to his sense of being trapped in a hybrid state that the artist was experiencing at this time; the still-fresh memory of a Japanese upbringing was influential too. Levin observed:

> The notion that Kuniyoshi had suffered enough fear to have taken seriously the superstitions alluded to in Japanese folk tales and toys is reinforced by his drawing *Boy Frightened by Lightning* (1921) and by *Child Frightened by Water* (1924).... Clearly, Kuniyoshi's choice of motifs suggests that he registered the fear of snakes, lightning, and the sea that was so common in Japan, making it likely that he also concerned himself with threats of disease, demons, and evil spirits which, along with ghosts, monsters, and dragons often populate Japanese legend and lore.[18]

Boy Frightened by Lightning, an ink drawing from 1921, conveys a sense of loneliness, passivity, and even stoicism. Wolf noted how "a boy expresses his anxiety more visibly, covering his ears and closing his eyes," and he cites a contemporary reviewer who described the pose as "someone stunned by momentary fear."[19]

What can be described as Kuniyoshi's period of fear and trembling included several other revelatory works. *Boy Fishing* (1921) reveals a glum

Figure 5.2   Yasuo Kuniyoshi, *Circus Performer Balanced on a Ball* (1930).

Whitney Museum of American Art. Estate of Yasuo Kuniyoshi. Licensed by VAGA at Artists Rights Society (ARS), New York, NY.

young man overshadowed by a haunting landscape and forbidding darkness. He stiffly, mechanically, pulls a fish out of the water, showing more resignation and discomfort than pleasure—someone clearly not in his element.

Sisters Frightened by a Whale (1923) invokes fear through the para-textual reference. The two nudes seem to display more self-consciousness, flattery at someone observing them, and even coquettishness rather than fright at the sight of a spouting, playful-looking whale. It receded into the background anyway. Similarly, a touch of irony shapes the painting titled *Child Frightened by Water* (1924). Wolf makes mention of the "artist's personal concerns with infancy and with fear."[20] But elsewhere he describes how Kuniyoshi turned the story of St. Christopher helping Jesus cross a river "into a painting of a serene mother carrying her uneasy child. A glimpse of a lighthouse in the background furthers the sense of protection."[21] If there is a reason to be fearful in this painting, it is that the infant with the puffed cheeks is straining to relieve itself.

Dread unmistakably takes on more palpable and explicit expressions in Kuniyoshi's pen-and-ink drawing *The Bad Dream* (1924). Taking its cue from the discovery of Freudian dream analysis, the drawing depicts grotesque dragons attacking vulnerable naked women. One subject in the artwork was dragged off by a demon, conjuring the imagery of the Biblical Last Judgment. The artist references both Japanese myths in the form of winged or smoking demons floating among broad-leafed plants but also American motifs as in the macabre form of the cow. Art critic Jane Myers believed that the drawing "offers dichotomous views of good and evil."[22] That represents a Manichean perspective traditionally used by its proponents to instill popular fear.

The mixed message about fear contained in the cycle of paintings and drawings of the early 1920s may, it can be argued, be related to Kuniyoshi's own unusual sense of dread. As already mentioned, fear originates in anxiety about the stranger, in attachment that a close relationship is about to be severed. But it was Kuniyoshi who was the alien in America in his quest for attachment. Insecurity breeds fear and the artist's increasingly heightened sense of it, especially after the Pearl Harbor attack, becomes the principal source for his artistic expressions of it and at times contains contradictory or ironic renderings. Insecurity together with the sense of exclusion from the host society combined to make fear salient in his early works.

Veering toward Racialized Art

In subsequent works during the 1930s, the painter approached cascading identitarian dilemmas in different ways but his angst may have been captured best by extrapolating his exhaustion onto the figure of a woman who declares *I'm Tired* (1938) (Figure 5.3).

ShiPu Wang, an art historian at the University of California at Merced, noted that after the 1920s Kuniyoshi increasingly "deployed emotive brushwork, suggestive of an unsettling mood, that belies his subjects' stoicism and inertness." Thickly layered brushstrokes became his "recurring pictorial device for creating a sense of instability that undercuts his depicted subjects' seemingly calm experience and hints at a deepening sense of unrest and uncertainty about the world."[23] Uncertainty about his own personal fate was much in the mix.

Figure 5.3 Yasuo Kuniyoshi, *I'm Tired* (1938).

Whitney Museum of American Art. Estate of Yasuo Kuniyoshi. Licensed by VAGA at Artists Rights Society (ARS), New York, NY.

His subsequent representational strategy involved figures and images that were largely detached from the surroundings around them. Wang observed:

Impassivity seems to function also as an artificial shield (which would later manifest itself in the motif of the mask) that guards the figures'— and to some extent the artist's—inaccessible interior world. This is perhaps indicative of the subterranean sense of dislocation caused by Kuniyoshi's diasporic experience, and he chose to express it in a pictorial language different from his fellow artists, including those who were Japanese immigrants like him.[24]

Meanings were encapsulated in his further artwork. At the height of World War II in 1943, Kuniyoshi painted on a large effusive canvas which was titled *Somebody Tore My Poster*. It both confronted new realities while harking back to earlier works.

In it, a centrally positioned woman stands in front of a torn poster. Her left hand holds on to a nearby railing as if to prevent herself from falling, while her right hand raises a burning cigarette that seems to block the sight of the desecrated poster. Turning away, she exudes an understated melancholy, typical of Kuniyoshi's figurative paintings from the 1930s, which mostly contained a lone, pensive female figure in a sparse space.[25]

Kuniyoshi resented the narrowing options he was given as the war went on. In a speech he delivered in 1942 archived by the Smithsonian Institution Archives of American Art, called "Civilization Besieged: The Artist's Role in War," he complained about the priority given to commercial work. Even though artists like himself were eager to make "propaganda and educational art," the government had given preference to "the work of the commercial artists, the illustrator, the cartoonist."[26] But even more of a concern was being commissioned to produce anti-Japanese war posters for the Office of War Information, a federal agency in charge of war propaganda.[27]

A personal motif and choice in a number of his paintings is the mask which merits further explanation. Levin noted that a mask first appeared in *Upside Down Table and Mask* completed in 1940. She contended: "That Kuniyoshi painted a mask at a time of mounting hostilities, just before the war, is significant."[28] Perhaps he had become aware of the stark choices that lay ahead as war clouds gathered on the horizon. He may have become particularly disturbed that the choice he had to make was to go over to the dark side, to be an artist instilling fear in others through racialized imagery of the enemy. In his pictorial representations, then, becoming cast as a propagandist for the American war cause may have persuaded him to reach for the mask symbol.

During the COVID pandemic where masks, in combination with social distancing, became all-important protective devices, we encounter questions about what the purposes of earlier periods of masking conveyed. In a Creole city such as New Orleans, masks during Mardi Gras are quintessential in obscuring one's personal identity and forging a different one. But an analysis by MIT in Cambridge, Massachusetts, suggests its pivotal role in many other social settings. In his account of "Masks as a Collective Cry for Justice," anthropologist Graham Jones underscored how "The mask is one of the most important human artifacts in all of anthropology. It is a tool of transformation that allows its wearers to transcend themselves, taking on timeless roles in ritual dramas, and as actors in a broader social drama." These would be obvious devices in Kuniyoshi's artistic toolbox.[29]

In turn, in an essay on "The Expressive Power of Masks," Sara Brown, director of design for MIT Theater Arts, proposed how "A performer in a mask is obscuring one's identity in order to embody another one. Often, masks for performances have meanings that can be instantly understood by an audience that is familiar with the specific codes embedded in a particular theater form." In the case of iconic Japanese Noh theater with which Kuniyoshi most likely have had become familiar, "a mask worn by the principal character can indicate the character's age and gender, and if the character is human or divine. Though the masks are static and cover the entire face, a skilled performer can invoke a range of expression through changing the mask's orientation and relationship to light."[30]

The last selection from the MIT Theatre Arts compendium I highlight is by Emma Teng, Professor of Asian Civilizations and director of MIT Global Languages. In "Masks as 公德心," she insisted that the wearing of face masks was dependent on aspects of differing cultures coming into play during the COVID pandemic. Teng referred to the "communitarian norms in East Asian countries" that stood behind the ethos that "doing something for the community good is good for me also. This value is known as 公德心 [public morality]; in Mandarin: *gongdexin*; in Japanese: *kootokushin*; in Korean: *Kongdokshim*; and in English: 'public spiritedness.'"[31]

For Kuniyoshi (Figure 5.4), aware of perhaps a few of these foreign language terms, masking appeared to be the most effective way to hide the inexorable fact he personally faced: that the US Supreme Court in 1922 had ruled

Figure 5.4 Yasuo Kuniyoshi, *Mask* (1948).

Philadelphia Museum of Art. Purchased with the Lola Downin Peck Fund from the Carl and Laura Zigrosser Collection, 1972. Courtesy of the Estate of the artist and Susan Teller Gallery, NY.

Japanese people were not the same as "free white persons" and therefore did not have the same rights to naturalization and to American citizenship.

Angst and Prejudice

American psychoanalyst Elisabeth Young-Bruehl has contended that "Studying prejudices requires the consciousness that all peoples have prejudices, and that any group will develop customs and ways of thinking that lead the group members to form prejudgments (and often leave them unable to take the next step and see their own prejudgments)."[32] As in the case of fear, recognition of one's prejudices marks the first step in making them harmless.

If loathing suggests aversion, abhorrence, disgust, and even hatred of a subject, prejudice implies similar feelings toward a group. It typically rests on a perverse relationship between one group, to which the subject feels she belongs, and another, which is perceived as different. The terms in-group and out-group accurately capture this relationship. To be sure, group relations take us away from the centrality of individual angst, the sensation that Kuniyoshi experienced and addressed in his art. The subject of group-based behavior counters his role as an individual artist but raises the "what if" question: what his experience could have been.

In his pioneering research on anti-Semitism, Canadian medievalist historian and anti-Semitism specialist Gavin Langmuir distinguished between garden-variety prejudice when groups simply did not like each other, and xenophobia when a group formed a negative opinion about another. He introduced a third category to map anti-Semitism: *chimera*—monsters, demons, and fantastical mythical creatures that became associated with an out-group. The genuine qualities of the out-group were conveniently ignored to make demonization easier.[33] Demonization of America's foe through enemy images of the Japanese surfaced in World War II as a Hobbesian choice that Kuniyoshi faced while working for a US government agency.

Stereotyping and scapegoating are central to prejudice. The expression "the victim is a scapegoat" implies the intent to have us reflect on not just the victim but the agency creating victimhood. French philosopher René Girard elaborated on this implicit logic: "Scapegoat indicates both the innocence of the victims, the collective polarisation in opposition to them, and the collective end result of that polarisation. The persecutors are caught up in the 'logic' of the representation of persecution from a persecutor's standpoint, and they cannot break away."[34]

Persecution and prejudice become the fabric, therefore, of in-group identity. More than that, the persecutor claims a natural right and moral imperative to be prejudiced against others: "In claiming to obey the imperatives of a responsibility that weighs more heavily upon him than anything else, he exonerates himself of any blame, when he does not simply create his own heroic reputation."[35]

Prejudices are functional for the group appropriating them. They bond group members together, provide a shared psychological experience, identify markers of membership, and delineate borders. They offer the necessary pretext for asserting that one's own group is better than another. Belief in a group's perfection brings elites and members together. As Young-Bruehl explained,

> Masses and elites that have nothing otherwise in common can find that the same ideology and the same organizing leadership unites them, relieves them of their rootlessness; the same apocalyptic and redemptive vision gives them a common future. They are relieved by it, enthused by it, feel swept into place by it, and they are glad to be all alike, uniform, in a historical process that asks no thinking of them but gives them the comfort of an obedience that does not feel passive to them.[36]

The product of such bonding can lead to the materialization of the enemy. Sociologist James Aho outlined the circuitous process by which an enemy becomes constructed. The enemy's territory is conceived of as a series of paradoxes in which apparently unbelievable notions become true. The first paradox is of evil's inseparability from good: violence emergences from a quest for good. The second is the unifying function of enemies: "There can be no harmony without chaos, no peace without war." The struggle against an adversary is not just about pursuing a group's interests but cementing its social solidarity. Finally, "the enemy is a *mysterium tremendum* ... a paradoxical duality that simultaneously revolts and attracts us."[37] These three stages help consolidate an enemy for a group, and we can see the contours of this process at work in contemporary politics at both the national or international level.

Polish sociologist Zygmunt Bauman summarized the nexus between fear and evil this way: "What we fear, is evil; what is evil, we fear."[38]

Predictably, then, redemptive violence is justified in the struggle between good and evil because the world can be redeemed by annihilating evil enemies who hatch demonic conspiracies and use immoral tactics. Particularly in times of crises, biblical images of peacemaking through waging holy war are invoked. The combination of enemy stereotypes, the mystique of violence, and a worship of one's own national, including religious, symbols makes holy war a just option.

This was what Kuniyoshi was expected to do while working for the Office of War Information. Eminent Washington-based psychiatrist Vamik Volkan explained how "Political propaganda intuitively makes use of the potential of large-group identity offered in adulthood to cover over or repair the damaged or conflicted personal identities. Because of this many individuals passionately cling to the 'new' large-group identity."[39] Kuniyoshi's aspirational large-group identity was to be an American even though his conflicted personal identity was holding him back.

Based on his theory concerning the death instinct, Freud was pessimistic about human nature and the role of psychoanalysis in preventing wars.[40] Volkan shared Freud's doubt about psychoanalysis and war prevention. Notionally, Kuniyoshi supported a just war against Japan. In the process, however, he was consumed by angst.

Return of the Artist

Kuniyoshi did not make use of motifs of redemptive violence in his wartime propaganda drawings. Instead, he enthusiastically embraced wartime employment with the War Information office and insisted "I'd like very much to do the 'Japanese enemy' poster."[41] His ensuing drawings "showed the viciousness of the Japanese military and his subject matter began to change and become more political and jarring. Paintings like *Torture, Rotting on the Shore, Little Girl Run for Your Life*, and *Headless Horse Who Wants to Jump* reflect a haunted sensibility that is in the grasp of both fear and the unknown."[42]

Apart from his criticism of commercial work being awarded commissions, there is little evidence that he regretted taking on the role of war propagandist. But at the subconscious level, the conflicted hybridity he embodied in this role had to have taken a toll. Kuniyoshi's recourse to masks became even more commonplace after the war.[43]

> [Kuniyoshi's] identity in crisis may have been behind the many masks that appear after the war in such paintings as *I Wear a Mask Today* (1946–1947); *The Clown, Charade, Clown with Mask*, and *Last Act* (1948); *Carnival* (1949); *Revelation* and *To the Ball* (1950); *Mask* and *Masquerade* (1951); and *Fakirs, Mr. Ace, Amazing Juggler*, and *The Juggler* (all 1952).[44]

"Losing face" is a cliché but it may furnish part of the explanation for his extensive use of the mask motif.

Compare this representational strategy to that which Kuniyoshi employed before hostilities between the United States and Japan broke out. In the summer of 1941, the artist sought relief from escalating tensions by traveling west to Colorado, New Mexico, Nevada, and California. "He drank in the wide, open landscape and the somber tonalities of the desert. He painted Western themes such as *Cow Girl*, *Colorado Landscape*, *Cripple Creek*, *Nevadaville*, and *Silver Gulch*. Perhaps by seeking out America's frontier, Kuniyoshi hoped to become more American in this troubled time."[45]

It provided a consoling interlude between two periods of terror. It evoked an observation made earlier by Edvard Munch (an artist cited earlier) who exhibited a unique skill for capturing sentiments of fear and dread in his works. In the 1890s, he completed a cycle of paintings that formed what he called *The Frieze of Life*. One of his most quoted remarks may fit the tormented life that Kuniyoshi had been living (Figure 5.5):

> From the moment of my birth, the angels of anxiety, worry, and death stood at my side, followed me out when I played, followed me in the sun of springtime and in the glories of summer. They stood at my side in the evening when I closed my eyes, and intimidated me with death, hell, and eternal damnation. And I would often wake up at night and stare widely into the room: Am I in Hell?[46]

Figure 5.5 Harry Sternberg, *Portrait of Yasuo Kuniyoshi* (1944).

Courtesy of the Estate of the artist and Susan Teller Gallery, NY.

Yet the eve of World War II marked a time when the artist was reaching new artistic heights: "Kuniyoshi's best work is what he produced from the late 1930s until his death. There is a sustained sense of loss, misfortune, fear, and disillusionment in many of his best works."[47] *Refugees* (1939) is especially noteworthy, depicting women fleeing from unidentified terror, victims of unexplained persecution. It coincided with the early years of the Sino-Japanese War. Accompanied by a ghostlike dog, women hurry along a road carved into a barren landscape. A dark-shrouded female figure leads the way as the father urges a reluctant child to hurry along. Figures of refugees further up the road heighten the "aura of tragedy."[48]

Wartime paintings of fear and foreboding—the so-called "atrocity images"—include *Rape* (1942), *Grandmother and Two Children* (1943), and *Murdered* (1944). All the subjects are women. Kuniyoshi completed even more gruesome drawings during the war years. But even after it ended, trauma remained palpable. *She Mourns* (1946) portrays a tearful head-scarfed woman holding a handkerchief to her closed eyes. *She Walks Among the Ruins* (1946) is of a younger woman seemingly asking herself how to cope with the chaos surrounding her.

Such figures "inhabit the postwar landscape of Kuniyoshi's late works, populated with ruined buildings, broken objects, and unintelligible fragments of words."[49] *Disturbing Dream* (1948) depicts an acrobat falling from a trapeze and missing her partner's hands. Absolute mortal fear and panic are etched on her face. *The Widow* (1948) suggests despair and grieving before a background of stark rectangular spaces. The supposition is that angst had been grafted onto postwar social conditions.

In 1942, Kuniyoshi had conveyed to imagined Japanese listeners the beliefs of "an artist of your race who lives in a much brighter place in every way than your own land. Whose eyes are opened on broader horizons than those who sit on one little island, seeing only one little sky."[50] His purpose in writing this letter was to suggest how human beings may be confined within borders but artists have none. The cosmopolitan claim was bound to rankle, however: not only did it indicate a sense of innate superiority of one country, culture, and civilization over another. It contrasted a universalism juxtaposed against a myopic nationalism. Prejudice, demonization, loathing, and self-loathing are contained in this textual reference.

Fortuitously for his artistic reputation, Kuniyoshi was not as *gauche* and klutzy in his works of art. Yet these combine to form a representation of angst that stem from the diverse stimuli across various contexts that punctuated his bifurcated life. In his study of war and relations between states, Thucydides largely overlooked the individual angst that shapes a citizen and a soldier.

Postscriptum

In 2017, English writer Kazuo Ishiguro won the 2017 Nobel Prize for Literature for "novels of great emotional force" in which he "uncovered the abyss beneath our illusory sense of connection with the world." Born in Nagasaki in 1954, at age five he and his family moved to Guildford in the south of England. He only returned to Japan twenty-nine years later and agreed that his Japanese language skills were "awful." His mother, however, was "a Japanese lady of her generation."

In his novel *The Remains of the Day* published in 1989, he writes of a butler named Stevens who, after three decades of service at Darlington Hall, questions whether he did well in serving the "great gentleman" Lord Darlington.

> What can we ever gain in forever looking back and blaming ourselves if our lives have not turned out quite as we might have wished? The hard reality is, surely, that for the likes of you and I, there is little choice other than to leave our fate, ultimately, in the hands of those great gentlemen at the hub of this world who employ our services. What is the point in worrying oneself too much about what one could or could not have done to control the course one's life took? Surely it is enough that the likes of you and I at least try to make our small contribution count for something true and worthy.

Kazuo Ishiguro, *The Remains of the Day* (New York: Vintage International, 1990), 244.

Notes

1 Søren Kierkegaard, *The Concept of Anxiety: A Simple Psychologically Orienting Deliberation on the Dogmatic Issue of Hereditary Sin* (Princeton: Princeton University Press, 1981).
2 Sigmund Freud, *Beyond the Pleasure Principle.* Authorized translation from the second German edn. by C. J. M. Hubback (1922), in *The International Psycho-analytical Press* (London and Vienna, MCMXXII), https://www.libraryofsocialscience.com/assets/pdf/freud_beyond_the_pleasure_principle.pdf.
3 Sigmund Freud, *The Problem of Anxiety.* Trans. Henry Alden Bunker (Mansfield Centre, CT: Martino Publishing, 2013).
4 Michael A. Milburn and Sheree D. Conrad, *The Politics of Denial* (Cambridge: MIT Press, 1996), 71.
5 Inge Bretherton, "The Origins of Attachment Theory: John Bowlby and Mary Ainsworth," *Developmental Psychology* 28, no. 5 (1992), 759–75.
6 Henri Parens, "Toward Understanding Prejudice—Benign and Malignant," in *The Future of Prejudice: Psychoanalysis and the Prevention of Prejudice*, eds. Henri Parens, Afaf Mahfouz, Stuart W. Twemlow, and David E. Scharff (Lanham: Rowman and Littlefield, 2007), 25–28.

7 Hans-Jürgen Wirth, "The Roots of Prejudice in Family Life and Its Political Significance as Discerned in a Study of Slobodan Milosevic," in *The Future of Prejudice*, 112.

8 Robert J. Sternberg and Karin Sternberg, *The Nature of Hate* (Cambridge: Cambridge University Press, 2008).

9 Antoni Kępiński, *Lęk* (Warsaw: Wydawnictwo Literackie, 2009).

10 Whitney Museum of American Art, https://whitney.org/collection/works/1367.

11 Smithsonian American Art Museum, "The Artistic Journey of Yasuo Kuniyoshi—April 2–August 29, 2015," New York, https://americanart.si.edu/exhibitions/kuniyoshi.

12 Adam Greenhalgh, "Yasuo Kuniyoshi's *Cows in Pasture*," *Gastronomica* 9, no. 3 (2009), 15–21, https://online.ucpress.edu/gastronomica/article-abstract/9/3/15/47161/Yasuo-Kuniyoshi-s-Cows-in-Pasture?redirectedFrom=fulltext.

13 Aaron Copland, "The Composer and His Critic," *Modern Music* 9, no. 4 (May–June 1932).

14 "Co-curators Joann Moser and Tom Wolfe Discuss Artist Yasuo Kuniyoshi," Smithsonian American Art Museum, April 2015, https://americanart.si.edu/exhibitions/kuniyoshi.

15 Gail Levin, "Between Two Worlds: Folk Culture, Identity, and the American Art of Yasuo Kuniyoshi," *Archives of American Art Journal* 43, nos. 3–4 (2003), 5.

16 William Murrell, *Yasuo Kuniyoshi* (Woodstock: William M. Fisher Publishers, 2012).

17 Jane Myers and Tom Wolf, "Kuniyoshi in the Early 1920s," in *The Shores of a Dream: Yasuo Kuniyoshi's Early Work in America* (Fort Worth: Amon Carter Museum, 1996), 26.

18 Levin, "Between Two Worlds," 2–17. Reprinted in Gail Levin, Yasuo Kuniyoshi, and Hirose Naruhisa, *Kuniyoshi in Japanese Collections* (Okayama Museum of Art, 2006), 328–42.

19 Wolf, "Kuniyoshi in the Early 1920s," 26.

20 Wolf, "Kuniyoshi in the Early 1920s," 32.

21 Tom Wolf, *Yasuo Kuniyoshi's Women* (Rohnert Park: Pomegranate Artbooks, 1993), ix.

22 Jane Myers and Tom Wolf, "Independent Creations: Kuniyoshi's Ink Drawings of 1921–25," in *The Shores of a Dream: Yasuo Kuniyoshi's Early Work in America* (Fort Worth: Amon Carter Museum, 1996), 60.

23 ShiPu Wang, *Becoming American: The Art and Identity Crisis of Yasuo Kuniyoshi* (Honolulu: University of Hawai'i Press, 2011), 36.

24 Wang, *Becoming American*, 38–39.

25 ShiPu Wang, "Prelude: Surviving Pearl Harbor," in *Becoming American*, http://www.jstor.org/stable/j.ctt6wqjw8.5.

26 Wang, *Becoming American*, 70–97. See also Smithsonian Institution Archives of American Art, Yasuo Kuniyoshi, "Civilization Besieged: The Artist's Role in War," https://edan.si.edu/transcription/pdf_files/36802.pdf.

27 ShiPu Wang, "Japan against Japan: U.S. Propaganda and Yasuo Kuniyoshi's Identity Crisis," *American Art* 22, no. 1 (Spring 2008), 28–51, https://www.journals.uchicago.edu/doi/abs/10.1086/587915?journalCode=amart.

28 Levin, "Between Two Worlds."

29 Graham Jones, "Masks as a Collective Cry for Justice," in "The Meanings of Masks," ed. Emily Hiestand, *MIT News*, September 20, 2020, https://news.mit.edu/2020/meanings-of-masks-shass-series-0924.

30 Sara Brown, "The Expressive Power of Masks," in "The Meanings of Masks."

31 Emma Tong, "Masks as 公德心," in "The Meanings of Masks."
32 Elisabeth Young-Bruehl, "A Brief History of Prejudice Studies," in *The Future of Prejudice: Psychoanalysis and the Prevention of Prejudice*, eds. Henri Parens, Afaf Mahfouz, Stuart W. Twemlow, and David E. Scharff (Lanham: Rowman and Littlefield, 2007), 219.
33 David Norman-Smith, "Anti-Semitism," in *Encyclopedia of Race, Ethnicity, and Society*, ed. Richard T. Schaefer (Thousand Oaks: Sage, 2008), 77.
34 René Girard, *The Scapegoat* (Baltimore: Johns Hopkins University Press, 1986), 39.
35 Lise Noël, *Intolerance: A General Survey* (Montreal: McGill-Queen's University Press, 1994), 127.
36 Young-Bruehl , "A Brief History," 352.
37 James A. Aho, *This Thing of Darkness: A Sociology of the Enemy* (Seattle: University of Washington Press, 1994), 15–17.
38 Zygmunt Bauman, *Liquid Fear* (Cambridge: Polity Press, 2006), 54.
39 Vamik D. Volkan, "A Look at Albert Einstein's Question 'Why War?' with a Focus on Large-Group Psychology," in *International Journal of Psychoanalysis* 103, no. 3 (July 2022), 455–66, https://www.tandfonline.com/doi/abs/10.1080/00207578.2022.2068774.
40 Sigmund Freud, "Why War?" *Standard Edition* 22 (London: Hogarth, 1933), 199–201.
41 Wang, *Becoming American*, 72.
42 Paul Yamada, "Yasuo Kuniyoshi," in *JACL Chicago Chapter Newsletter*, January/February 2007, http://www.discovernikkei.org/en/journal/2010/1/5/yasuo-kuniyoshi/
43 Wang, *Becoming American*, ch. 5.
44 Levin, "Between Two Worlds."
45 Levin, "Between Two Worlds."
46 Wendy Gray, "The Frieze of Life by Edvard Munch," *Daily Art Magazine*, January 8, 2022, https://www.dailyartmagazine.com/edvard-munch-and-the-frieze-of-life/.
47 Yamada, "Yasuo Kuniyoshi."
48 Wolf, *Yasuo Kuniyoshi's Women*, xv.
49 Wolf *Yasuo Kuniyoshi's Women*, xviii.
50 Wang, *Becoming American*, 51.

Chapter 6

INTERSTATE FEARS: AUSTRALIA'S LINKAGES TO CHINA

The next case study is of both domestic and interstate fears: Australia's running confrontation with China. Thucydides had an unusual, rarely used term for this phenomenon, *hypopsia*, as he sketched the fear-encrusted relations that existed between Athens and Sparta in the fifth century BCE. The term he employed in his catalog of fear, *hypopsia*, entails searching beneath the surface of things in order to identify a general fear of a rather distant threat.

Australian research has spotlighted the significance of achieving a sense of social cohesion in its society. A corollary of this is ascertaining whether protectionist, nativist, and even anti-foreigner attitudes in a society will undermine this objective. But Australia's relevance to China is more than just the possible impact on domestic policy caused by large-scale demographic shifts and immigration. It also can create an interstate fear in foreign policy that contrasts two states which are distant from each other but one of whose populations is around twenty-five million and the other's is approaching 1.5 billion. Interstate fear thereby overlaps with a domestic threat.

Ethnic minorities often experience uneasiness when they live alongside earlier-settled societies; this is especially applicable to Indigenous First Peoples. Interstate distrust can also be rooted in countries separated from each other which develop mutual suspicions, for example, security threats emanating from one or the other—or both as in the case of ancient Athens and Sparta. *Hypopsia* becomes even more precarious when one state holds strategic advantages compared to the other, in other words, arising during a shaky imbalance of power.

Racial makeup regularly constitutes a factor that shapes fear of strangers. In the studies examined in this book, I also highlighted cultural racism where religious, educational, and/or behavioral factors not linked to the color of a person's skin comes to the fore. When Brexit forces used a culturally racist argument to undermine the free movement principle established by the EU and now available to enlargement states, it was a clear instance of discrimination against strangers.

In Australia, it was argued how privileged the country had been for a long time due to skin color. Its White population rarely experienced systemic prejudice against it while sometimes it has been responsible for sowing prejudice against non-Whites. Generally, it enjoyed the benefits of racial advantage, as other colonized states had done. Carmen Lawrence, the first popularly elected president of the Australian Labor Party selected in 2004, underscored how "Under federation, the nation incorporated the same values of racial superiority and exclusion." An "invasion anxiety" with "racial overtones" led to a fear that "Chinese immigrants would 'swamp the whole European community of these colonies' and 'obliterate every trace of British progress and civilization.' "[1]

Furthermore, an enduring contrast has arisen between later settlers in the country and Aboriginal First Peoples unable to shake off their subaltern postcolonial status. A series of mainly half-measures has tried to incorporate Indigenous Peoples into, ironically, a more recently constructed settler society. Thus a 2023 referendum on a constitutional amendment was to determine whether a "Voice to Parliament" instituting a federal advisory body on Indigenous affairs would be approved. I briefly consider their presence below. But it has been "invasion anxiety" that historically evoked wider concerns and took precedence over the extension of rights to an already-existing ancient civilization.

In-migration to Australia

Are there distinctive features about Australia's selection of immigrants which helped shape its future society? Elaborating on his classic book titled *The Big White Lie*, Melbourne security studies professor John Fitzgerald noted that while other former British colonies—Canada, the United States, and New Zealand—discriminated against people of Chinese origin and invoked salient racial ideologies which inspired them,

> none of these countries constituted themselves as sovereign states on the back of arguments about preserving national purity by restricting Asian immigration: Australia did. For a good 70 years from its founding moment in 1901 Australia was White Australia. There was no other Australia going. Australia's effort to restrict Chinese immigration was distinguished by a number of features but above all by its association with nation building.

Indeed, declared Fitzgerald, "In Australia an ideal of racial purity converged with a triumphalist rhetoric of self-conscious nation building to yield a particular vision of a brand new country able to demonstrate its independence by shutting its gates to all but Whites."[2]

In the 1980s, this type of prejudice changed as people from foreign countries applied for and received Australian residency permits and very often subsequently, citizenship. With the exception of New Zealanders who migrate across the "nearby" Tasman Ditch—approximately one-fifth of Kiwis are lured to Australia mainly due to higher wages offered here—geographically mobile populations arrived from distant shores, held different religious faiths and cultural pathways, and were often Brown or Black or Yellow.

It made sense that multiculturalism became the main strategy for managing growing diversity. Migrants were given considerable autonomy in organizing their lives and assimilationist or monocultural models were duly discarded. An alternative policy might have included interculturalism—a diversity strategy recognizing a state's majority peoples and the primacy of its spoken language over those of minority cultures but the one expectation was that minorities would be tasked with making reasonable accommodation so as to adjust to the country's majority. What is understood as reasonable itself became a matter of push-and-shove debates.

Australian migration policy is both different from and similar to other immigrant-receiving societies. It is different because "Australia's history as a geographically defined nation with control over its borders has pushed successive governments to place migration law and policy at the forefront of the political agenda."[3] It is similar because, as its Prime Minister Malcolm Turnbull underscored in 2017, the country has had the most successful multicultural policies anywhere in the world.[4]

If multiculturalism focuses on protecting the cultural rights of minorities, and if interculturalism insists on paying greater attention to the rights of a majority while respecting minority rights, does each promote a different set of values? For example, do they differ in their support for language diversity, or for entry into the labor market, or for improving educational skills? What of other considerations such as obtaining affordable housing, applying for family unification of loved ones living abroad, or affirming their cultural and linguistic legacies in Australia? In spite of Turnbull's claim, does the multicultural paradigm remain unchallenged in Australia?[5]

As this study has highlighted, migration continues to be a polarizing issue in world politics. Receiving societies are expected to integrate migrants from around the world and achieve social cohesion. This entails promoting trust in and legitimacy for the state, furthering migrants' inclusion and belonging in a society while overcoming their marginalization.[6] But what if a country thousands of miles away has developed into an economic powerhouse, its minorities become economically dominant in countries of the region, and a still distant threat of it becoming economically and politically dominant appears palpable?

Two Australian scholars considered that "There is limited research on social cohesion and refugees in Australia."[7] In their yearly iterations, the bellwether Scanlon Foundation surveys recognized that "there is no agreed definition of social cohesion."[8] The humanitarian dimension of migration comes into play: do some migrants even get as far as arriving in a country and being welcomed by it? Migration analysts argue that "While Australia is a leading provider of humanitarian settlement, priding itself on dedicated resettlement programs to assist those legitimately channeled through United Nations programs, people arriving by boat are often described as 'queue jumpers'"—a term bandied about in Australia's political discourse.[9]

Australia's Navy seeks to control the high seas and wishes to prevent queue jumpers from arriving on the mainland. It has set up a system of offshore processing where migrants never reach the country's shores. Has this process anything in common with constructing a socially cohesive society? International publicity about the Christmas Island detention center nearer to Indonesia than Australia, and the Nauru and Manus Islands locations in Papua New Guinea gave the country a black eye about the handling of refugees. Such harsh measures have gradually been scaled down.

Research on different aspects of migration has exploded over the last few decades. Social cohesion as an explanatory independent variable is justifiable in enhancing migration studies. Multiculturalism, interculturalism, integration, assimilation, post-nationalism, and other adaptive processes may be allotted secondary importance in conceptual frameworks. Moreover, social cohesion is of concern to many disciplines whether it is politics, sociology, anthropology, psychology, history, demography, semiotics, or other fields. Highlighting cohesion has a practical aspect too; it has the potential to preempt incidents of violence, crime, lawlessness, xenophobia, anomie, moral panic, and social disintegration.

But a society with deep suspicions of particular ethnic communities may likely find building social cohesion elusive. In-migration "is unleashing the most profound changes to Australian society since the gold rushes of the 1850s."[10] In some seventy years, Australia has been transformed from a mainly White, Anglo-Irish society to one in which nearly half the population is born overseas or has one parent who was born abroad. Religiosity is also affected: the Australian Bureau of Statistics reported in 2022 that fewer than half of Australians (forty-four percent) identify as Christian; a little over fifty years ago the proportion was about ninety percent. Although Christianity remains the single largest faith, it is now followed by those with no religion at all (thirty-nine percent). To be sure, Hinduism and Islam are the fastest-growing religions but each makes up about three percent of the population.[11]

For the Scanlon Institute, which has been based at Monash University in Melbourne, a multicultural Australia has been constructed on ever-increasing public acceptance of this phenomenon; I present survey results later in this chapter.[12] During the early 1990s' recession, opposition to immigration reached nearly seventy percent but dramatically declined since and was under fifteen percent in 2020. But the rival Lowy Institute poll has cautioned that for the very first time a slight majority of Australians—fifty-four percent, a sharp climb from forty percent in 2017—responded that the number of migrants remains too high.

Distrust of the Chinese influence in Australia, specifically, for those in the know the part played by the Chinese Communist Party (CCP) in bringing alleged political shills into the country, masks "the broader issue of a perceived increase in racist abuse against Asian people in Australia, driven in part by the coronavirus pandemic."[13] Many non-Chinese are victims of Sinophobia because it is difficult to identify the differences between one Asian person and another. Language spoken is usually the cue.

This study focuses on Chinese arrivals in Australia partly over *la longue durée* but mainly focusing on recent years. It is crucial to acknowledge that broader Asia-phobic sentiments not specifically targeting Chinese-speaking communities (whether Mandarin, Cantonese, or another dialect) may be involved. The term Sinophobia should be invoked only where necessary and unmistakable evidence exists that the phobia is directed at the Chinese population. To sum up, close to 1.4 million people with Chinese ancestry live in Australia today with forty-one percent having been born in mainland China. A hypopsic attitude toward this growing community arises because of suspicion of what mainland China's motives are likely to be in the country.

Indigenous Peoples—The Racialized Always-Other

A comparative study by Justine Dandy and Rogelia Pe-Pua explored "refugee perspectives on integration in Australia through the lens of Jenson's dimensions of social cohesion…. To what extent do refugees feel like they 'fit in' and/or are accepted, and what are the factors that enhance or detract from their inclusion in Australian society?"[14] Five conditions were set out by Canadian political scientist Jane Jenson when building social cohesion:

1. belonging: the sense of connectedness to and pride in the community or nation;
2. inclusion: equal access to resources including education, employment, health care, and housing;
3. participation: engagement in politics, civics, society, and local community;
4. recognition: the extent to which mutual respect and tolerance exist;
5. legitimacy: institutionally grounded issues such as policies promoting pluralism and public confidence in the political system and government.[15]

For Jenson, social cohesion becomes problematic, particularly in ethnically diverse societies, where migrant communities arrive with different values and priorities than the settler societies preceding them. In welcoming foreigners, belonging confronts nativism reflected in the conviction that self-ascribed locals are the nation's keepers of tradition. Unless socialized to void bias, a nativist backlash is likely in most societies experiencing an inflow of immigrants whose ethnic, racial, cultural, and religious loyalties are dissimilar to those of established residents. Views about "unmeltable" differences are fueled by the attachments newcomers have to their own traditions and identities, regarded as at odds with those of receiving societies.

Yet in the case of Indigenous Peoples across the globe, it is colonialism, neocolonialism, and xenophobia that manifest themselves in the legal and extrajudicial discrimination they suffer. First Nations are descendants of those who were there before settlers arrived and re-defined their societies, land laws, and economic system. Early Indigenous inhabitants are shaped partly by descent, partly by distinctive pathways, and typically by language, ways of life, and hunting-and-gathering skills. Indigenous Peoples were those who controlled borderless lands until stripped of them by later arrivals, then succumbed to their domination and suffered from their neglect. Consequently, the law of discovery attributed to settlers arriving in "no man's land" is bogus, as is the doctrine of *terra nullius*.

Aboriginal Peoples are not expected to integrate into societies they fashioned; they lived on these lands for millennia. Recognition of that fact has gained ground in much of Australian society—and other states with Indigenous populations as well. Modern societies recognize majority over minority rights but also multiculturalism over monoculturalism. Yet for centuries settler societies ignored the fate of First Peoples even though the land, lakes, rivers, rocks, forests, fauna, and flora had belonged to them.

Leaders of Indigenous communities believe that in addition to ethical claims about being able to hold on to their culture, land, and language, First Peoples can empower a return to the ecological and spiritual values they held long ago (Figure 6.1). Without returning to these values, the world could be at serious risk. Some environmentalists go further and insist that only Indigenous ways of life can save the globe from a not-so-distant climate catastrophe.

Changing demographics add to the complexity of immigrant-receiving societies such as Australia. Over a quarter of the country's population was born in non-English-speaking countries or are the progeny of such people. However, as Michael Clyne, director of the Coalition for Inclusive Capitalism, pointed out, "Prior to the first European settlement, Australia was a multilingual continent in which most people needed several languages to communicate.

Figure 6.1 An Indigenous Australian playing a eucalyptus didjeridu, a sacred musical instrument hollowed out by termites whose resonating vibration results from the musician's vocal tracts.

Some of the communities in Australia practiced compulsory exogamy, where the men of one community had to marry women from another and the children learned a different language from their father and mother."[16] These are fascinating observations needing corroboration and awareness.

Clyne noted that today's immigrant offspring coming from different linguistic backgrounds were returning to historic bilingualism, even multilingualism (theoretically, the term polyglots is reserved for those who speak six languages or more). The author insisted that "Today's Australia is a multilingual nation in a multilingual world in which there are far more plurilinguals (those using two or more languages) than monolinguals."[17] But since English throughout the country is the *lingua franca*, the pressure is to use this language even if "according to 'liberal nationalist' principles... [it is] a desirable feature of diversity within unity which entailed recognizing plurilinguals as every bit as Australian as monolingual English speakers."[18] Thus in many societies there is pushback on the part of a unilingual majority to embrace plurilingual speakers as their own.

Of main non-English languages spoken at home, Mandarin, Hindi, and Korean have gained considerably. For Clyne, "A high degree of language shift from the community language to English is indicative of assimilation. A low degree of shift can reflect multiculturalism or a desire to segregate but does not necessarily indicate a reluctance to integrate, since it is comparable with a high degree of bilingualism."[19] Consequently, "The symbolic significance of language choice in relation to identity also varies. It may express solidarity with non-English-speaking relatives (e.g., in Taiwan, Chinese and Lebanese communities."[20] This could lead to grievances about these communities' "divisiveness—too much 'sticking together'"—identified by majority groups as impacting negatively on social diversity.[21]

Excepting the preeminence of Indigenous Peoples living "in country"—as it is termed by Aboriginal groups—Australia's contemporary demographics has changed as much as those of other immigrant-receiving societies. One person in ten is now born in Asia. In cities like Melbourne and Sydney, about one in three people speaks Mandarin or Cantonese at home. Aboriginal Peoples represent no threat to society but supposedly far-off Chinese communities do.

The PRC Ascendant

Influential and well-off minorities attract resentment just about everywhere. But when these minorities differ ethnically and are highly visible, resentment rises. It feeds ethnic competition and, possibly, subsequent animosity. The Chinese presence is reflected in Australia through language use: Mandarin is now the second most common tongue spoken. Before COVID, over 200,000 Chinese students were registered in Australian universities and colleges. Before the pandemic, 1.5 million Chinese short-term tourists spent over $12 billion contributing to the country's economy. Privileged economic elites from the People's Republic of China (PRC) include those managing direct foreign investments. The Investment Facilitation Arrangement in Canberra provided a concession allowing a project company registered in Australia but with fifty percent Chinese ownership to bring Chinese workers to the country to work on infrastructure development projects. This happens regularly.

Hypopsia, a suspicion or distrust of Chinese motives in moving *en bloc* to Australia, has resulted in disquieting relations between the two states. Australia reneged on parts of the Belt and Road Initiative—a massive global Chinese development initiative—that might have brought the two countries closer together. Just as importantly, longstanding liberal values such as pluralism, tolerance, and multicultural coexistence have come under challenge in their interstate relationship.

A review of writer Clive Hamilton's much-cited book *Silent Invasion* observed how "From politics to culture, real estate to agriculture, universities to unions, and even in our primary schools, he [Hamilton] uncovered compelling evidence of the Chinese Communist Party's infiltration of Australia." The book was triggered by an earlier revelation that wealthy Chinese businessmen linked to the CCP had become the biggest donors to both of Australia's major political parties.[22] An essay by a journalist also sparked further suspicion about China's motives: "Australia and China have got rich together. For Australia, that is quite enough. But China's government wants more. As much power and influence over Australia as it can possibly get, using fair means or foul."[23]

A dissenting view about the PRC was advanced by David Brophy, an expert on modern Chinese history at the University of Sydney. In an insightful book titled *China Panic*, he lay the blame for panic on Australian leaders. It began with Prime Minister Turnbull's "The Australian People Have Stood Up" speech in 2017, to his successor, Scott Morrison's call in 2020 for an international inquiry into the origins of the COVID-19 virus. He suggested that World Health Organization officials be given powers similar to those of United Nations' weapons inspectors to investigate health and safety crises in the PRC.[24]

Brophy critiqued both states' policies and the United States was not spared either. A reviewer of *China Panic* highlighted how the book "offers an insightful antidote to the sometimes hysterical analysis and commentary emanating from Australian politicians of all stripes, intelligence agencies, the media, think tanks, journalists, and commentators." At the center of foreign policy should be peoples' well-being, not economic or security priorities.[25]

Deepening Chinese involvement in Australian economics, politics, and international relations, reflected by the urgency on the part of the United States to sign the 2021 Aukus security pact comprising the United States, the United Kingdom, and Australia—all members of the anglosphere—produced suspicious reactions in Australia. A critical issue affecting the newfound alliance was whether the United States or the United Kingdom would supply nuclear submarines to the country that was closest to China. The Labor Party in government since 2022 was more open-minded in seeking to reset relations with the PRC. But Australia could not reject the security interests of its closest security partner.

For some time China has comprised the second-largest economy in the world; it is forecast to overtake the United States by the end of the 2020s. Its economic power is matched by its political reach: its strength and involvement extend from Greenland and Iceland to the Caribbean (Barbados reputedly replaced the Queen as monarch under pressure from China) and Peru and Argentina; and from South Africa, Zimbabwe, and a host of other African states to Pakistan and Mongolia. Moreover, Southeast Asia is replete with sizeable, powerful Chinese diasporas. Even interests in Antarctica have not been overlooked by Beijing. Looking retrospectively at his country, Chinese dissident artist and filmmaker Ai Weiwei, now resident in the United Kingdom, remarked: "The West should really have worried about China decades ago." He now believed that China uses its immense economic power to impose political influence.[26]

An expanding role for China's influencers is found in the venerable example of Cambridge University. One journalist suggested that "China is adept at directing funding towards areas of research which it sees as strategically important and it has targeted a range of British institutions. Few have allowed themselves to be so comprehensively compromised as Cambridge." For China observer Ian Williams, author of *Every Breath You Take: China's New Tyranny*, "Cambridge is often seen to be the pinnacle of Britain's liberal education system. But it has also shown itself to be truly world-beating when it comes to accepting Chinese money with few questions asked."[27]

Australian universities, like many others in the world, are as eager to collaborate with Chinese counterparts in order to obtain funding. A Four Corners-Background Briefing in 2019 "uncovered widespread collaborations between Australia's leading universities and Chinese entities involved in Beijing's surveillance apparatus." In fact, according to the Briefing, "Australia's top universities could be aiding the Chinese Communist Party's mission to develop mass surveillance and military technologies, amid rising concerns from Australian intelligence agencies that they are putting national security at risk."[28]

A former chairman of the Department of Foreign Affairs and Trade's Australia-China Council emphasized that Chinese companies were capitalizing on Australia's expertise: "Australia's science and technology priorities are being set by the Chinese Government because we enter into collaborations that have really been designed to support China's goals, not ours." Artificial intelligence was high on the list. Following Cambridge, the twin enticements of money and prestige were involved in the decisions to collaborate with Western universities.[29]

Amy Chua published a seminal book in 2003 that framed the West's relations with the PRC. In *World on Fire: How Exporting Free Market Democracy Breeds Ethnic Hatred and Global Instability*, the Yale University law professor believed that an ethnic minority with economic dominance, such as China, can engender ethnic conflict and violence. Over the decades across Southeast Asia, disproportionate economic power was accumulated by Chinese market-dominant minorities. If some Chinese migration took place more recently, a better term might be an "alien elite."

Chua put it bluntly: "In the Philippines, millions of Filipinos work for Chinese: almost no Chinese work for Filipinos."[30] In Australia, it would be inaccurate to call China a market-dominant minority, let alone a ruling economic class. But has it not already created blowback directed at its commercial activities and its political influencers resident in the country?

The beginnings of Chinese settlement in the country are fascinating. In the 1840s, the first settlers arrived, soon numbering about 10,000, and began work in the gold mines mainly in the eastern regions of the country. Their role was contextualized in an award-winning 2022 book by Columbia University scholar Mae Ngai who drew comparisons of Californian, South African, and Australian gold mining by Chinese emigrants in the second half of the nineteenth century. She rebuked the notion of a coolie myth: "The 'coolie' myth is insidious because it alleges that Chinese immigrants were pitiably oppressed, without individual personality or will, and pawns of big capitalists. Chinese were deemed a special, *racialized* version of 'cheap labor.'" In the United States, this background justified Chinese exclusion laws.[31]

Mae stressed how in her research in these far-off countries anti-Chinese politics emerged differently, in line with contrasting political and economic conditions. At the same time "politics also travel and borrow from each other, so that by the late-19th and early-20th centuries, there emerged a common racist theory grounded in White-settler colonialism."[32] Accordingly, after the gold rush began in Australia, "a typical White racist 'moral panic' focused on the Chinese as diseased, corrupt and morally decayed (e.g., opium addiction)."[33] In this chapter's Postscriptum, I relate the nature of the interactions between a Chinese headman in a gold mine town in Victoria State and a White designated-protector of Chinese workers.

What was on the table several decades later in clarifying the status of Chinese migrants was a brutal Sinophobic backlash evidenced in Australian migration legislation enacted by the 1901 Immigration Restriction Act. Its objective was to halt further influx of the fearsome Yellow Peril.

Skip forward more than a hundred years. A wave of non-Europeans began arriving in Australia in the late 1970s comprised of refugees. Chief among them were the Vietnamese fleeing the American-led war. Half of the Vietnamese seeking refuge were ethnic Chinese. Much later, in 2019, the Australian government established a task force to investigate Chinese interference, attempts to bribe politicians, and efforts to fund political campaigns in favor of Chinese Australians. This came on the heels of an investigation into Chinese-born federal Member of Parliament Gladys Liu whose links to the CCP propaganda machine came under scrutiny.

About 170 years after the gold rush, the Chinese population in Australia includes well-off groups such as those involved in direct foreign investments: Just before the pandemic started in 2020, according to the Department of Foreign Affairs and Trade China ranked fifth in direct foreign inward investment in the country. According to the OECD, Australia was home to the second largest temporary migrant workforce in the world behind the United States. Before the COVID outbreak, international education of foreign students ranked as the country's third largest export industry; according to the Department of Education and Training, Chinese students led the way. Australia is second (after the United States) as the destination most favored by Chinese students. Chinese entrepreneurs' preferences of sending their offspring abroad for higher education indicated that Australia (fourteen percent) ranked only behind the United States (thirty-seven percent) and Britain (twenty-five percent) in student intake.

In his alarmist *Silent Invasion*, Hamilton predicted that Chinese in-migration would catapult the PRC to broader economic and political clout in interstate relations. Foreign policy controversies such as over a 2015 Chinese lease on the port of Darwin for ninety-nine years made Canberra aware that the country's security needs were coming into play. Not just the Northern Territory was at risk, but so was its southernmost state—Tasmania. Chinese leader Xi Jinping's 2014 visit to Hobart initiated Chinese tourist growth in the island state; more ominously, Tasmania was becoming caught up in China's rapid expansion of its interests in Antarctica. An Antarctic gateway and resupply port was crowned by the maiden voyage of a new icebreaker, the *Xue Long 2*, which docked in Hobart on its way to the PRC's fifth Antarctic base in Terra Nova Bay on the Ross Sea.

Explaining its rapid growth, a Chinese law expert at the University of Adelaide pointed to a mix of national pride that it could set up bases in remote parts of the world while exemplifying its broad scientific and geopolitical interests. Both polar regions (the Antarctic and Arctic), deep sea beds, and outer space exploration were strategic new frontiers where the PRC would have a say in governance regimes. Not surprisingly, in 2019 China and Russia voted against Australia's efforts to have parts of the eastern Antarctic declared a marine sanctuary.[34]

Victoria State had planned to take part in China's Belt and Road project, deemed as a twenty-first-century Silk Road that would include new ports, highways, and railways across the globe. It would have boosted Victoria's economy while, from China's perspective, it would lay the basis for infrastructure firms to establish a presence in Melbourne so as to bid on major projects.[35] In the end, perhaps setting fear aside, Australia pulled out of this venture.

Survey Research on Attitudes to China

Survey data indicating that Australian respondents express distrust of China's intentions and motives have significantly increased in recent years. Concerns about the creation of a market-dominant Chinese minority as Amy Chua cautioned have been taken to heart by average Australians. Extensive data are available as I selectively present below. My focus is on replies to questions asked in three major surveys that bear on Australian attitudes toward the PRC. China's population includes those who are established settlers and foreign investors to short-term visitors and students.

Lowy Institute Data

Based in Sydney, the Lowy Institute is an independent research center that serves as an influential think tank and policy analysis hub, attracts important visiting speakers, includes a core staff investigating many aspects of Australian society, and publishes regular public opinion surveys on the country's changing attitudes. The 2021 annual survey taken to heart by Australia's political class reported the following results on citizen attitudes to China, in many ways a low point in public views of the PRC:

- Trust in China dropped to a new record low: Eighty-four percent of respondents claimed they had very little trust and only sixteen percent said they trusted China to act responsibly in the world. The first figure represented a seven-point drop from 2020 and an even larger decrease of a third recorded in 2018 when a majority of Australians (fifty-two percent) said they trusted China.
- One in ten Australians claimed they had "some" or "a lot" of confidence in China's President Xi Jinping to "do the right thing regarding world affairs." This halved since 2020 and declined 33 points since 2018.

On intersecurity concerns between the two countries, the survey found:

- The majority of Australians now regarded China as "more of a security threat to Australia" (sixty-three percent), a dramatic 22-point increase from the preceding year.
- The belief that China was "more of an economic partner to Australia" declined and fell to thirty-four percent, 21 points lower than in 2020.
- More than half (fifty-six percent) of respondents viewed China as "more to blame" than Australia for tensions in the Australia-China relationship.

On questions related to social cohesion resulting from impressions that Chinese people had made on Australians, the results included this:

- Three-quarters (seventy-six percent) believed that Chinese people they met positively influenced their view of China, a welcome exception from negative data.
- In the same vein, nearly seven in ten Australians (sixty-eight percent) reported that China's culture and history have a positive influence on their view of China. Nevertheless, this represented an 11-point decline from 2016.

In terms of its economic achievements, findings showed:

- Nearly half the population (forty-seven percent) thought that China's economic growth had a positive influence on their view of China, a dramatic 28-point fall since 2016.
- Just one in five indicated that Chinese investment in Australia had a positive influence on their view of China, a 17-point decline from the high point in 2016.

Worst of all was respondents' assessment of China's political system and its military activities:

- Merely six percent noted that China's system of government had a positive influence on their views of China; ninety-two percent disagreed this was so.
- Few Australians (five percent) thought that China's military activities in the region had a positive influence on their views of China.
- Concern about Chinese military activities contributed to a substantial increase in the number of Australians who viewed a military conflict between the United States and China over Taiwan as a critical threat to Australia's vital interests over the next ten years (up 17 points to fifty-two percent).[36]
- On the other hand, in the case of a US-China military conflict, fifty-seven percent of Australians remained neutral while under half (forty-one percent) backed the United States.

Overall, positive impressions of China were in free fall and *hypopsia* was developing into a majority view: "The sharp decline in the Australia-China relationship in recent years has been clearly mirrored in Australian public opinion, as seen in successive Lowy Institute Polls. Trust, warmth and confidence in China and China's leaders started to decline in 2017, and this year's results present another record low for Australians' views of China."[37] An array of economic and political disputes between Australia and China have left its mark.

An innovative approach taken by the Lowy Institute was tabulating a "feelings thermometer" describing Australians' sentiments toward other nations. The thermometer measured Australians' perceptions about other countries on a scale of 0° (coldest feelings) to 100° (warmest feelings). For the first time ever China slipped to the bottom of the table and registered a near-frigid 32°—a steep 26-degree decline since 2018 when Saudi Arabia and Iran were ascribed the most frigid feelings.

Scanlon Foundation Report

In its recent surveys, the prestigious, much-cited Scanlon Foundation Report at Monash University in Melbourne took up the question of COVID and discrimination against minorities. Directed by venerable political analyst Andrew Markus, its results were reported in its publication *Mapping Social Cohesion 2021.*

- The survey found that a majority of Australians were optimistic about the future while twenty-nine percent were pessimistic. True to its generally pollyanish findings, it represented a lower proportion in 2021 than in 2019 when 36 percent indicated pessimism although COVID lockdowns had not begun.
- Perceptions of racism in COVID-hit societies were measured. One survey question asked, "How big a problem is racism in Australia?" In 2020, the proportion indicating that it was a very or fairly big problem was stable at forty percent. In 2021, however, it was substantially higher at sixty percent: The survey recognized that "An increase of 20 percentage points in response to a general question of this nature is almost unprecedented in Scanlon Foundation surveys."
- A higher proportion of overseas-born people saw racism as a big problem including sixty-nine percent of respondents who were born in an Asian country; fifty-seven percent of Australian-born citizens agreed too.[38]

In past Scanlon surveys, which were first conducted in 2007, the largest number of people feeling discriminated against was reported by Australians of non-English-speaking backgrounds. This worrying finding remained consistent in the 2021 findings.

- In response to the question "Have you experienced discrimination in the last twelve months because of your skin color, ethnic origin or religion?" eleven percent of those born in Australia claimed that they had experienced discrimination; about the same percentage applied to those born overseas but in an English-speaking country; but a much higher percentage (thirty-four percent) affected overseas-born non-English-speaking countries. For Asians, a slightly higher figure (thirty-eight percent) was cited by those born in China, Hong Kong, or Taiwan. Overall, forty percent of all respondents born in Asia said they experienced discrimination.[39]

Even the multiculturalism-friendly Scanlon Report acknowledged that Asians generally and Chinese-born communities in particular expressed a feeling of being discriminated against.

When factoring in people's nationality, the report focused on attitudes toward ten specified national and faith groups living in Australia. Again the Chinese topped the list in negative responses (forty-seven percent) to the 2021 survey question: "Would you say your feelings are positive, negative, or neutral?"[40]

A research fellow at an Australian think tank on China singled out variations in the perception of anti-Chinese discrimination. He noted how 500 individuals surveyed in simplified Mandarin on WeChat (the Chinese equivalent of US Facebook or the Russian *V kontakte*) painted a picture in May and June 2020 of growing apprehension and discrimination:

- Twenty-seven percent indicated they experienced discrimination because of their appearance, ethnicity, or national origin over the last twelve months. A further twenty percent declined to answer the question suggesting underreporting the problem.
- Forty-one percent indicated experiencing more racism during the COVID pandemic.
- Thirty-nine percent agreed with the statement: "I feel conscious/nervous in public, particularly when I'm alone."[41]

This survey suggests how a small sample of Chinese felt about being discriminated against, harassed, or otherwise marginalized in their encounters with Australians.[42] Seen as outsiders and ferreting out whether they were happy or distressed by their encounters with the majority culture are crucial indicators of whether they feel they belong in the receiving country. To be sure, "feeling discriminated against" has also been used in some European surveys and can result in skewed or not accurate indications of discriminatory attitudes.[43]

Australia-China Relations Institute Survey

The third major social survey on attitudes toward China was carried out by the Australia-China Relations Institute (ACRI) based at the University of Technology Sydney (UTS). This latecomer Institute was initially established in 2014 and in 2021 conducted its first survey. In their executive summary, authors Elena Collinson and Paul F. Burke underlined the important caveat of differences that Australian elites and the public have on attitudes toward China:

> the presentation of the Australia-China relationship through a binary lens or a zero-sum prism does not completely align with perceptions in the wider community. There remains a divide between government views and much analytical commentary on the one hand, and popular attitudes on the other. However, in tracking the change in attitudes in some areas between this year and the last, it might also be said that the dominance of the elite narrative does appear to be slowly becoming more entrenched in the public consciousness.[44]

The following results were taken from the 2022 survey. I identify only those bearing on attitudes toward China's intentions.

- First, the majority of Australians (seventy-three percent) expressed mistrust of the Chinese government; three-quarters claimed that "China is a security threat to Australia."
- Over half (fifty-eight percent) expressed support for a harder line to be adopted by the Australian government with respect to its policies dealing with China.
- On surveillance questions, sixty-eight percent argued that "The Chinese government is monitoring the communications of Australians closely with apps such as WeChat"; forty-seven percent believed that "Australia should ban Chinese-owned apps such as TikTok and WeChat."

China's economic achievements, once heralded as spectacular, underwent a hardening.

- More Australians (fifty-seven percent) now believed that "The Australian government is right not to sign up to participate in China's Belt and Road Initiative."
- General support for foreign investment from China is fairly low, with forty-nine percent thinking that "Foreign investment from China is more detrimental than beneficial to Australia."
- Regarding higher education, sixty-seven percent agreed that "International students from China provide a major economic benefit to Australia." But that represented a nine-point decrease from 2021. Three-quarters were also concerned that "Australian universities are too financially reliant on international students from China," a six-point fall from 2021 when it was eighty-one percent.
- Perceptions of China's meddling, interference, and influence in Australia have risen. Two-thirds said that "Foreign interference in Australia stemming from China is more concerning than foreign interference from other countries" (a little less, sixty-five percent, claimed that "Foreign interference stemming from Russia is a major problem").
- Underscoring *hypopsia*, forty-two percent of respondents believed that "Australians of Chinese origin can be mobilized by the Chinese government to undermine Australia's interests and social cohesion."[45]

Qualitative data are also figured in the 2022 ACRI report. "Fallout from political friction between the two countries continues to be felt across a number of Australian sectors including, but not limited to, government, business and industry, media, and academia and research. People-to-people links have come under strain, and the Australian-Chinese community continues to feel the effects of tensions." Views on the Australia-China relationship within the government remain bleak, for example, when Coalition Defense Minister Peter Dutton was asked whether Australia was already "in a cold war with China at the moment." He refused to rebut the question.[46]

The Labor government elected in 2022 undertook some policy changes differing from the previous Liberal-National Coalition. New Minister for Foreign Affairs Penny Wong became the first Asian-born to hold an Australian Cabinet post. She had come to Australia from Malaysia as an eight-year-old and spent time serving as leader of the Australian Senate before her Cabinet appointment.

Prime Minister Anthony Albanese himself differed from all his predecessors in that he did not have an anglo name. But his relationship with China was not much warmer than that of past leader Scott Morrison. Indeed, a *China Daily* editorial described Albanese as "ill-informed," "ignorant," and letting NATO "fill his head with nonsense."[47]

Former Labor Prime Minister Kevin Ruud, who served as Prime Minister from 2007 to 2010 and briefly in 2013, was unusual in speaking fluent Mandarin and was regularly a welcome guest in the PRC. But on the return of the Labor government, he became as contentious as other Australian politicians in attacks on the PRC.

A tentative conclusion can be, then, that if having suspicions about and distrust toward peoples of different nationalities amount to *hypopsia*, then those of Chinese origin are at the top of the list in Australia's book. Moreover, this is likely as true of political elites as of average citizens.

China Bashing

Attitudinal surveys alone are not enough to show that a distrust of China has set in, never mind that it may be long-lasting. But depictions of a series of political events in the relationship between the two countries over the past decade can be stronger evidence of a breakdown of trust.

In 2013, a Chinese football team had reported abuses and racist chants hurled at them on Australia Day. It was followed by anti-Chinese graffiti scrawled in universities in Sydney and Melbourne where many Chinese students were registered. In 2017, Sinophobic posters appeared warning students, in Mandarin, that they could not enter university premises or they would face deportation. COVID caused a further spike in hostility toward the Chinese presence.

In comparing two Asian states in an article published in 2021, scholars Sylvia Ang and Val Colic-Peisker described a renewed Sinophobia emerging in both Singapore and Australia but with different historical and contemporary origins. In Australia, a historically grounded fear depicted the Chinese as the Yellow Peril; in Singapore, anxiety about incoming mainland Chinese was construed as the Other in Singaporean-Chinese relations.[48] For these authors, the turbulence of migration "causes intense anxieties in many nation-states over changing racial and ethnic population compositions and their potential to gradually shift political power away from hitherto dominant ethnic groups." White-majority countries were still the most attractive migrant destinations but the authors explored a different angle:

> The much debated decline of the "West" and the rise of Asia and China are reconfiguring global ethno-racial power constellations. Yet, studies of racism are still concentrated on Western racism. The extant histories of racism focus on its origin in early-modern European colonialism and its encounter with people of color, combined with the (Western) "scientific" penchant for classifying people and societies.[49]

Furthermore, a paramount issue concerned Australia's rebranding itself: "This whole phenomenon brings to the fore some deep, but often concealed, vulnerabilities in Australia's national psyche. This is a country that has never, until recently, had to conceive of itself as an Asian one, despite its geographical location."[50]

Tensions between Beijing and Canberra simmered after 2016 when Australia rejected bids by two Chinese companies for purchasing electricity distributor Ausgrid over national security concerns. Telecoms firm Huawei was banned from developing its 5G network in 2018. Legal issues arose over Chinese trade measures that interpreted the rules of the World Trade Organization and the China-Australia Free Trade Agreement in its favor.[51]

Bias could go in the opposite direction. Key findings of the 2018 Australian Human Rights Commission Report examined the background of chief executive officers of ASX 200 companies, federal ministers, heads of federal and state government departments, and vice chancellors of universities. The authors found that

> about 95 per cent of senior leaders in Australia have an Anglo-Celtic or European background. Although those who have non-European and Indigenous backgrounds make up 24 percent of the Australian population, such backgrounds account for only 5 per cent of senior leaders. Cultural diversity is particularly low within the senior leadership of Australian government departments and Australian universities.[52]

Without a stronger commitment to diversity among Australia's leaders, the Report admonished, problems would persist undermining the country's strongly held perception of being a "fair go" society.

Research resulting from the COVID pandemic took Sinophobia into uncharted waters. Discrimination against Chinese was associated with stereotypical associations of where the coronavirus pandemic originated. A "triple conflation" emerged in which the health, racial, and political/national status of Chinese people became intermingled. Political claims unfavorable to China and Chinese were constructed based on the pandemic's origins. COVID metaphors created imaginaries depicting Chinese people as suspect biopolitical subjects. The result was a geopolitics of belonging in which Chinese peoples' rights to social and physical spaces were contested either through administrative means (such as travel restrictions) or through mental representations such as recurring images of Chinese as alien people.[53]

The issue of unrepresentative government in Australia took hypopsic perceptions further. According to Juliet Pietsch's seminal book, Australia lagged behind the United States and Canada in the representation of immigrants and ethnic minorities in federal politics. While she completed research on this topic in 2018, the 2022 elections nevertheless highlighted that ninety-six percent of federal lawmakers were White even though a common belief is that Australia ranks as one of the most multicultural nations in the world.

A theme among Australian political representatives is the enduring influence of ties that immigrants and ethnic minorities retain with their countries of origin. These in turn, it is claimed, affect their levels of political interest and participation in Australian politics. Comparing levels of interest in Australian as opposed to home-country politics may reveal not just political attitudes and behavior but political knowledge. Pietsch's dismal conclusion was that "Asian immigrants have struggled to enter formal national-level political institutions to a degree not experienced by other groups."[54]

Tests of loyalty to Australia and not China were introduced in different ways under Morrison's government. A Senate committee hearing in 2020 examining attitudes to the CCP raised quintessential questions on diversity. A Liberal (conservative) Senator in his government, Eric Abetz, asked three Chinese-Australian witnesses to respond to questions about their loyalty. He introduced the Senate inquiry by emphasizing that "There are other factors a lot more important to be considered than skin color and ethnic origin.... Can I ask each of the three witnesses to very briefly tell me whether they are willing to unconditionally condemn the Chinese Communist Party dictatorship?"

The answer given by Wesa Chau, at that time Labor Party candidate for deputy Lord Mayor in Melbourne, was typical: Australia should "defend human rights and speak up against it." But it was grossly unfair to insist that witnesses "publicly declare their allegiance to Australia by condemning a foreign government."

Jieh-Yung Lo, director of the Centre for Asian Australian Leadership at the Australian National University, observed that the country had a long way to go in instituting genuine multiculturalism: "If the Senator does believe that it is our duty to condemn foreign dictatorships and autocratic governments, then it should be all foreign dictatorships and autocratic governments, not specific ones that are seemingly associated with our ethnicity." As the hearing bluntly asserted, "multiculturalism and inclusion should be more than just food and festivals."[55]

Securitization

Contradictory narratives regularly occur when comparing leaders' public discourses. For example, in January 2023 Prime Minister Albanese visited independent Papua New Guinea, a population of just under ten million, intent on furthering the Labor government's campaign to combat Chinese influence. He spoke of the Pacific region as a "Pacific family" linked together by "Pacific mateship." Not long afterward, PRC President Xi insisted that Chinese-Australian relations were heading in the right direction. As with reciprocal attitudes, so too politicians' discourses can be confusing.

A keen observer of China's engagement in "a new world disorder" has been Canadian journalist Joanna Chiu. In a 2021 book, she explained why in recent years "China's volley of attacks against Australia was meant to deter others, such as Canada, the European Union, and Japan, from siding with America to counter China's rise."[56] An even less optimistic narrative was spun by controversial French novelist Michel Houellebecq. A cynic-prone observer on matters of fear across Europe, he reached further to address threats emanating from China and framed his argument from a continental perspective:

> The truth is that French obsession with the idea of decline is far from new. Jean-Jacques Rousseau asserts somewhere (or is it Voltaire? I'm too lazy to check; these authors are tedious to read. Anyway, it is one of the two), that sooner or later—"the thing is certain": we will be enslaved by the Chinese…. When Joe Biden claims that "America is once again ready to lead the world" (here again, I am too lazy to find the exact quotation; Biden is even more tedious than Voltaire), I immediately interpret this as:
>
> • America will not be long in embarking on a new war;
> • As always, she will wind up conducting herself like a piece of shit;
> • She will waste a lot of money, while reinforcing the near-universal loathing of which she is the target; this will allow China to strengthen its position.[57]

Houellebecq's remarks were political realism at its most distressing—and even accurate.

In June 2020, the Ministry of Culture and Tourism in Beijing issued a warning discouraging Chinese travel to Australia. Allegedly a significant increase in racist attacks on Chinese and Asian tourists in the country had sparked the warning. Totaling 1.4 million in 2019, Chinese nationals represented the largest inbound market for Australian visitor arrivals.[58] *The Global Times*, a CCP-linked newspaper, accused Australia of conducting an anti-China strategy and cautioned that the travel ban could be "just the tip of the iceberg." China felt it was "smeared" over the COVID outbreak and it criticized the Morrison government for calling for an independent inquiry into the origins of the pandemic.[59] Australia was accused of being a fellow traveler of the United States in plotting its anti-China strategy; Chinese human rights abuses included the mass detention of Uyghurs in Xinjiang. Beijing retaliated by imposing higher tariffs on Australian barley and banning imports from its abattoirs, accounting for thirty-five percent of beef exports to China.

As Ang and Colic-Peisker reported, "Simmering political and diplomatic tension between Australia and China, for years based on the difference in political systems and political values, has reached its zenith in 2019–2020 based on suspicions of undue Chinese influence in Australia and digital attacks."[60] Under Morrison's leadership, the dispute continued unabated.

Examining the securitization dilemma helps frame interstate rivalries between Australia and China. Applying a well-known analytical framework popularized by Barry Buzan, Ole Waever, and Jaap de Wilde in 1998, the process of securitization begins with a "securitizing move" like a speech act declaring that an existential threat confronts a valued referent object. Identifying the speech act allows emergency actions to occur outside the normal rules of democratic politics: these include the use of force, covert government activities, surveillance of citizens, and reductions in civil liberties. The securitizing move has been successful if this occurs.[61] Australia's sweeping tranche of national security legislation passed by Parliament in 2018 was an obvious example of securitization.

For security analyst Andrew Chubb, the classic security dilemma sketched above ran amok when characterizing Australia-China relations:

> The securitization of "Chinese influence" has had both intended and unintended effects on Australia's political landscape and society. On one hand, the emergency legislation advocated by the original securitizers became law; on the other hand, the discourse has unleashed divisive social forces and created a 'toxic environment' for Chinese-Australians, especially in public and political life. The securitization process... also dramatically worsened Australia's relations with the PRC, setting the scene for a further deterioration into open acrimony following the COVID-19 pandemic.[62]

Interpreting this on a practical level, Australian public sentiments toward China had gone into a tailspin after 2017. The term used in public discussions was changed from foreign interference to Chinese influence. But Osmond Chiu correctly weighs in: "How we talk about China has unintended consequences on the everyday lives of more than 1.3 million Australians with Chinese heritage, and many more of East Asian heritage. Avoiding such issues or claiming they are only propaganda talking points does us no favors."[63] Distrust in Beijing's policies is hard to overcome.

This chapter signals that growing mistrust of China has been spreading across many sections of Australian society. Australia's leaders, whether Liberal or Labor, accepted this fact and prioritized security alliances with US-led institutions such as the ANZUS Treaty of 1951, "Five Eyes" (monitoring and sharing internet use so as to protect the national security of four Commonwealth countries and the United States), and most recently Aukus. Skeptical analysts may claim that all three institutions are rooted in the anglospheric bloc. They may go even further and indicate that an explicit "White Australia" alliance system has not been dislodged.

Postscriptum

Set in Victoria's Central Highlands in 1855, the star of the 2021 Australian TV series *New Gold Mountain* is a charismatic Chinese headman at a gold-mining camp whose often unethical policies nevertheless further the interests of Chinese arrivals. The headman, Wei Shing, stumbles across a valuable seam on the state's frontier. He struggles to reconcile a fragile harmony between Chinese and European diggers and their respective authorities. The series was written by Peter Cox and directed by Corrie Chen and features numerous bilingual-speaking characters. The dialogue from this scene set in Season 1, Episode 1, is entitled "Propriety" and features an acerbic discussion between the Chinese headman and the designated "British protector of the Chinese."

Wei Shing: The Chinese tax, you're adding another.
Protector: I was coming to see you.
Wei Shing: There's no way we can pay more than we already are.
Protector: I'm sorry but the diggers see the Chinese as a problem.
Taking land, wasting water.
Wei Shing: We don't waste it.
Protector: Working on a Sunday, spreading disease, general lack of
Christian moral fibre. Not my argument, by the way.
Wei Shing: I've been doing my job. I need something in return.
Protector: You get paid. And about this job - what's this Brotherhood
I've been hearing about? *Hing Dai Wu*, is it?

Wei Shing: Well, some are called that. Most are just people from the same village helping one another. It's not easy being alone.

Protector: The secret societies they have in California. Importing opium illegally, gambling. We cannot have them here.

Wei Shing: People turn to them if they do not feel safe.

Protector: How are they not safe?

Wei Shing: Three mining accidents just last week. One dead. Ropes were cut in the night.

Protector: Do you have proof?

Wei Shing: The word of my people.

Protector: Oh, well, in that case…

Wei Shing: You're the Chinese Protector.

…

Protector: What about this Party of yours?

Wei Shing: The Mid-Autumn Festival.

Protector: Whites and Chinese together. That's the idea, right?

Wei Shing: I was hoping it would help to build relations, yes.

…

Protector: Truth is you've got one job. The Chinese keep to their camp, the Whites will keep to theirs. No fuss, no problems. Pay your taxes. If you can't, I'll find someone who can.

Notes

1   Carmen Lawrence, *Fear and Politics* (Melbourne: Scribe Short Books, 2006), 43.

2   John Fitzgerald, *Big White Lie: Chinese Australians in White Australia* (Randwick, NSW: University of New South Wales Press, 2007), 1–2.

3   Marianne Dickey, "Introduction," in *Unintended Consequences: The Impact of Migration Law and Policy*, eds. Marianne Dickey, Dorota Gozdecka, and Sudrishti Reich (Canberra: ANU Press, 2016), 2.

4   Geoffrey Brahm Levey, "The Turnbull Government's 'Post-multiculturalism' Multicultural Policy," *Australian Journal of Political Science* 54, no. 4 (July 2019), https://www.tandfonline.com/doi/abs/10.1080/10361146.2019.1634675?journalCode=cajp20.

5   Michael Clyne and James Jupp (eds.), *Multiculturalism and Integration: A Harmonious Relationship* (Canberra: ANU Press, 2011). See also Juliet Pietsch and Haydn Aarons (eds.), *Australia: Identity, Fear and Governance in the 21st Century* (Canberra: ANU Press, 2012); Tim Watts, *The Golden Country: Australia's Changing Identity* (Melbourne: Text Publishing, 2019).

6   OECD, *Perspectives on Global Development 2012: Social Cohesion in a Shifting World* (Paris: OECD, 2011) http://dx.doi.org/10.1787/persp_glob_dev-2012-en.

7   Justine Dandy and Rogelia Pe-Pua, "The Refugee Experience of Social Cohesion in Australia: Exploring the Roles of Racism, Intercultural Contact, and the Media," *Journal of Immigrant & Refugee Studies* 13, no. 4 (2015), 341.

8   Andrew Markus, *Mapping Social Cohesion: The Scanlon Foundation Surveys 2016* (Melbourne: Monash University, 2016).

9   Cheryl M. R. Sulaiman-Hill, Sandra C. Thompson, Rita Afsar, and Toshi L. Hodliffe, "Changing Images of Refugees: Australian and New Zealand Print Media, 1998–2008," *Journal of Immigrant & Refugee Studies* 9, no. 4 (2011), 359.

10 George Megalogenis, *The Australian Moment: How We Were Made for These Times* (Penguin Books Australia: Melbourne, 2017).

11 Australian Bureau of Statistics, "Snapshot of Australia 2021," https://www.abs.gov.au/statistics/people/people-and-communities/snapshot-australia/2021.

12 James Button (narrator), "A Changing Australia: How Immigration is Changing the Nation." Scanlon Institute for Applied Social Cohesion Research, September 2018, 5–6.

13 Iris Zhao, Erin Handley, and Michael Walsh, "China is Attacking Australia over Racism—But Ordinary People are Getting Stuck in the Middle," *ABC News,* July 18, 2020, https://www.abc.net.au/news/2020-07-18/china-australia-coronavirus-racism-affects-on-ordinary-people/12469092.

14 Dandy and Pe-Pua, "The Refugee Experience," 340.

15 Jane Jenson, *Mapping Social Cohesion: The State of Canadian Research* (Ottawa: Canadian Policy Research Networks, 1998).

16 Michael Clyne, "Multilingualism, Multiculturalism and Integration," in *Multiculturalism and Integration: A Harmonious Relationship*, eds. James Jupp and Clyne (Canberra: ANU Press, 2011), 53.

17 Clyne, "Multilingualism," 54.

18 Clyne, "Multilingualism," 56–57.

19 Clyne, "Multilingualism," 62.

20 Clyne, "Multilingualism," 69.

21 Clyne, "Multilingualism," 73.

22 Clive Hamilton, *Silent Invasion: China's Influence in Australia* (Melbourne: Hardie Grant Publishing, 2017).

23 Peter Hartcher, "Red Flag: Waking Up to China's Challenge," *Quarterly Essay* 76 (November 2019), https://www.quarterlyessay.com.au/essay/2019/11/red-flag.

24 David Brophy, *China Panic: Australia's Alternative to Paranoia and Pandering* (Melbourne: Black, Inc., 2021).

25 John West, "Book Review: *China Panic: Australia's Alternative to Paranoia and Pandering*," Australian Institute of International Affairs, September 11, 2021, https://www.internationalaffairs.org.au/australianoutlook/book-review-china-panic-australias-alternative-to-paranoia-and-pandering/.

26 John Simpson, "Ai Weiwei: 'Too Late' to Curb China's Global Influence," *BBC News*, September 29, 2020, https://www.bbc.com/news/world-asia-china-54321598.

27 Ian Williams, "How China Bought Cambridge," *The Spectator,* July 10, 2021, https://www.spectator.co.uk/article/how-china-bought-cambridge?utm_medium=email&utm_source=CampaignMonitor_Editorial&utm_campaign=WEEK%20%2020210710%20%20AL+CID_cd7e2e30f4b6cf5a60234315a134ffef.

28 Sean Rubinsztein-Dunlop, Mario Christodoulou, Sashka Koloff, Lauren Day, and Echo Hui, "Are Australian Universities Putting our National Security at Risk by Working with China?" *ABC News*, October 14, 2019, https://www.abc.net.au/news/2019-10-14/chinese-communist-party-gtcom-connection-australian-universities/11586118.

29 Rubinsztein-Dunlop et al., "Are Australian Universities?"

30 Amy Chua, *World on Fire: How Exporting Free Market Democracy Breeds Ethnic Hatred and Global Instability* (New York: Anchor, 2004).

31 Ngae Mae, *The Chinese Question: The Gold Rushes and Global Politics* (New York: W.W. Norton, 2022).

32 Caroline Harting, "Uncovering the Origins of Racism Against Chinese Immigrants Around the Globe," Interview with Professor Mae Ngai, *Columbia News*, August 26, 2021, https://news.columbia.edu/news/mae-ngai-chinese-question.

33 Ang and Colic-Peisker, "Sinophobia," 6.

34 Emily Baker and Annah Fromberg, "China has Become Tasmania's Biggest Trading Partner, but has the State been Left 'Vulnerable?'" *ABC News*, November 18, 2019, https://www.abc.net.au/news/2019-11-18/tasmania-china-trade-links/11708012.

35 Richard Willingham and Bill Birtles, "Victoria Deepens Engagement with Beijing's Controversial Belt and Road Initiative," *ABC News*, October 24, 2019, https://www.abc.net.au/news/2019-10-24/victoria-deepens-links-with-china-controversial-belt-and-road/11636704.

36 Natasha Kassam, *Lowy Institute Poll 2021: Understanding Australian Attitudes towards the World, 2021* (Sydney: Lowy Institute, November 2021), 4–5.

37 Kassam, *Lowy Institute Poll 2021*, 12.

38 Andrew Markus, *Mapping Social Cohesion 2021* (Melbourne: Scanlon Foundation, Monash University, November 2021), 11, https://www.monash.edu/__data/assets/pdf_file/0007/2762080/mapping-social-cohesion-national-report-2021.pdf.

39 Markus, *Mapping Social Cohesion 2021*, 13.

40 Markus, *Mapping Social Cohesion 2021*, 61.

41 Osmond Chiu, "Negative Feelings towards Chinese Immigrants Show Our Debates Do not Happen in a Vacuum," *The China Story.org*, February 23, 2021, https://www.thechinastory.org/negative-feelings-towards-chinese-immigrants-show-our-debates-do-not-happen-in-a-vacuum/.

42 For a survey of Chinese-Australians' public opinion on their place in Australia, see Jennifer Hsu, *2023 Being Chinese in Australia: Public Opinion in Chinese Communities* (Sydney: Lowy Institute, 2023).

43 European Union Agency for Fundamental Rights, "Survey on Minorities and Discrimination in EU (2016)," https://fra.europa.eu/en/publications-and-resources/data-and-maps/survey-data-explorer-second-eu-minorities-discrimination-survey.

44 Elena Collinson and Paul F. Burke, "The Australia-China Relationship: What do Australians Think?" UTS:ACRI/BIDA Poll, May 2022, 7, https://www.australiachinarelations.org/content/utsacribida-poll-2022. Opinionated political elites taking a more xenophobic position than average citizens toward a purportedly adversarial state was my conclusion in accounting for perceptions in Poland of Russia in 2014; Ray Taras, "Russia Resurgent, Russophobia in Decline? Polish Perceptions of Relations with the Russian Federation 2004–2012," *Europe-Asia Studies* 66, no. 5 (July 2014), 710–34.

45 Collinson and Burke, "The Australia-China Relationship," 8–12.

46 Collinson and Burke, "The Australia-China relationship," 17.

47 "Albanese must not be Misled by Alliance," *chinadaily.com.cn*, June 29, 2022, https://global.chinadaily.com.cn/a/202206/29/WS62bc3f13a310fd2b29e695bb.html.

48 Sylvia Ang and Val Colic-Peisker, "Sinophobia in the Asian Century: Race, Nation and Othering in Australia and Singapore," *Ethnic and Racial Studies* 45, no. 4 (June 2021), https://www.tandfonline.com/doi/abs/10.1080/01419870.2021.1921236.

49 Ang and Colic-Peisker, "Sinophobia," 719.

50 Kerry Brown, "Why China's Rise Exposes Australian Vulnerabilities," *BBC News*, November 7, 2019, https://www.bbc.com/news/world-australia-50299783.

51 Weihuan Zhou and James Laurenceson, "Demystifying Australia-China Trade Tensions," *Journal of World Trade* 56, no. 1 (2022), 51–86, https://opus.lib.uts.edu.au/handle/10453/155697.

52 Iyanatul Islam, "Australia's Immigration Policy: Political And Economic Lessons for Europe," *Social Europe*, May 1, 2018, https://socialeurope.eu/the-politics-and-economics-of-australias-immigration-policy-lessons-for-europe.

53 Zhipeng Gao, "Sinophobia during the Covid-19 Pandemic: Identity, Belonging, and International Politics," *Integrative Psychological and Behavioral Science* (October 2021), 1–19, https://link.springer.com/article/10.1007/s12124-021-09659-z.

54 Juliet Pietsch, *Race, Ethnicity, and the Participation Gap: Understanding Australia's Political Complexion* (Toronto: University of Toronto Press, 2018), 156.

55 Bang Xiao and Stephen Dziedzic, "Senator Eric Abetz's Controversial Questions about Loyalty Rattle Chinese Communities in Australia," *ABC News*, October 21, 2020, https://www.abc.net.au/news/2020-10-22/senator-abetz-questions-about-loyalties-rattle-chinese-community/12797638.

56 Joanna Chiu, *China Unbound: A New World Disorder* (Toronto: House of Anansi Press, 2021), 160.

57 Michel Houellebecq, "The narcissistic fall of France," *UnHerd*, June 8, 2021, https://unherd.com/2021/06/the-narcissistic-fall-of-france/.

58 Max Walden, "Australia says China Travel Warning 'Unhelpful' amid Escalating Diplomatic Row," *ABC News*, June 7, 2020, https://www.abc.net.au/news/2020-06-08/china-coronavirus-travel-ban-australia-diplomatic-row/12332016.

59 *The Global Times*, cited in Walden, "Australia."

60 Ang and Colic-Peisker, "Sinophobia," 4.

61 Barry Buzan, Ole Waever, and Jaap de Wilde, "Security Analysis: A Conceptual Apparatus," in *Security: A New Framework for Analysis*, eds. Barry Buzan, Ole Waever, and Jaap de Wilde (Boulder: Lynne Reinner 1998), 5.

62 Andrew Chubb, "The Securitization of 'Chinese Influence' in Australia," *Journal of Contemporary China*, March 21, 2022, https://www.tandfonline.com/doi/full/10.1080/10670564.2022.2052437.

63 Chiu, "Negative Feelings towards Chinese immigrants."

Chapter 7

IDENTITY FEARS: THE UNITED STATES AND TRIBAL POLITICS

Malaise or Remedy

Many troubling questions requiring hardheaded solutions have been asked about today's America. Among key issues are managing control over migration on the border with Mexico; repairing infrastructure in American cities; curbing outlandish profit-making by US corporations particularly in the oil and gas industry; reducing unparalleled socioeconomic inequalities instead of creating incentives to take them higher; halting the decline of the US middle class; making changes to the prevailing low and even zero tax rates assessed to American companies that are too big to fail; resolving persistent structural racism which is not solved merely by impact-less concessions to disadvantaged people; weakening the dominance of a glorified celebrity culture linking arms with cynical politicians; doing something about a not-free press and social media that are owned by mega-oligarchs; reducing incestuous nepotism; putting an end to absurd gerrymandering; and plus a sundry of other issues. The most serious and intractable problem of them all, climate change, is a universal problem. Many of these needed policy decisions result from predatory rather than free-market capitalism. With regard to foreign policy, the country's status as a once-enviable superpower is now under attack.

Diversity and inclusiveness sweeping across US institutions are paradoxes since most of the problem areas listed above seriously constrain inclusivity and go beyond its symbolic dimensions. For French-born journalist Raoul de Roussy de Sales writing in 1939, the answer to the question what makes an American was straightforward: "to become an American is a process which resembles a conversion. It is not so much a country one adopts as a new creed. And in all Americans can be discerned some of the traits of those who have, at one time or the other, abandoned an ancient faith for a new one."[1]

Staying with the notion of a distinctive creed, recent years have, by contrast, been characterized by sweeping identity politics and, at their core, the centrality of both distinctiveness and inclusiveness. Encouraged by an ideological state apparatus—in the United States there is one if we look hard enough—its main purpose is in practice to divide Americans into notional tribes of people. The goal of forging national unity is treated, then, as worthy of disdain and scorn when weighed against identity.

A large segment of American society still believes that tweaking democracy and its constitution is all that is needed to address the superpower's difficulties. At the basic level that can mean changing its leaders whether they sit on the Supreme Court—difficult to pull off when there is no limit on members' age; Congress—where tiny states like Rhode Island hold the same number of Senate seats as California; or the Presidency—where the Electoral College sometimes produces a result contrary to the wishes of the majority of American voters.

At the grassroots level, this picture reflects an increasing skepticism of the federal government. Public trust in it remains low: only two in ten Americans say they trust the government to do what is right "just about always" (two percent) or "most of the time" (nineteen percent). Disaggregating by ethnicity, thirty-seven percent of Asians trust the government "most of the time" or "just about always." Hispanics (twenty-nine percent) and African-Americans (twenty-four percent) are less sold on trusting it. But the most startling data involve White folks who trust the government the least. Commanding a majority of the US population, this group's level of trust is significantly below other ethnicities at sixteen percent.[2]

Since the 1970s, the level of trust in the government has largely been reflected along partisan divides. It has been consistently higher among members of the party that controls the White House than among the opposition party. Partisanship regularly leads to vote-rigging, gerrymandering, scandals in office, and nepotism—which is underplayed when discussing governance issues in the United States. Frustrated that they can do little to change this ossified system, many Americans have opted for a change that they can control—identity politics.

Global journalist James Meek, who views American politics from the British Isles, regards identity politics as a deliberate repositioning of American priorities. It minimizes "secondary-level" arguments over capitalism, economic policy, inequality, climate change, institutional decay, and corruption. For former US President Jimmy Carter, all these pathologies added up to "an oligarchy with unlimited political bribery."[3]

Meek elaborated: "If you frame 'identity politics' as a self-indulgent distraction from the vital business of creating a shared vision of America that all Americans can believe in, you're not only taking identities of gender or race or sexuality out of play; you are also taking for granted what it means to be 'American.'"[4] *E pluribus unum* stands unity on its head, we can derive from these arguments, when identity politics dominate. As we see later in this chapter, an American political scientist as critical of identity politics as Meek is Mark Lilla.

This chapter connects burgeoning identity politics to American politics; the phenomenon exists in other Western countries too with Britain's special relationship with the United States providing a lockstep mechanism. To be sure, identity politics are not inherently a malaise and they can help resolve problematic questions in the country. Moreover, some identity politics are more justifiable than others; the consequences of slavery, for instance, require exceptional identity politics. But when it becomes a pervasive dogma and is treated as a cure-all panacea for many different problems, it is likely to generate a new set of difficulties and compound deep-seated problems. In this final case study, I deploy Thucydides' interconnected terms *ekplexis* and *kataplexis* to assay the salience of identity politics.

Fear and Trembling in the USA

Some two decades ago, American sociologist Barry Glassner asked what appeared to be a rhetorical question: "Why are there so many fears in the air, and so many of them unfounded?" He offered a largely tautological answer: "One of the paradoxes of a culture of fear is that serious problems remain widely ignored even though they give rise to precisely the dangers that the populace most abhors." As examples, he pointed to how conditions of poverty are thought to correlate strongly with other pathologies such as child abuse, crime, and drug abuse. But his blunt conclusion on the cost-benefits question was accurate: "immense power and money await those who tap into our moral insecurities and supply us with symbolic substitutes."[5] In short, the culture-of-fear narrative provides enticing possibilities to opportune entrepreneurs.

This last case study finds that, along with many other countries, the United States is not exceptional in facing a gradual breakdown and weakening of political authority. In earlier periods of American history, the most vivid example was the American Civil War fought from 1861 to 1865. A more recent but sometimes overlooked instance was in the 1960s with the assassination of multiple political figures from the US President and his brother to civil rights activists including Martin Luther King and Malcolm X; even John Lennon was shot down in the heart of New York City in this vicious era. Following its Russian designation for the 1990s, this abbreviated period in US history earns the title of a time of troubles for America.

In the 2020s, the trajectory forward reached a new watershed. Gun violence was worse than ever but excluded elites. But an even more ossified and now polarized two-party system had emerged and was at the root of the political system. Its spread has produced consequences not only in Congress but the US Supreme Court. In a matter of two weeks in June 2022, the landmark 1973 *Roe v Wade* decision legalizing abortion was overturned by an activist Supreme Court seeking to make laws rather than interpreting them. It struck down as unconstitutional a New York law requiring applicants wishing to carry a gun outside the home to have "proper cause" to do so. It also limited the ability of the Environmental Protection Agency to reduce the carbon output of power plants, thus dealing a blow to efforts seeking to combat climate change. In June 2023 it struck down affirmative action.

For the United States, *sic transit Gloria*—in essence, "how glory fades"—may be a sign that it was not just Nero who fiddled while Rome burned. The two-party-dominant system was at the heart of many controversies. For the Democratic Party, the January 6, 2021 "invasion" of Congress (the term itself is disputed) represented a benchmark and *caesura* in American history. The armed assault on Russia's Parliament building in Moscow by forces loyal to President Yeltsin in 1993 was small beer, for many Democrats, even though casualties were much higher than in Washington; hundreds had been left dead ushering in a brief period of unchecked neoliberalism when gangsters and mafia groups took over leading Russian industries and services. Not so with the hours-long event in DC that Democrats blamed on Republican Party conspirators, above all, former President Donald Trump.

In turn, for many Republicans, the November 3, 2020 elections were viewed as stolen from the incumbent President. By tiny majorities, a number of swing states voted against Trump in places as far apart as Georgia, Arizona, and Wisconsin. Not conceding defeat—unlike Democrat Al Gore who humiliatingly did after the 2000 election to George W. Bush in arguably the most disputed election ever in US history—Trump was able to perpetuate the myth of a stolen election even though he lost the popular vote by seven million votes, as tabulated by the 538 electors making up the Electoral College.

Each of these political claims proved highly polarizing and schismatic. It may have fostered a moral panic in the minds of Democratic and Republican voters. It branded rival political identities as important for the ages. Easily overlooked was that in both cases gerontocracies at the head of each party seemed comforted by the polarization that followed.

A fragmenting national identity suggests that again we need to reach for Thucydides' understandings of fear. From his contrasting meanings, we can extrapolate that the preferable word choice for breakdown of national identity is *ekplexis*—consternation, moral panic, and even terror evoked by a general breakdown in the natural order. Solid evidence that this is the appropriate term to use comes from a Dutch art historian; Caroline van Eck's study of the sublime led to the Greek rhetorician Hermogenes, a close friend of

Socrates, to the rescue: *"Ekplexis* is derived from *ekpletto,* which means to strike, confound, paralyze, or render somebody besides themselves with fear, surprise, or amazement."[6]

This term raises questions about the identity of a society that may be descending into a spiral of moral panic. Although overly used, moral panic consists of "a mass movement based on the false or exaggerated perception that some cultural behavior or group of people is dangerously deviant and poses a threat to society's values and interests. Moral panics are generally fuelled by media coverage of social issues."[7] The expression is out of proportion to its initial, banal use by sociologist Stanley Cohen in the 1960s who used it to apply to the British mods and rockers as "tribes" who frequently clashed swords in English coastal towns.[8]

Panic itself connotes a lack of control spiced with a modicum of irrationality. But it has repercussions on institutional crumbling as well. In the American case, this is ironic given that the United States boasts of being such a powerful country that it is too big to fail. Paradoxically, then, the main concern is how the country appeared to be unraveling as its own national identity faded. Irrational forces may hone in on some evil person or behavior or element that threatens longstanding values, interests, and the well-being of a social order. These forces can combine to undermine a well-established national identity.

Ekplexis is connected and, in places, overlaps with another word group used by Thucydides. *Kataplexis* can be translated as: "to confound, paralyze, render somebody beside themselves." The English word cataplexy literally signifies a "fixation of the eyes," or stupefaction, usually caused by an extreme emotional stimulus. This rendering captures the sensation of not merely being fearful but also surprised, amazed, and astonished.

Moral panic entrepreneurs frequently use virtue signaling—for Cohen "right-thinkers" and simplistic "holier than thou" adherents—as their go-to code of behavior. They have been joined by mass media and social networks unofficially carrying out self-selected policing and surveillance work across society. Fifty years ago, renowned communications guru Stuart Hall was convinced that moral panics following a rise in crime rates or gun violence can detonate a fuse mobilizing public support in favor of the need to "police the crisis."[9]

Caution is required, therefore, when employing the term moral panic. Frank Furedi, a specialist on the culture of fear, seemed lost when trying to define it: "in everyday language the term moral panic tended to be attached to anxieties that were related to uncertainties about values." Which was it, then, anxieties, uncertainties, or values?[10]

A further explanation for schismatic aberrations in American society can be the emergence of narcissistic attitudes across the country.[11]

Christopher Lasch, a University of Rochester professor and critic of modern liberalism, argued in his 1979 book that narcissistic behavior was not simply an individual ailment but now a part of a wider social epidemic affecting many Americans. Unending expansion of the manic narcissistic self was becoming the norm with each passing generation. Lasch insisted that diminishing reservoirs of patriotism and the absence of reciprocal obligations characterized the upwardly mobile social class which was prone to narcissistic behavior. In my view, close on its heels would be the spread of political fear.

Such approaches suggest that deepening recalcitrant behavior patterns have emerged in American society. It served as a contrast to the earlier conviction, canonized in the adoption of a constitution ratified in 1788, that the United States would constitute "the first new nation."[12] Has this not-so-new nation today been torn to shreds? Have Americans become confounded and splintered as a society? Is identity politics, understood at times as symbolic politics, replacing class struggle with tribal struggle? The ease with which the politics of identity has displaced socioeconomic class offers evidence *sui generis*.

Both US political parties engaged in indulging particular identities whether related to ethnicity, gender, national origin, body type, disability, medical condition, or other characteristics. Indeed, identity politics vehemently claims to have displaced ideological politics making it a positive thing.[13] A supposition is that neoliberalism's mission imposes its priorities in order for the political class to prolong and thrive and bask in their economic successes while neglecting the rest of society. For those not part of this class, being drawn into this game suggests either a subconscious predisposition to elitist priorities or blatant false consciousness, plain and simple.

Applying Thucydides' terms of *ekplexis* and *kataplexis* as panic and stupification allows us to dig deeper and unravel cleavages affecting the breaking up of American national identity. There are few signs that identity politics will disappear soon—it seems firmly lodged among its advocates—so the road to a refashioned, recast national identity may be vanishing.

Identities and Culture

According to data provided by the 2020 census, the US population was becoming more diverse even if caveats exist. Over the ten years since the 2010 census, people who identified as Hispanic, Asian, or more than one race (the multiracial category was added to the census twenty years ago) was the fastest growing category in the country. By contrast, the share of people who identified as White has continued to decline since the 1960s when the United States opened its doors to immigrants from outside Europe. Between 2010 and 2020, significantly, the total number of White people fell for the first time. Simultaneously, during these years, the overall US population grew at its slowest rate in nearly a century.[14]

Demographic changes usher in differing cultures. But the impact of any one culture can also vary. For pioneering sociologist Nathan Glazer, culture in different societies makes a difference but "It is very hard to determine what in culture makes the difference."[15] As it melts into American life, a culture's grand traditions may not necessarily rise to the fore.

> Ethnic and racial groups in the United States are not randomly drawn from the large populations that bear or are characterized by a culture. The million Chinese in the United States do not represent a China a thousand times larger; and similarly with the million Asian Indians in the United States. This is the case with every ethnic or racial group in the United States.[16]

Writing on ethnicity and nationalism, Israeli political scientist Azar Gat accepted that the United States is different from older nations in Europe, Japan, China, or others. These comprise dominant historic ethnic cores and strong kinship sentiments that bind their political communities: "The American nation was created by immigrants, its population is multiethnic, and immigration remains central to the nation's experience, ethos, and identity." Going further, Gat was convinced that "The new people's self-perception as a community of culture and, to some degree, also kinship (intermarried, adopted) becomes very recognizable" so that new kin-culture national communities should be classified in ethnic terms.[17]

Gat accepted that immigrants typically replace their language, values, and much else with those of the majority culture: "Within a few generations, they merge into a shared, amalgamated American culture, to which they also variably contribute." Yet the commendable rhetoric of multiculturalism, multi-ethnicity, and diversity that applauds immigrants' transitions nevertheless does not obscure a distinct American culture and identity widely shared by the large majority of Americans. Not just the English language is acquired but other cultural characteristics: "These encompass mores, symbols, social practices, public knowledge, and a sense of common historical tradition; popular tastes, images, and heroes; music, sports, cuisine, public holidays, and social rituals. It is a fusion culture drawing from many different immigrant sources, traditions, and kinship networks."[18]

The Israeli author concluded that the majority identity in America is American. It bridges over their original ethnic identities because members lose touch with their countries of origin and ancestral identities. Americans, he insisted, are bound together by citizenship, allegiance to their adopted country, and adherence to its Constitution. However, Gat ignored the notion of identity politics that can fracture national identity. Little scope is allowed for Samuel Huntington's thesis that, for instance, in the case of Mexican immigrants in past years who accounted for a substantial majority of people arriving in the United States, their transition to an American way of life from a Mexican one was not dented but prolonged even after four generations of being settled here.[19]

The degree of social and labor market integration or full cultural acculturation and assimilation into American society by immigrant groups is much-debated. Is it the case that all these ethnic communities absorb an American identity after a given period of time? Or does this differ from one group to another depending on how much social (intracultural) and how much cross-cultural bonding takes place? With the emergence of tribal politics that can weaken or displace the allure of national identity, is the United States in the process of unmaking nationhood? Are long-settled "nativist" Americans splintering, giving cues to recent immigrants?

International relations can also be affected on the basis of American identity politics. Huntington asserted: "How Americans define themselves determines their role in the world, but how the world views that role also shapes American identity." Of significant importance is American religiosity, in particular, Christianity: "Those countries that are more religious tend to be more nationalist."

For the Harvard professor, it remained uncertain whether America would choose a cosmopolitan, imperial, or national path; his book was published in 2004, three years after the 9/11 attacks on the United States. Political elites were generally divided over assuming a cosmopolitan or imperial role: "The overwhelming bulk of the American people are committed to a national alternative and to preserving and strengthening the American identity that has existed for centuries."[20] In other words, national identity remained the residual one.

Sneaking up on these options and rendering them over time mostly irrelevant has been the clout of identity politics. Key questions to ask include whether identity politics are carved out of exclusively minority—not majority—preferences. And is there now a fight back against such distorted dismantling of what used to be thought of as US national identity?

Diverse Critiques of Identity Politics

In their pivotal book published in 2014 on *American Identity and the Politics of Multiculturalism*, Jack Citrin and David Sears made one reference only to identity politics. That was to left-leaning scholars who were stating the obvious: "Identity politics and demands for group rights based on ethnicity would undermine a sense of common identity and individual rights." Yet a consensus developed across different political leanings that ethnic awareness is clearly discernable in the United States: "There is a surprising similarity in the degree to which liberals, moderates, and conservatives in every minority ethnic group express a strong sense of ethnic consciousness."[21]

When debating the appeal or dislike of identity politics, disagreement tends to arise across the majority-versus-minority divide. Perhaps this is a case of mistaken identity but some reputed "leftists" and radical liberals are branded as strongly endorsing identity politics. In fact, a liberal-versus-conservative ideological approach on the subject is difficult to sustain.

Regarded as liberal on a range of topics, Mark Lilla's series of hard-hitting critiques of identity politics underscores how difficult it is to place its supporters and dissenters on a continuum. For the Columbia University political scientist, such politics consist of "a pseudo-politics of self-regard and increasingly narrow and exclusionary self-definition."[22] Lilla took apart the American two-party system:

What's extraordinary—and appalling—about the past four decades of our history is that our politics have been dominated by two ideologies that encourage and even celebrate the unmaking of citizens. On the right, an ideology that questions the existence of a common good and denies our obligation to help fellow citizens, through government action if necessary. On the left, an ideology institutionalized in colleges and universities that fetishizes our individual and group attachments, applauds self-absorption, and casts a shadow of suspicion over any invocation of a universal democratic *we*.[23]

Ironically, as rare as bipartisanship became in the 2020s, it reached into the foundations of what comprised identity politics.[24]

Whether willing endorsers of identity politics or their opponents, Americans are increasingly categorized by the pursuit of narrow identity-related interests. In the 1960s and 1970s, massive anti-Vietnam War demonstrations and civil rights marches brought about solidarity on the basis of ideology. But today large rallies and demonstrations about an existential threat such as climate change are not that commonplace. Instead, a schism has occurred, possibly an objective of some identity politics enthusiasts, to engage in divide-and-rule tactics while preserving the status quo ante.

A dilettante approach that rejected identity politics was taken by Yale professor Amy Chua (discussed in Chapter 6 in the context of a Chinese ethnically dominant minority emerging in Australia). She claimed that for the first time in US history, White Americans are faced with the prospect of becoming a minority in their own country. She claimed that "While many in our multicultural cities may well celebrate the 'browning of America' as a welcome step away from 'White supremacy,' it's safe to say that large numbers of American Whites are more anxious about this phenomenon, whether they admit it or not." Chua pointed to a 2012 study showing how more than half of White Americans believed that "Whites have replaced Blacks as the 'primary victims of discrimination'"[25]

The dynamics of identity politics was laid bare by this controversial author: "When groups feel threatened, they retreat into tribalism. When groups feel mistreated and disrespected, they close ranks and become more insular, more defensive, more punitive, more us-versus-them." There is pervasive dispersal of such politics: "In America today, every group feels this way to some extent. Whites and Blacks, Latinos and Asians, men and women, Christians, Jews, and Muslims, straight people and gay people, liberals and conservatives— all feel their groups are being attacked, bullied, persecuted, discriminated against."

Chua elaborated on her understanding of tribes: "One group's claims to feeling threatened and voiceless are often met by another group's derision because it discounts their own feelings of persecution—but such is political tribalism." The war on cultural appropriation by one group of another's supposed eminent domain is rooted in the belief that groups have exclusive rights to their own histories, symbols, and traditions.

The implication for Chua of the rise of identity politics was that "almost no one is standing up for an America without identity politics, for an American identity that transcends and unites all the country's many subgroups." She pointed, perhaps ironically, to Great Society liberals of the 1960s who captured the moment in American society when deep divisions over civil rights and the Vietnam War were transcended by the language of national unity and equal opportunity.

She reserved a final dig at the unreformed left and radical liberals who had invented and sponsored identity politics. Chua inveighed that "The anti-capitalist economic preoccupations of the old Left began to take a backseat to a new way of understanding oppression: the politics of redistribution was replaced by a 'politics of recognition.' Modern identity politics was born." But rather than highlighting a politics of inclusion, its premise was to carry out a politics of exclusion that pinpointed which identity groups would be insiders and which would become outsiders. Chua was thus dismissive of the anti-capitalist left and the identity politics that they institutionalized. Her incidental praise of Great Society liberals also appeared to be disingenuous.

Reading identity politics in Chua's doctrinaire way proved not just contentious but vulnerable to blowback. Several other authors have taken aim at this approach. Conservative writer Vivek Ramaswamy, author of

Woke, Inc., argues that Big Tech encourages corporate wokeism because appearing to embrace social justice suits these firms' commercial interests, both in terms of recruitment and appeal to their clients. While it expresses allegiance to identity politics it simultaneously rejects the alleged left's critique of capitalism.[26] Rock-solid endorsement of the capitalist order goes hand-in-hand in many cases with shoring up identity politics.

A different take is offered in a book entitled *The Coddling of the American Mind*. Authors Greg Lukianoff and Jonathan Haidt posit that overprotective parenting in the shadow of the war on terrorism that began with 9/11 produced a phenomenon dubbed safetyism. It manufactured a belief that safety, including above all emotional safety, trumps all other practical and moral concerns.[27] The recession of 2008 in which the disadvantaged suffered deep setbacks while economic elites seemed untouched and even received federal bailouts provided evidence of this approach. Finding safe spaces for people is often praiseworthy. But at times this has been associated with passionate identity seekers where no greater good exists than identity and other disadvantaged groups are excluded.

It remains unclear where identity politics fits on a left-right scale but explosive rhetoric comes from both sides. *The Spectator* contributor James Allan (for its Australian edition) in 2021 opened up a litany of grievances. He remarked how "Everything is about groups not individuals. Now, though, it's not groups defined by wealth and their relation to the means of production. Instead, it's groups defined by such things as skin pigmentation, type of reproductive organs, sexual preferences and date of arrival in the country. It's intellectual wankery and you know it."[28] Collectivities are mainly built on individual wants and desires although the phenomenon of groupthink exists where group rights take pride of place over individual rights. It is a subject I do not discuss here.

Exaggerating what identity politics signifies has become the favorite tool of some conservative thinkers. Sometimes referred to as a pundit rather than a historian, Niall Ferguson, fellow at the Hoover Institution at Stanford, took the criticism one step further: the infiltration of woke culture "was just a case of the old problem: that liberals defer to progressives. And progressives defer to outright totalitarians."[29] This logic made no sense. To be on the safe side, he made no explicit references to senior university administrators as totalitarians even though *The Economist* provided data on how this group had been filling jobs at universities in much greater proportions than research and teaching staff. It was what the late anthropologist David Graeber would have called "bullshit jobs"—"jobs which even the person doing the job can't really justify the existence of but they have to pretend that there's some reason for it to exist. That's the bullshit element. A lot of people confuse bullshit jobs and shit jobs, but they're not the same thing."[30]

A briefing in *The Economist* in 2021 developed the linkage between identity politics and wokeness more directly. Again vilifying the left, the British magazine argued that randomness and caprices brought together

> a loose constellation of ideas that is changing the way that mostly White, educated, left-leaning Americans view the world. This credo still lacks a definitive name: it is variously known as left-liberal identity politics, social-justice activism or, simply, wokeness. But it has a clear common thread: a belief that any disparities between racial groups are evidence of structural racism; that the norms of free speech, individualism and universalism which pretend to be progressive are really camouflage for this discrimination; and that injustice will persist until systems of language and privilege are dismantled.[31]

For *The Economist*, "These notions were incubated for years in the humanities departments of universities (elite ones in particular), without serious challenge. Moral panics about campus culture are hardly new, and the emergence of a new leftism in the early 2010s prompted little concern."

If this constituted new leftism, Ferguson was off the mark claiming "students began scouring the words of academics, administrators and fellow students for micro-aggressions, the oppressive slights embedded in everyday speech." This represented an injustice to the activities of most students.

To reiterate, critiques of the left suggesting it had nourished identity politics have no resemblance to either old or new left. Pathologies associated with leftist liberals—even those in privileged humanities departments—became muddled by the new-thinking conservative right. References to 1960s writers such as Brazilian pedagogue Paolo Freire or German philosopher Herbert Marcuse, both of whom supposedly influenced the soon-to-be left while in their student days, missed the mark. Instead, conservatives retrenched capitalist relations of production while placing all the blame on *gauchisme*.

Terms like "woke," micro-aggression," "trigger warnings," and "safetyism" serve as neologisms conceived in recent years to obscure and put out of mind older, grounded terms such as class conflict which singled out the progressive left. Bashing the left when it represented a swiftly disappearing phantom was duplicitous.

Economic Divides and Tribalism

The United States is an economically poorly divided society, another reason given for why the country is herded into identity concerns while flouting the deep fissures of socioeconomic cleavages. Seventy percent of countries have more equal income distribution patterns than the United States and the top one percent of income groups in America account for well over twenty percent of total income. There is a difference, too, in terms of societal perceptions: the average American estimates that the current ratio of CEO-to-unskilled-worker pay is thirty-to-one and their preference is to have about a seven-to-one ratio. Yet the actual CEO-versus-unskilled wage ratio in America is 354-to-one.[32] The extraordinary policymaking gulfs on US income inequality have been handed down to a shrinking class of sociologists to figure out. They should be making national headlines with their results.

Former US President Jimmy Carter published a book that was controversial by the standards of presidential autobiographies. His focus rested on the consequences of inequality:

> Millionaires, billionaires can put in unlimited amounts of money directly into the campaign. In a way, it gives legal bribery a chance to prevail, because almost all the candidates, whether they're honest or not, and whether they're Democratic or Republican, depend on these massive infusions of money from very rich people in order to have money to campaign.[33]

The bribery of politicians in order to further particular programs and policy goals has fractured a sense of national unity. Given uniform opposition to gun control measures, for example, makes the choice of a political candidate to support have little relevance or impact.

Does analyzing different forms of discrimination help construct a composite index of identity objectives, thereby putting identity to practical use? Intersectionality is a well-known sociological theory that describes multiple threats of discrimination when an individual's identity overlaps with differing points of disadvantage. These include race, gender and sexual orientation, age, ethnicity, and health, among others. The idea of intersectionality recognizes that multiple forms of oppression and exploitation exist. At times it encourages the importance of far-reaching solidarity across identity categories. But just as often it becomes absorbed with the plight of special identities at the price of ignoring graver ones. A crucial example in America is the politics of the African-American community.

To begin, the United States is exceptional in forging a high degree of physical separation between Black people and White. Racial categories shape migrant opportunities but also the way that they look at themselves and the way that they are viewed by others. Separation goes beyond physicality: "African Americans typically raise their children to protect themselves against a presumed hostility from White teachers, White police officers, White supervisors, and White co-workers."[34]

Whether immigrant or native-born, Black people are frequently residentially segregated from Whites in contrast to cohorts in Western Europe. Rates of Black-White intermarriage are lower in the United States than in countries such as Britain, France, or the Netherlands. It is not only those classified as Black who are seen through the prism of color-coded racism.[35]

President Barack Obama was defensive about such forms of racism and implored his Black audiences to turn mainstream. According to commentator Ta-Nehisi Coates, "For much of his presidency, a standard portion of Obama's speeches about race riffed on Black people's need to turn off the television, stop eating junk food, and stop blaming White people for their problems."[36] Latinos and Asians, when viewed as nonwhite or people of color, also suffer from similar stereotypes.

Racial roles briefly changed when a Black President was inaugurated in 2009. Coates' insightfulness how "The symbolic power of Barack Obama's presidency—that Whiteness was no longer strong enough to prevent peons taking up residence in the castle—assaulted the most deeply rooted notions of White supremacy and instilled fear in its adherents and beneficiaries."[37] Coates' book, *Eight Years in Power*, implied that Obama turned one of America's greatest fears into a reality. Referring to Reconstruction-era Black political leaders, writer W.E.B. Du Bois asserted: "If there was one thing South Carolina feared more than bad Negro government, it was good Negro government." That was what Obama assured—for Coates and liberals in America. But it did not anticipate the backlash to a sitting Black President that followed his years in office.

When out of office, President Obama warned about the pitfalls of woke culture and argued that it did not represent activism or progress for minority groups.[38] His interpretation of identity politics was directed at events occurring on university campuses in the United States (which his daughters were attending at the time) where cancel culture was harnessed to negate the academic freedom of public speakers who were controversial and not well-liked. But growing attention to woke culture put Obama himself at its center, according to dilettante author Norman Finkelstein. In *I'll Burn That Bridge When I Get to It! Heretical Thoughts on Identity Politics, Cancel Culture, and Academic Freedom*, Finkelstein bemoaned the lack of intellectual substance to superficial woke culture, accused Obama of helping institutionalize it at the expense of social-class-based radical thinking personified by Democratic Party progressive Bernie Sanders, and generally abandoning the struggle for wider social and economic justice on behalf of African-Americans.[39] These were harsh criticisms of a President popular with this minority group.

A critical moment in advancing what came to be known as identity politics took place several decades before Obama's election. In 1977, a group of Black feminist lesbian activists who became known as *The Combahee River Collective* (recalling a battle fought in 1782 during the American Revolutionary War) underscored selfregarding activism while paying respect to earlier intersectional feminism. Their statement read how "focusing upon our own oppression is embodied in the concept of identity politics. We believe that the most profound and potentially most radical politics come directly out of our own identity, as opposed to working to end somebody else's oppression."[40]

In other words, identity politics emerged from the Black feminist movement of the 1970s but, after that, it was taken in many different directions, some of them problematic.

Alicia Garza, an American civil rights activist and writer who co-founded the international Black Lives Matter movement, fully welcomed the emergence of identity politics (Figure 7.1). In contrast to President Obama's more cautious politics, she underscored how "The term 'identity politics' was first coined by Black feminist Barbara Smith and the Combahee River Collective in 1974. Identity politics originated from the need to reshape movements that had until then prioritized the monotony of sameness over the strategic value of difference." Going further, Garza's objective has been to explore the Black feminist origins of identity politics: "Identity politics is not only widely misunderstood, but intentionally distorted in order to avoid acknowledging the ways in which 'identity' shapes the economy, our democracy, and our society." Furthermore, she added that "Another fallacy from critics of identity politics is that identifying and addressing differences somehow prevent people with different histories, backgrounds, ethnicities, identities, or experiences from finding commonality."[41]

Figure 7.1 An intrinsic identity in its own right extends beyond narrow tribal politics and displays solidarity with other disadvantaged groups.

Aware of this caveat, Garza makes solidarity a defining characteristic and *sine qua* non of identity politics. She challenges the contrived premise of identity politics that frequently seeks to hush up all debate. It does this by claiming that conservative, White supremacist, and right-wing groups are neutral on this subject:

> The fight over identity politics is a false one; it forces false choices and even worse, inauthentic ones. Conservative movements have identified race and gender in particular as arenas where neutrality is strategic to maintain white, heterosexual, male, cisgendered power, at the expense of everyone who does not occupy those social positions. They have identified that inequality resulting from race and gender, and other social indicators that have economic implications, is best left undiscussed.

For those who oppose identity politics, the result has been to achieve no real substantive change in the relationships of power or the outcomes obtained. Yet according to a senior fellow of the right-wing Heritage Foundation, behind identity politics stand "Some of the wealthiest families in America— such as the Soros, Buffett, and Rockefeller families—and much of corporate America are involved in this effort.[42] The tentative conclusion is that either rich people or corporate America represent the politics of the left or they are subversive and only pose as the left.

Garza convincingly identified what stakes were involved in the 2016 elections won by Trump:

> In the lead up to the 2016 Presidential election, Donald Trump ran on the slogan of "Make America Great Again." Making America great again insinuated that America was great before, leaving one to ask: "What are we trying to restore America to, and what are we trying to change it from?" Throughout the campaign, the answer became clear—America, apparently, was great before its demographics changed, before women had rights, before Black people could stand up for their rights, and so on. The America invoked by Trump was an America run and dominated by white, Christian, heterosexual men. That America was powered by blue-collar manufacturing jobs, and in that America, people of color, women, and others did not have equal rights to white men.

Her arguments offer an antidote to *prima facie* criticism of all forms of identity politics. Nuanced White-supremacy politics may represent a sufficient though not necessary feature of identity politics debates. Protecting existing racial hierarchies are often the teleological endpoints of identity politics. At the same time, however, differences in identity politics are underscored, in many instances linking these to structural features that produce socioeconomic inequalities. In sum, Garza pleads for equality of opportunity and less for the Biblical injunction that the last shall be first and the first last. Trepidation and stupification, terms implied by Thucydides, should have no place, in her view, with meaningful debates addressing identity politics.

The politics of identity subsumes not just marginalized groups sharing an experience of injustice, such as Black identities, but also White communities. For Ashley Jardina, a political science professor at Duke University, concerns over America's mushrooming diversity initiatives have caused White Americans to view the political world through the lens of racial identity. Whiteness, historically a hegemonic position a few decades ago, has made a comeback while some argue it never went away. White people in America actively identify with their racial group and, predictably, also support policies seeking to protect their status and power.[43]

Drawing on data from American National Election Studies surveys, Jardina has argued that White Americans—roughly thirty to forty percent of them—profess racial solidarity with Whiteness. Equating the two does not invariably overlap, however, with White racist attitudes. Whites do favor their own racial in-group over outgroup ones but, crucially, defending White identity does not mean embracing White supremacist policies. In sum, White racial prejudice in American politics and White identity politics represent two separate forces pushing in the same direction but, for Jardina, capturing two different subsets of White Americans.[44] Hers is an aspirational understanding of White identity politics.

Anxiety about privileges, status, and power slipping from their hands, to be replaced by other advancing ethnicities, remains an important calculation. The prospect that Whites will cease to be a majority by the middle of this century has become a distant fear, not just a suspicion. For Huntington's writing in 2004, a rock-solid bulwark against minority groups' rise to influence was made up of White Anglo-Saxon Protestants (WASPs). For him, members of minorities need not be WASPs themselves but they should lend support to the culture and values sowed by WASPs over several centuries of American history.[45]

White identity, expressing solidarity with non-White populations, can serve as a resource. Its concern for a deepening sense of belonging to America is indispensable so that other ethnicities and racial communities can follow suit. To be sure, major exceptions to inclusivity have included Native Americans who were exploited and marginalized for centuries. Africans brought to this continent as slaves have also suffered from exclusionary politics. While a turn to identity politics is not in itself a panacea for resolving multiple problems afflicting the United States, a sense of resilient solidarity coupled with a common desire to march together to protest injustices are pivotal steps to regaining true national identity.

Postscriptum

The 1993 Nobel Prize in Literature was awarded to Toni Morrison "who in novels characterized by visionary force and poetic import, gives life to an essential aspect of American reality." She was the first native-born American to win since John Steinbeck in 1962 and was followed by laureate Bob Dylan in 2016 "for having created new poetic expressions within the great American song tradition," and Louise Glück "for her unmistakable poetic voice that with austere beauty makes individual existence universal."

Toni Morrisson, an African-American, died in 2019. This excerpt from her *Song of Solomon* teaches us what love should be and what it should not.

> You think because he doesn't love you that you are worthless. You think that because he doesn't want you anymore that he is right—that his judgment and opinion of you are correct. If he throws you out, then you are garbage. You think he belongs to you because you want to belong to him. Don't. It's a bad word, 'belong.' Especially when you put it with somebody you love. Love shouldn't be like that…. You can't own a human being. You can't lose what you don't own. Suppose you did own him. Could you really love somebody who was absolutely nobody without you? You really want somebody like that? Somebody who falls apart when you walk out the door? You don't, do you? And neither does he. You're turning over your whole life to him. Your whole life, girl. And if it means so little to you that you can just give it away, hand it to him, then why should it mean any more to him? He can't value you more than you value yourself."

Toni Morrison, *Song of Solomon* (New York: Alfred A. Knopf, 1977), 306.

Notes

1 Raoul de Roussy de Sales, "What Makes an American," *The Atlantic* (March 1939).
2 Pew Research Center, "Public Trust in Government: 1958–2022," https://www.pewresearch.org/politics/2022/06/06/public-trust-in-government-1958-2022/.
3 Jimmy Carter, *Our Endangered Values: America's Moral Crisis* (New York: Simon and Schuster, 2005).
4 James Meek, "Against Passion," *London Review of Books* 39, no. 23 (November 30, 2017), https://www.lrb.co.uk/the-paper/v39/n23/james-meek/against-passion.

5 Barry Glassner, *The Culture of Fear: Why Americans are Afraid of the Wrong Things—Crime, Drugs, Minorities, Teen Moms, Killer Kids, Mutant Microbes, Plane Crashes, Road Rage, and So Much More* (New York: Basic Books, 1999), xi, xviii.

6 Caroline van Eck, "The Petrifying Gaze of Medusa: Ambivalence, Ekplexis, and the Sublime," *Journal of Historians of Netherlandish Art* 8, no. 2 (Summer 2016), https:// jhna.org/articles/petrifying-gaze-medusa-ambivalence-explexis-sublime/.

7 Overview, "Moral Panic," *Oxford Reference* (2022), https://www.oxfordreference.com/ view/10.1093/oi/authority.20110803100208829.

8 Stanley Cohen, *Folk Devils and Moral Panics: The Creation of the Mods and Rockers*, 3rd edn (London: Routledge, 2011) [London: MacGibbon and Kee 1972].

9 Stuart Hall, Chas Critcher, Tony Jefferson, John Clarke, and Brian Roberts, *Policing the Crisis: Mugging, the State and Law and Order* (New York: Palgrave Macmillan, 2013) [1978].

10 Frank Furedi, *How Fear Works: Culture of Fear in the 21st Century* (London: Bloomsbury Continuum, 2019), 107–108.

11 Christopher Lasch, *The Culture of Narcissism: American Life in an Age of Diminishing Expectations* (New York: W.W. Norton, 2018) [1979].

12 Seymour Martin Lipset, *The First New Nation: The United States in Historical and Comparative Perspective* (New York: W.W. Norton, 1979).

13 Daniel Bell, *The End of Ideology: On the Exhaustion of Political Ideas in the Fifties*. 2nd edn. (Cambridge: Harvard University Press, 2000).

14 "A Changing Country," *New York Times*, August 13, 2021, https://www.nytimes. com/2021/08/13/briefing/census-2020-diversity-united-states.html.

15 Nathan Glazer, "Disaggregating Culture," in *Culture Matters: How Values Shape Human Progress*, eds. Lawrence E. Harrison and Samuel P. Huntington (New York: Basic Books, 2000), 230.

16 Glazer, "Disaggregating Culture," 222.

17 Azar Gat, *Nations: The Long History and Deep Roots of Political Ethnicity and Nationalism* (Cambridge: Cambridge University Press, 2012), 268.

18 Gat, *Nations*.

19 Samuel P. Huntington, *Who Are We? The Challenges to America's National Identity* (New York: Simon and Schuster, 2004), ch. 9.

20 Huntington, *Who Are We?* 362–63, 365–66.

21 Jack Citrin and David O. Sears, *American Identity and the Politics of Multiculturalism* (Cambridge: Cambridge University Press, 2014), 238.

22 Mark Lilla, *The Once and Future Liberal: After Identity Politics* (New York: Harper, 2018).

23 Lilla, *The Once and Future Liberal*.

24 Mark Lilla, "The End of Identity Liberalism," *New York Times*, November 18, 2016, https://www.nytimes.com/2016/11/20/opinion/sunday/the-end-of-identity-liberalism.html.

25 Amy Chua, "How America's Identity Politics Went from Inclusion to Division," *The Guardian*, March 1, 2018, https://www.theguardian.com/society/2018/mar/01/ how-americas-identity-politics-went-from-inclusion-to-division; see also Chua, *Political Tribes: Group Instinct and the Fate of Nations* (London: Penguin Press, 2018).

26 Vivek Ramaswamy, *Woke, Inc: Inside Corporate America's Social Justice Scam* (New York: Center Street, 2021).

27 Greg Lukianoff and Jonathan Haidt, *The Coddling of the American Mind: How Good Intentions and Bad Ideas Are Setting Up a Generation for Failure* (London: Penguin Press, 2019).

28 James Allan, "The New Religion of Diversity," *Spectator Australia*, July 17, 2021, https://www.spectator.com.au/2021/07/the-new-religion-of-diversity/.

29 Briefing, "The Illiberal Left: How did American 'Wokeness' Jump from Elite Schools to Everyday Life?" *The Economist*, September 4, 2021, https://www.economist.com/briefing/2021/09/04/how-did-american-wokeness-jump-from-elite-schools-to-everyday-life?utm_medium=cpc.adword.pd&utm_source=google&utm_campaign=a.22brand_pmax&utm_content=conversion.direct-response.anonymous&gclid=CjwKCAjwo_KXBhAaEiwA2RZ8hJd_MklB6FW7USyeoHokE0PXxj1Yc-BfoqPUzh_Lwblb_QBcDHOMCRoCG58QAvD_BwE&gclsrc=aw.ds.

30 Sean Illing, Interview with David Graeber, "Bullshit Jobs: Why They Exist and Why You Might Have One," *Vox*, November 9, 2019, https://www.vox.com/2018/5/8/17308744/bullshit-jobs-book-david-graeber-occupy-wall-street-karl-marx; for a complete, humorous read, see Graeber, *Bullshit Jobs: A Theory* (London: Penguin Press, 2019).

31 Briefing, *The Economist*.

32 "Why is America More Tolerant of Inequality than Many Rich Countries?" *The Economist*, December 18, 2017, https://www.economist.com/blogs/democracyinamerica/2017/12/capital-question?cid1=cust/ddnew/email/n/n/20171218n/owned/n/n/ddnew/n/n/n/nNA/Daily_Dispatch/email&etear=dailydispatch.

33 Interview with John Humphrys, "Jimmy Carter: US Campaign Funding is 'Legal Bribery,'" *BBC News*, February 3, 2016, http://www.bbc.co.uk/programmes/p03hd981.

34 Ta-Nehisi Coates, "My President was Black," *The Atlantic*, January-February 2017, https://www.theatlantic.com/magazine/archive/2017/01/my-president-was-black/508793/.

35 Franklin D. Gilliam, *Farther to Go: Readings and Cases in African-American Politics* (Fort Worth, TX: Harcourt, 2002).

36 Coates, "My President."

37 Ta-Nehisi Coates, *We Were Eight Years in Power: An American Tragedy* (New York: One World, 2017).

38 Video, "Barack Obama Takes on 'Woke' Call-out Culture: 'That's not Activism,'" October 30, 2019, https://www.theguardian.com/us-news/video/2019/oct/30/barack-obama-calls-out-politically-woke-social-media-generation-video.

39 Norman Finkelstein, *I'll Burn That Bridge When I Get to It! Heretical Thoughts on Identity Politics, Cancel Culture, and Academic Freedom* (New York: Sublation Media, 2023).

40 Combahee River Collective Statement, *Blackpast*, primary document, 1977, https://www.blackpast.org/african-american-history/combahee-river-collective-statement-1977/.

41 Alicia Garza, "Identity Politics: Friend or Foe?" Berkeley: Othering and Belonging Institute, September 24, 2019, https://belonging.berkeley.edu/identity-politics-friend-or-foe.

42 Mike Gonzales, "The Long Shadow of the Identity Politics 'Constitution,'" *Heritage Foundation*, December 18, 2020, https://www.heritage.org/civil-society/commentary/the-long-shadow-the-identity-politics-constitution.

43 Ashley Jardina, *White Identity Politics* (Cambridge: Cambridge University Press, 2019).

44 Sean Illing, "White Identity Politics is about More than Racism," Interview with Ashley Jardina, *Vox*, April 27, 2019, https://www.vox.com/2019/4/26/18306125/white-identity-politics-trump-racism-ashley-jardina.

45 Huntington, *Who Are We?*

Chapter 8

MUSINGS ON POLITICAL FEAR: METHODS AND THEORIES

Meditating on Methods

Thucydides' different approaches to the concept of fear provide us with a better grasp of how we can operationalize it across a wide set of case studies. Located in six countries where I undertook fieldwork, the depth of the analytical framework extends to a set of comparative stories which inform us about the fallout resulting from distinguishable notions of fear that arise in Western-positioned states, that is, if we agree that in-migration to western parts of Russia qualifies as a Western phenomenon.

Admittedly, coupling Thucydides' classification with culturally dissimilar countries may have a hit-or-miss character to it. For example, it would be possible for *orrodia*, a rhetorical device, to be applied to all the six cases examined. However, choosing only Russia's President as rhetorician-in-chief singles out its explanatory breath. Identifying six different terms to ferret out supporting evidence for the types of fear characteristic of a country is a plausible paradigm that augurs in best practices and optimizing analyses.

Ben Judah's book *This Is London* begins with a fine-tuned understanding of what method he will be using before he plunges into micro-analyses of the roads and rail stations and street corners of London on the eve of the Brexit referendum: "I have to see everything for myself. I don't trust statistics. I don't trust columnists. I don't trust self-appointed spokesmen. I have to make up my own mind. This is why I am shivering again, in Victoria Coach Station, at 6 am."[1] This method comprises, paradoxically, an ideal-type framework for conducting empirical research. It is admirable that Judah flaunts his brass-knuckles approach when digging for empirics.

For my part, an obligation presented itself to investigate surveys and their inferences in addition to examining self-appointed rhetoricians and the inner workings of angst so as to unsheathe latent and manifest explanatory variables. All manner of data was included in the mix: interpretations of opinion polls and of election results; inferences drawn from policy debates and political rhetoric; and analyses of one-sided biased opinion and editorial commentaries. An asymmetrical investigation across case studies is advantageous so long as the dependent variable—political fear—remains constant.

Nevertheless, there are a host of appropriate questions to ask about research outcomes. One is whether a country is more fear-fixated than another; Russia's history and real-time quandary come to mind. Assaying supposedly self-confident states—here Germany and Japan serve as examples—may cut through well-worn images and national brands and ultimately can reveal insecurities and complexes. I have not posed these questions in my study because applying Thucydides' pliable framework may not produce a fully reliable answer.

Where sufficient skepticism emerges about the value of taking Thucydides at his word and focusing on six contemporary cases of fear, my response would be that this research can be treated as a plausibility probe (mentioned in Chapter 1). In light of political scientist Stephen van Evera's query about how to frame, assess, and apply theories in the social sciences, his suggestion is to do this working backward: from the proposition ("the answer") to collecting evidence-based proof. The sequence he proposes leads from: a proposition "to data exploration ('plausibility probe') to revised hypothesis to prediction to larger data exploration to conclusion." Deeper and thicker analysis, then, will result in a robust in-depth case study.[2]

Plausibility means more than passing a validity test for which rigorous testing is required. A plausibility probe attempts "to determine whether potential validity may reasonably be considered great enough to warrant the pains and costs of testing."[3] Deciding whether to employ such a probe is the result of a cost-benefit analysis surveying research options available. In fact, investing in an analysis of likely outcomes is generally preferable to investing in less likely ones. A plausibility probe is therefore preferable to a rudimentary pilot study.

The sequencing of a plausibility probe indicates—but it does not confirm— "answers" to contrasting understandings of fear. A chapter-by-chapter resumé suggests that *deos* represents an intangible fear of a distant, ill-defined threat, as in the case of England's "national" fear which opposes the free movement of people from Europe but privileges Englishness. *Phobos* signifies a direr, irrational fear of a present threat, as evidenced in the "regional" fear of Muslim migrants settling in Saxony. *Orrodia* are speech acts entailing expressions of fear; a "likely" actor making extensive use of this notion was Russia's President, capturing the ethnic concerns Russians have of becoming outnumbered by non-Russians.

Angst is not a word employed by Thucydides but reflects an accurate substitute for capturing individualistic aspects of fear. This was applied to the case of a Japanese artist working in the US bureaucracy caught between divided loyalties during World War II. *Hypopsia* signifies suspicion and mistrust of a general threat and fits Australia's domestic as well as inter-state concerns about the rise of China. Finally, *ekplexis* and *kataplexis*, terms that spell out moral panic and paralysis, bring out the stages at which the United States has reached in replacing national identity with an avowal of tribal politics.

Further complications in the research enterprise may arise when comparing country studies even if all but Russia are regarded as Western states. Empirical, evidence-based research relies on historical factors incorporating a country's past path dependence. A separate issue is to become familiar with survey research carried out in these states by their own analysts. That is because public opinion surveys capture a snapshot of political attitudes at a specific moment in time that limits their applicability. Some polls offer contradictory findings about the state of public opinion while others do not even pass a validity test.

Political discourse is connected with fear and becomes more crudely fear-mongering when leaders deliberately employ it to arouse people's basic instincts. In such cases, the spread of fear requires exploring it at an individual level of analysis in order then to construct collective groupthink, if it exists.

Participant observation can also help frame the context of particular time periods. Value-free objective analyses written by historians, political sociologists, and intellectuals (who guard these cultural and historical domains) can reflect a participatory framework. In contrast, an array of influencers uncommitted to objectivity can reify fear and even inflame it. American journalist Walter Lippmann's books on public opinion written a hundred years ago merit a fresh look.[4]

Let me pose two counterfactuals—what if's—to suggest which scenarios could be sketched for Thucydides as alternative analytical frameworks. The first would assume that he was deeply troubled by fear and war in which case he would not have delivered an unblemished Funeral Oration to Pericles glorifying him for inciting the citizens of Athens to back the war effort against Sparta and give their lives so as to protect their freedom. This alternative was patently untrue, of course.

Would Thucydides' history be blunter, starker, and reaching into darker spaces if he described how the Athenian alliance had evolved into an empire that included most of the northern and eastern shores of the Aegean Sea? Would Sparta be vindicated for not being a liberal democracy as well as for attacking preemptively if Athenians had already been accused of amassing a war chest from tribute paid by their empire and conquered territories?

The second "what if" is this: what if the historian had not survived the plague that killed 100,000 people in Athens? The history of the Peloponnesian war would not have been written and we would remain ignorant about his catalog of words denoting fear. Or a long-shot counterfactual thought experiment could be introduced: Thucydides had decided to collaborate with Herodotus and discovered that co-authoring a trippy Mediterranean Odyssey with him had greater appeal than a dire study of war.[5]

These what-if questions are hypothetical but have no certain answers. The preponderance of evidence presented in this book suggests that for the historian who wrote about the Peloponnesian war, close-call or long-shot hypotheses are far-fetched. On the other hand, second-order counterfactuals exist when a researcher believes that the predicted events almost happened. For international relations specialist Ned Lebow, then, good history needs to be sharpened by a series of counterfactual perspectives.

Meditating on Theories

Thucydides, a good and ethical man, was an admirer of the Athenian form of government. In examining his account of the conflicts that occurred between it, Sparta, and their respective alliances during the Peloponnesian wars, fears became reciprocal and could be viewed as an early example of the security dilemma. This is a situation where the actions taken by a state to increase its own security cause reactions from other states. This reaction ultimately leads to a decrease rather than an increase in the initial state's security.

Thucydides did not spell this dilemma out so clearly. But did we need to wait nearly 2,500 years to understand the big theory underscoring the concept? Anders Wivel was part of the Copenhagen School which argued that security rests upon a symbiotic relationship between actor and audience and an issue is only securitized when an audience accepts it as such. He intuited that "The logic of the security dilemma was first described by Herbert Butterfield in 1949. The term was coined by John Hertz in 1950." This is far removed from 400 BCE.

The Cold War, perhaps looked back upon fondly compared to the disastrous consequences of the Great War of 1914–1918, the murderous Second World War from 1939–1945, or even the Ukraine-Russia War initiated in 2022 that took in both nearby and distant parts of the globe, may be presented as a security dilemma: "the logic seems to fit particularly well with the security competition between the United States and the Soviet Union," today's Russia. It "reflects the fundamentally tragic nature of international life: state actors strive for peace and stability, but end up in military conflict. Thus, even if all states are status quo powers wishing only peace and security, war may occur, because of the fear and insecurity following from the anarchic structure of the international system."[6]

If the Peloponnesian war triggered reciprocal fear and a near-inevitable security dilemma arising between two alliances, could the war be framed by Athens calling itself a democracy and Sparta not? Was the existence of democracy relevant in distinguishing between the two city-states? Would tacking on the adjective "liberal" democracy make it more justifiable for supporters of Athens? Or was that irrelevant? Divergent theories of what constitutes liberalism come to the fore.

American political theorist Patrick Deneen accepted that liberalism has always been "a foundation of contradictions."[7] However, for the writer, its earlier proclaimed successes in achieving a near-limitless expansion of the liberal state were now spawning its own failures. Regular conferences of wealthy and notionally liberal states are cases in point. The G-7, the G-20, the Davos Economic Forum, a military pact like NATO, and even trade pacts signed by "liberal" countries such as NAFTA raise questions about liberal thinking today and its regular refrain, a "rules-based order." A tautological phenomenon emerges: when Western institutions gather, the rallying cry is for more liberalism elsewhere. Predictably, then, when searching for the presence of liberalism in organizational structures around the world, only those exclusively Western institutions claim they possess it.

Contesting liberal ideas expounded by political theorists underscores how a disconnect exists between liberalism's stated ideals and its actual practices. When the focus is on practices, the overuse of the concept of fear by elites awakens the public's consciousness of liberalism's fundamental contradictions. Almost by definition, illiberal regimes are equated with the authoritarian rule; states branded as illiberal, like Hungary and Russia in Europe or Myanmar and China in Asia, are *ipso facto* depicted as autocratic even if we can quickly list pro-Western countries that are forgiven their illiberalism.

Modern liberalism has little in common with nineteenth-century liberal theories other than a focus on furthering individual will and individual rights. Back then, as John Stuart Mill had stressed, people were free to do what they wanted so long as they met the thin requirement of not breaking the law or causing immediate physical harm to others. I return to Mill's exception below when describing "cruelty" and "violence" occurring in modern societies dubbed liberal; these frequently target outsider groups and expose liberalism's latent duplicity. But first I review theories about democracy and conditions under which clampdowns are needed on undemocratic forces so as to safeguard liberal democracy.

A Fool's Errand

On its 175th anniversary, *The Economist* wrote: "It is the moment for a liberal reinvention. Liberals need to spend less time dismissing their critics as fools and bigots and more fixing what is wrong. The true spirit of liberalism is not self-preserving, but radical and disruptive."[8] Indirectly, this is a warning to the EU to stop dismissing EU critics as fools and bigots. Until the EU's self-interests become less self-preserving, there will be countries that will be tempted by an EU exit.

What contingency plans are postulated when democracy and liberalism are eroded and instead democratic and liberal backsliding occur? The key variable becomes the significance of tolerance.

When Democracies are Rattled: Tolerance

We can return to Thucydides to discover what a democracy should do when it is rattled by dissent and opposition. This estimable classical Greek scholar preferred a mixed constitution that blended elements of a democracy with oligarchy while avoiding the extremes of both, in order to salvage compromise.[9] But while those times reflected on democratic and liberal thought, they have become gargantuan subjects since and we skip ahead to the nineteenth century and John Stuart Mill.

Mill was a strong believer in the virtue of tolerance.[10] In his view, the state may only interfere with people expressing their views if those views cause harm to others. Even then, it should only interfere if doing so would be more beneficial than not doing so. There should be "absolute freedom of opinion and sentiment on all subjects, practical or speculative, scientific, moral, or theological," however, immoral or dishonest the opinion or sentiment may seem.[11] He continued: "The peculiar evil of silencing the expression of an opinion is that it is robbing the human race... If the opinion is right, they are deprived of the opportunity of exchanging error for truth; if wrong, they lose, what is almost as great a benefit, the clearer perception and livelier impression of truth produced by its collision with error."[12]

This view embraces the spirit of tolerance. Mill asked: "Should we not censor those opinions that we think are, not false, but dangerous to society?" He gave two responses: "First, the belief that an opinion is dangerous can be disputed—as above, we cannot be certain that the view is in fact dangerous to society unless we allow free debate on the matter. But for this, we must allow the 'dangerous' view to be discussed, and cannot censor it."

The second holds that if the view to be censored is true, then the view that opposes it must be false. Many people have argued that no belief that is false can, in the end, be useful. So, for Mill, it is never in the best interests of society to defend a false belief against the "dangerous truth."[13] In sum, a democracy has limited occasions on which to censor dangerous views or lock down dissent. Today locking down dissent happens in many states, democracies included. Yet the argument I am making is that tolerance can reduce fear.

Many theorists arrive at the view that unlimited tolerance must lead to the disappearance of tolerance. If we are not prepared to defend a tolerant society against the onslaught of the intolerant, then the tolerant will be destroyed, and tolerance with it. Showing intolerance to those who are branded as intolerant is a question easily answered in political systems that are viewed as authoritarian: they impose an authoritarian rule to end opposition agitation. But Western theorists have also regularly held to the idea that not tolerating those regarded as intolerant, those who possess dangerous ideas, and those whose ideologies are plain wrong-headed should not benefit from living in a tolerant society. I call this obfuscation limiting tolerance smokescreen liberalism; it can be liberal in form but illiberal in substance.

This dilemma bedeviled Karl Popper and shaped his views when writing *The Open Society and Its Enemies* in 1945. His book was regarded as a spirited "defense of the open society against its enemies." He charged Plato, Hegel, and Marx for relying on historicism to underpin their particular political philosophies, turning them into advocates of totalitarianism. He, therefore, unleashed his critique of historicism, his defense of the open society, and his admiration for liberal democracy. But "what if" there may be a good reason to tolerate those with whom we disagree? What if, in that disagreement, they may be proved right and we find ourselves in the wrong?

Popper's apprehensions revolved around the "paradox of tolerance." It claimed that if a society is tolerant without limits, its ability to remain tolerant will eventually be seized or destroyed by the intolerant. Popper arrived at the paradoxical conclusion, therefore, that in order to maintain a tolerant society, society must be intolerant of intolerance. To be sure, some of the intolerant would use rational arguments when confronting their opponents. But not everyone listens to rational arguments and, for Popper in such cases, suppression would be needed, even using force. Smokescreen liberalism can therefore run amok.

A more persuasive political philosopher than Popper is John Rawls who theorized that liberty precedes social justice. He was nuanced about claiming, in the name of tolerance, the right not to tolerate the intolerant. In his 1971 book called *A Theory of Justice*, he asserted that a just society must tolerate the intolerant, otherwise society would then itself be shown to be intolerant, and therefore unjust.

Like Popper, Rawls was certain that society reserves a reasonable right of self-preservation that overrides the principle of tolerance. He argued: "While an intolerant sect does not itself have title to complain of intolerance, its freedom should be restricted only when the tolerant sincerely and with reason believe that their own security and that of the institutions of liberty are in danger."[14] This is a complex problem to resolve.

In 1997, another acclaimed American philosopher, Michael Walzer, was asked the question pointblank: "Should we tolerate the intolerant?" He replied that in the case of religious tolerance most minority religions benefiting from tolerance are themselves intolerant. However, in a tolerant system, such followers may learn themselves to tolerate, or at least act as if they possessed this virtue. He added that intolerant speech should be subject to a different, less penalizing, standard of justification than violent, repressive behavior. Again, judging the differences between the two is not always straightforward.

Communitarian theorist Michael Sandel was more forgiving of dissent in a liberal democracy: "It is a mistake to see only the bigotry in populist protest, or to view it only as an economic complaint…. For those left behind by three decades of market-driven globalization, the problem is not only wage stagnation and the loss of jobs; it is also the loss of social esteem. It is not only about unfairness; it is also about humiliation."

For Sandel, liberal neutrality, by avoiding rather than engaging with moral disagreements, "misses the anger and resentment that animate the populist revolt… the cultural estrangement, even humiliation, that many working class and middle class voters feel; and it ignores the meritocratic hubris of elites." He concluded, ambiguously, how "Donald Trump is keenly alive to the politics of humiliation."[15]

Peter Jones, a Classics professor at Newcastle University, offered significant contributions to the debate on tolerance: He cleared up fundamental misunderstandings of what it comprised: "Toleration in its orthodox sense entails disapproval or dislike. We tolerate only that to which we object; if we find something unobjectionable, we have no occasion to tolerate it." Furthermore, "We can tolerate only what we are able to prevent. If we object to x, but are powerless to prevent it, we cannot tolerate x. Toleration exists only when intolerance is an option."[16] That seems a convincing argument to make.

For this classicist, a tolerant political arrangement is one that upholds an ideal of toleration rather than one that itself engages in toleration. A neutral state grounded in a commitment to toleration must be committed to the promotion and maintenance of the ideal of toleration.[17] Therefore, "We understand a tolerant regime as one that upholds an ideal of toleration rather than one that itself tolerates the population whose lives it regulates." Indeed, in order to deconstruct the concept of toleration Jones raised the issue of

> overextended complaints of intolerance in which groups or individuals juggle with the idea of toleration so that they can represent themselves as victims of intolerance. Most of the conduct that we do not tolerate, routinely and rightly, has nothing to do with intolerance. Murder, rape, assault, intimidation, theft, and exploitation are not, in the ordinary run of cases, expressions of intolerance. We should not, therefore, feel obliged always to characterize the intolerable as intolerant.[18]

Again, this persuasive argument makes clear what exceptions exist to the general rule of not harassing the intolerant.

Let me consider an approach taken by the late political philosopher Glen Newey. Known as oppositional, combative, yet furnishing penetrating critiques on toleration, he crafted trenchant and original critiques of the phenomenon. He was convinced that tolerating the intolerant "is the normal state of affairs. When disputes arise amongst a population, the parties to the dispute typically regard one another's demands as intolerable and, when the government responds to their conflicting demands, it inevitably indulges the intolerance of one or other party."[16]

Newey associated democratic governance with political toleration,

> an idea that makes no sense in contemporary democratic circumstances. It makes no sense precisely for those liberal democratic societies that conceive themselves as embodiments of the ideal of toleration. Rather than engage in toleration, the real task of government in those societies is to decide what they should *not* tolerate. "Democratic toleration" is a "rubber duck."[19]

Remaining contrarian, Newey believed that toleration and intolerance were two sides of a single coin. Thus to "identify a particular type of society as 'tolerant', or as 'more tolerant' than another, must be an illusion. Every instance of political toleration must have intolerance as its flip-side." Not only that,

> "Tolerant" and "toleration" are frequently used as commendatory terms, while "intolerant" and "intolerance" are often used pejoratively. Perhaps then we should accept that the language of toleration is inescapably value-loaded and that "tolerant" cannot be used merely to *describe* a society; rather, "tolerant" is a term we should use only if we mean to *endorse* it.[20]

Liberalism's embrace of toleration can be circumspect but nevertheless intriguing and clever. Yet no overview of liberalism can be exhausted without reference to a principled libertarian. A Malaysian-born Australian political theorist who views himself as a contrarian liberal, Chandran Kukathas insists that classical liberalism, rightly understood, should favor "pure toleration." He investigated what the "principled" basis of a free society marked by cultural diversity and group loyalties is and his answer was this:

> A free society is an open society and, therefore, the principles which describe its nature must be principles which admit the variability

of human arrangements rather than fix or establish or uphold a determinate set of institutions within a closed order. Such principles should take as given only the existence of individuals and their propensity to associate; they need not and should not assume the salience of any particular individuals or of any particular historical associations. Granted this, the fundamental principle describing a free society is the principle of freedom of association.[21]

We arrive at the heart of libertarianism. For Kukathas, "a society is free to the extent that it is prepared to tolerate in its midst associations which differ or dissent from its standards or practices." Moreover, "The principles of a free society describe not a hierarchy of superior and subordinate authorities but an archipelago of competing and overlapping jurisdictions. A free society is sustained to the extent that laws honor these principles and authorities operate within such laws."[22]

Debating tolerance is critical to unscrambling democratic theory. For the purposes of this study, tolerance can prove pivotal in reducing political fears among its citizens since it accommodates a big-tent approach enticing a broad spectrum of viewpoints. I conclude this book by examining liberal theory and its erstwhile opponent, illiberalism.

Liberalism Sparking Fear?

A consensus in politics suggests that a liberal society is not one in which liberties and protections are extended only to those groups favored by liberals. Dissenters too should enjoy such liberties and protections and not be marginalized or altogether removed from political society. By the same token, the treatment of diaspora communities finding their place in new societies should be fair, not stigmatizing outsider groups for their possibly politically incorrect preferences or singling out insider groups for their correct viewpoints. The pledge that "liberals argue that toleration should not extend to the intolerant, where that can undermine the civility and reciprocity on which liberal democracy depends" is effectively intolerance, that is, smokescreen liberalism.[23]

Other advocates of liberalism say that liberal politics must squeeze into the gap opening up between being too narrowly self-regarding yet simultaneously barring unwelcome groups that have deep stakes in their communities. One such theorist asked a simple and perhaps naïve question. "Is it possible for liberals to re-appropriate for themselves the theme of community without giving in to the nationalists, or worse still to the nativists?"[24]

In her pathbreaking essay, "The Liberalism of Fear" published in 1989, political theorist Judith Shklar distinguished her approach from that of Rawls, her Harvard colleague who called for a liberalism of rights. She noted that "Realists and non-ideal theorists currently criticize Rawlsian mainstream liberalism for its inability to address injustice and political conflict." Moreover, for Shklar "contemporary liberalism is incapable of conceptualizing genuinely political notions such as power and conflict due to its reliance on a specific conceptualization of rationality and the resulting subordination of political philosophy to moral philosophy."[25]

Some thirty years after the publication of her article, Katharina Kaufmann returned to this thorny subject. She argued that "the liberalism of fear represents a genuinely realist version of liberalism;" it represents "a theory highly sensitive to the concerns of marginalized persons, and therefore a reinvigoration of liberalism's emancipatory and progressive thrust."[26]

Shklar's paradigm shift was to argue that liberal theory was inspired not by a *summum bonum*, or ultimate good, but by a *summum malum*, an ultimate evil—something that at all costs has to be avoided: "That evil is cruelty and the fear it inspires, and the very fear of fear itself. To that extent the liberalism of fear makes a universal and especially a cosmopolitan claim, as it historically always has done."[27] Its emphasis on restraint needs to be underpinned by "the distinctive political evil of living in fear of state violence and cruelty."[28]

What did Shklar mean by a term so vague as cruelty? "It is a deliberate infliction of physical, and secondarily emotional, pain upon a weaker person or group by stronger ones in order to achieve some end, tangible or intangible, of the latter."[29] In an earlier book she acknowledged the reality and the harm of moral cruelty while subordinating it to that of physical cruelty: "It is not just a matter of hurting someone's feelings. It is deliberate and persistent humiliation, so that the victim can eventually trust neither himself nor anyone else."[30] Put differently, such moral fear knows no limits.

Shklar's most lasting innovation was linking the political and the moral back into the center of liberal political theorizing. Toleration was re-introduced to the agenda: liberalism "has its historically 'deepest grounding' in the convictions of the defenders of toleration. But liberalism is not equivalent to toleration; rather, the affinity here lies in the sense of horror that liberals and the early defenders of toleration share at what Shklar calls 'cruelty.'"[31]

The sublime connection between fear and liberalism was put into practice by McGill professor Jacob Levy's research. In *The Multiculturalism of Fear*, he states: "I aim to develop a political and social theory of multiculturalism and nationalism which pays primary attention to the dangers of violence, cruelty, and political humiliation which so often accompany ethnic pluralism and ethnic politics." This is fear writ large, with liberalism mustering its forces to extinguish it.

> the danger of bloody ethnic violence, the reality that states treat members of minority cultures in humiliating ways, the intentional cruelty of language restrictions and police beatings and subtler measures which remind members of a minority that they are not full citizens or whole persons, these are the focus of attention [of a multiculturalism of fear].[32]

For Levy, the practice of multiculturalism gels into a normative theory positing how states can respond to the existence of cultural pluralism; when they should set aside special accommodation for ethnic minorities; stipulating conditions under which breaking up states and secession is justifiable; and explaining the types of reasonable accommodation that can reach cultural communities. Multiculturalism prevents a society from slipping away toward authoritarianism:

> Persons identify and empathize more easily with those with whom they have more in common than with those with whom they have less. They rally around their fellow religionists; they seek the familiar comforts of native speakers of their native languages; they support those they see as kin against those they see as strangers. They seek places that feel like home, and seek to protect those places; they are raised in particular cultures, with particular sets of local knowledge, norms, and traditions, which come to seem normal and enduring. These feelings, repeated and generalized, help give rise to a world of ethnic, cultural, and national loyalty, and also a world of enduring ethnic, cultural, and national variety.[33]

Yet Levy is resigned to the fact that "Nothing in the modern world is more prone to generate political violence and cruelty than the claimed ties of ethnicity and culture. Surely, then, the last thing liberalism should do is encourage persons to see themselves as parts of tribes rather than as individuals."[34] The inference is that non-cruelty, non-humiliation, and genuine tolerance are possible on condition that respect and recognition are selective and given to some ethnic communities and not others: "Ethnocultural groups develop in contrast to others; all too often a particular trait is valued precisely because it makes members seem better than some neighboring group. To recognize what a group values in its own culture is to accept a standard by which some other groups fail to be worthy of respect."[35]

As a result preference-making, whether of extant cultures or makeshift diasporas, in effect asserts that toleration should not extend to non-liberals.

I return to Shklar's liberal theory of fear which insists that it must encompass all who suffer cruelty and humiliation most often caused by the all-powerful state. In the early 1990s, she was not aware that multicultural policies could fit the bill and offer a solution. This was before the growth in the size of diverse communities that followed mass migration. Admittedly, preexisting established hierarchies determining who gets what in any society are inevitable; the interests of the majority community typically come first, then come traditional minority groups together with state-preferred diasporas, and at the bottom of the totem pole have always been Indigenous Peoples. But for Shklar no group should suffer humiliation or cruelty whether by the state or, in pluralist societies, by competing groups.

Coupling liberalism with democracy in a state can be an uphill struggle and is not as easy as invoking the mantra of liberal democracy. Thucydides sometimes thought that he lived in a city-state that had succeeded. Today the link between the two is murkier:

> Without the institutions of representative democracy and an accessible, fair, and independent judiciary open to appeals, and in the absence of a multiplicity of politically active groups, liberalism is in jeopardy. It is the entire purpose of the liberalism of fear to prevent that outcome. It is therefore fair to say that liberalism is monogamously, faithfully, and permanently married to democracy—but it is a marriage of convenience.[36]

In Thucydides' time, the classical conception of liberalism was to educate citizens in character and virtue so as to liberate them from their base desires and instincts. This is an understanding of liberty lost on many theorists of liberalism today. In many countries, liberty has even degenerated into populist slogans so that "liberal populists" advocate for mass consumption, hedonistic and narcissistic behavior patterns, and wrath and violence toward groups labeled as outsiders.

Deneen's book *Why Liberalism Failed* highlights the slippery slope and misleading meanings of this concept: "Liberalism is built on a foundation of contradictions: it trumpets equal rights while fostering incomparable material inequality; its legitimacy rests on consent, yet it discourages civic commitments in favor of privatism; and in its pursuit of individual autonomy, it has given rise to the most far-reaching, comprehensive state system in human history."[37]

Liberalism no longer forms the guardrails by which fear can be controlled, let alone extinguished. Together with a backsliding democratic system that is neither representative nor responsible,[38] liberalism opens up opportunity structures to mistreat the disadvantaged by inseminating fear in society. Separating a well-intentioned daring liberalism imbued with toleration from a self-seeking smokescreen one is urgent when seeking to reduce or altogether remove fear from our lives.

Notes

1 Ben Judah, *This is London: The Stories You Never Hear. The People You Never See* (London: Picador, 2016), 1.
2 Stephen van Evera, *Guide to Methods for Students of Political Science* (Ithaca: Cornell University Press, 1997), 105.
3 Harry Eckstein, "Case Study and Theory in Political Science," in *Regarding Politics: Essays on Political Theory, Stability, and Change*, ed. Eckstein (Berkeley: University of California Press, 1991), 147.
4 Walter Lippmann, *Public Opinion* (St. Paul: Wilder Publications, 2018) [1922]; *The Phantom Public* (St. Paul: Wilder Publications, 2021 [1925]).
5 Richard Ned Lebow, *Counterfactuals and International Relations* (Princeton: Princeton University Press, 2010).
6 Anders Wivel, "Security Dilemma," in *International Encyclopedia of Political Science*, eds. Bertrand Badie, Dirk Berg-Schlosser, and Leonardo Morlino. (Thousand Oaks: Sage, 2011), https://www.researchgate.net/profile/Anders-Wivel-2/publication/320211391_Security_dilemma/links/59d4e777a6fdcc181adc5d66/Security-dilemma.pdf
7 Patrick J. Deneen, *Why Liberalism Failed* (New Haven: Yale University Press, 2018).
8 "A Manifesto for Renewing Liberalism," *The Economist*, September 13, 2018, https://www.economist.com/leaders/2018/09/13/a-manifesto-for-renewing-liberalism?utm_medium=cpc.adword.pd&utm_source=google&utm_campaign=a.22brand_pmax&utm_content=conversion.direct-response.anonymous&gclid=CjwKC Ajw6fyXBhBgEiwAhhiZss8Nv45hfq3OyoF9G0G5BtfCWzt_oGMKhP4l2_zd4eXSnrHWhoUn4xoCLp0QAvD_BwE&gclsrc=aw.ds
9 Kurt A. Raaflaub, "Thucydides on Democracy and Oligarchy," in *Brill's Companion to Thucydides*, eds. Antonis Tsakmakis and Antonios Rengakos (Leiden: Brill, 2006), 189–222.
10 John Stuart Mill, *On Liberty* (Garden City: Dover Publications, 2002), ch. 2. See also Michael Lacewing, "Moral Philosophy," in *Philosophy*, eds. Elizabeth Burns and Stephen Law (London: Routledge, 2004), 44–93.
11 Mill, *On Liberty*, 71.
12 Mill, *On Liberty*, 76.
13 Mill, *On Liberty*, 82.
14 John Rawls, *A Theory of Justice* (Cambridge: Harvard University Press, 1999), 193.
15 Michael J. Sandel, "Populism, Trump, and the Future of Democracy," *openDemocracy*, May 9, 2018, https://www.opendemocracy.net/en/populism-trump-and-future-of-democracy/
16 Peter Jones, *Essays on Toleration* (Lanham Rowman & Littlefield, 2018), 29.
17 Jones, *Essays on Toleration*, 33.
18 Jones, *Essays on Toleration*, 48–49.
19 Glen Newey, *Toleration in Political Conflict* (Cambridge: Cambridge University Press, 2013), 38–39.

20 Newey, *Toleration*, 39.

21 Chandran Kukathas, *The Liberal Archipelago: A Theory of Diversity and Freedom* (Oxford: Oxford University Press, 2003), 4.

22 Kukathas, *The Liberal Archipelago*, 4.

23 Email correspondence with Geoffrey Levey, Professor at UNSW, Sydney, July 1, 2022.

24 Francesco Ronchi, "Liberals, Year Zero," *openDemocracy*, May 22, 2018, https://www.opendemocracy.net/en/liberals-year-zero/

25 Katharina Kaufmann, "Conflict in Political Liberalism: Judith Shklar's Liberalism of Fear," *Res Publica* 26, no. 4 (November 2020), 577, https://link.springer.com/article/10.1007/s11158-020-09475-z

26 Kaufmann, "Conflict in Political Liberalism," 583, 593.

27 Judith Shklar, "The Liberalism of Fear," in *Liberalism and the Moral Life*, ed. Nancy L. Rosenblum (Cambridge: Harvard University Press, 1989), 29. For a focus on injustice and rights, see Sklar's related book *The Faces of Injustice* (New Haven: Yale University Press, 1990).

28 Jacob T. Levy, "Who's Afraid of Judith Shklar?" *Foreign Policy*, July 2018, https://foreignpolicy.com/2018/07/16/whos-afraid-of-judith-shklar-liberalism/

29 Shklar, "The Liberalism of Fear," 29.

30 Judith Shklar, *Ordinary Vices* (Cambridge: Harvard University Press, 1984), 37.

31 Anonymous blog, "Judith Shklar: "The Liberalism of Fear," February 25, 2016, https://politicalnotmetaphysical.wordpress.com/2016/02/

32 Jacob T. Levy, *The Multiculturalism of Fear* (Oxford: Oxford University Press, 2000), 12, 35.

33 Levy, *The Multiculturalism of Fear*, 6.

34 Levy, *The Multiculturalism of Fear*, 27.

35 Levy, *The Multiculturalism of Fear*, 32.

36 Anonymous blog, "Judith Shklar."

37 Deneen, *Why Liberalism Failed*, https://www.goodreads.com/book/show/34746473-why-liberalism-failed

38 A. H. Birch, *Representative and Responsible Government* (London: George Allen and Unwin, 1964).

BIBLIOGRAPHY

Aho, James A. *This Thing of Darkness: A Sociology of the Enemy*. Seattle: University of Washington Press, 1994.

Alba, Richard, Peter Schmidt, and Martina Wasmer, eds. *Germans or Foreigners? Attitudes Toward Ethnic Minorities in Post-Reunification Germany*. London: Palgrave, 2003.

Alexievich, Svetlana. *Secondhand Time: The Last of the Soviets*. New York: Random House, 2016.

Alexievich, Svetlana. *The Unwomanly Face of War: An Oral History of Women in World War II*. New York: Random House, 2018.

Allport, Gordon. *The Nature of Prejudice*. Cambridge: Perseus Books, 1954.

Badie, Bertrand, Dirk Berg-Schlosser, and Leonardo Morlino, eds. *International Encyclopedia of Political Science*. Thousand Oaks: Sage, 2011.

Barnier, Michel. *My Secret Brexit Diary: A Glorious Illusion*. Cambridge: Polity Press, 2021.

Bauman, Zygmunt. *Liquid Fear*. Cambridge: Polity Press, 2006.

Bell, Daniel. *The End of Ideology: On the Exhaustion of Political Ideas in the Fifties*. Cambridge: Harvard University Press, 2000.

Birch, A. H. *Representative and Responsible Government*. London: George Allen and Unwin, 1964.

Brophy, David. *China Panic: Australia's Alternative to Paranoia and Pandering*. Melbourne: Black, Inc., 2021.

Buckley, Mary. *The Politics of Unfree Labour in Russia: Human Trafficking and Labour Migration*. Cambridge: Cambridge University Press, 2018.

Buzan, Barry, Ole Waever, and Jaap de Wilde, eds. *Security: A New Framework for Analysis*. Boulder: Lynne Reinner, 1998.

Calabrese, Brian E. *Fear in Democracy: A Study of Thucydides' Political Thought*. Ann Arbor: ProQuest, UMI Dissertations Publishing, 2008.

Carter, Jimmy. *Our Endangered Values: America's Moral Crisis*. New York: Simon and Schuster, 2005.

Chiu, Joanna. *China Unbound: A New World Disorder*. Toronto: House of Anansi Press, 2021.

Chua, Amy. *World on Fire: How Exporting Free Market Democracy Breeds Ethnic Hatred and Global Instability*. New York: Anchor, 2004.

Chua, Amy. *Political Tribes: Group Instinct and the Fate of Nations*. London: Penguin Press, 2018.

Citrin, Jack, and David O. Sears. *American Identity and the Politics of Multiculturalism*. Cambridge: Cambridge University Press, 2014.

Clarke, Harold D., Matthew Goodwin, and Paul Whiteley. *Brexit: Why Britain Voted to Leave the European Union*. Cambridge: Cambridge University Press, 2017.

Clyne, Michael, and James Jupp, eds. *Multiculturalism and Integration: A Harmonious Relationship*. Canberra: ANU Press, 2011.

Coates, Ta-Nehisi. *We Were Eight Years in Power: An American Tragedy.* New York: One World, 2017.

Cohen, Stanley. *Folk Devils and Moral Panics: The Creation of the Mods and Rockers.* London: Routledge, 2011.

Deneen, Patrick J. *Why Liberalism Failed.* New Haven: Yale University Press, 2018.

Denisenko, Mikhail, Salvatore Strozza, and Matthew Light, eds. *Migration from the Newly Independent States: 25 Years After the Collapse of the USSR.* Cham, Switzerland: Springer, 2020.

Dickey, Marianne, Dorota Gozdecka, and Sudrishti Reich, eds. *Unintended Consequences: The Impact of Migration Law and Policy.* Canberra: ANU Press, 2016.

Dostoyevsky, Fyodor. *The Possessed.* Translated by Constance Garnett. New York: Macmillan Company, 1948.

Dugin, Alexander. *The Foundations of Geopolitics: The Geopolitical Future of Russia.* 2020. Kindle.

Eckstein, Harry, ed. *Regarding Politics: Essays on Political Theory, Stability, and Change.* Berkeley: University of California Press, 1991.

Evans, Geoffrey, and Anand Menon. *Brexit and British Politics.* Cambridge: Polity Press, 2017.

Ferguson, Kate, and Andy Fearn, *A Gathering Storm? Assessing Risks of Identity-Based Violence in Britain.* Lambeth: Protection Approaches, 2019.

Finkelstein, Norman. *I'll Burn That Bridge When I Get to It! Heretical Thoughts on Identity Politics, Cancel Culture, and Academic Freedom.* New York: Sublation Media, 2023.

Fitzgerald, John. *Big White Lie: Chinese Australians in White Australia.* Randwick: University of New South Wales Press, 2007.

Freud, Sigmund. *Beyond the Pleasure Principle.* Translated by C. J. M. Hubback. The International Psycho-analytical Press: London and Vienna, 1922.

Freud, Sigmund. *A General Introduction to Psychoanalysis.* Edited by Tom Griffith. London: Wordsworth Edition, 2012.

Freud, Sigmund. *The Problem of Anxiety.* Translated by Henry Alden Bunker. Mansfield Centre: Martino Publishing, 2013.

Fukuyama, Francis. *Trust: The Social Virtues and the Creation of Prosperity.* New York: Free Press, 1996.

Furedi, Frank. *How Fear Works: Culture of Fear in the 21ˢᵗ Century.* London: Bloomsbury Continuum, 2019.

Gat, Azar. *Nations: The Long History and Deep Roots of Political Ethnicity and Nationalism.* Cambridge: Cambridge University Press, 2012.

Gilliam, Franklin D. *Farther to Go: Readings and Cases in African-American Politics.* Fort Worth: Harcourt, 2002.

Girard, René. *The Scapegoat.* Baltimore: Johns Hopkins University Press, 1986.

Glassner, Barry. *The Culture of Fear: Why Americans are Afraid of the Wrong Things—Crime, Drugs, Minorities, Teen Moms, Killer Kids, Mutant Microbes, Plane Crashes, Road Rage, and So Much More.* New York: Basic Books, 1999.

Gleason, Gregory. *Federalism and Nationalism: The Struggle for Republican Rights in the USSR.* Boulder: Westview Press, 1990.

Goodwin, Matthew, and Caitlin Milazzo. *UKIP: Inside the Campaign to Redraw the Map of British Politics.* Oxford: Oxford University Press, 2015.

Graeber, David. *Bullshit Jobs: A Theory.* London: Penguin Press, 2019.

Hall, Stuart, Chas Critcher, Tony Jefferson, John Clarke, and Brian Roberts, *Policing the Crisis: Mugging, the State and Law and Order.* New York: Palgrave Macmillan, 2013.

Hamilton, Clive. *Silent Invasion: China's Influence in Australia.* Melbourne: Hardie Grant Publishing, 2017.

Harrison, Lawrence E., and Samuel P. Huntington, eds. *Culture Matters: How Values Shape Human Progress.* New York: Basic Books, 2000.

Hedetoft, Ulf. *Paradoxes of Populism: Troubles of the West and Nationalism's Second Coming.* London: Anthem Press, 2020.

Helmus, Todd C., Elizabeth Bodine-Baron, Andrew Radin, Madeline Magnuson, Joshua Mendelsohn, William Marcellino, Andriy Bega, and Zev Winkelman. *Russian Social Media Influence: Understanding Russian Propaganda in Eastern Europe.* Santa Monica: Rand Corporation, 2018.

Henderson, Ailsa, and Richard Wyn Jones. *Englishness: The Political Force Transforming Britain.* Oxford: Oxford University Press, 2021.

Huntington, Samuel P. *Who Are We? The Challenges to America's National Identity.* New York: Simon and Schuster, 2004.

Jardina, Ashley. *White Identity Politics.* Cambridge: Cambridge University Press, 2019.

Jenson, Jane. *Mapping Social Cohesion: The State of Canadian Research.* Ottawa: Canadian Policy Research Networks, 1998.

Jones, Richard Wyn, Guy Lodge, Ailsa Henderson, and Daniel Wincott. *The Dog that Finally Barked: England as an Emerging Political Community.* London: Progressive Policy Think Tank, 2012.

Jones, Peter. *Essays on Toleration.* Lanham: Rowman & Littlefield, 2018.

Judah, Ben. *This is London: The Stories You Never Hear. The People You Never See.* London: Picador, 2016.

Jupp, James, and Michael Clyne. *Multiculturalism and Integration: A Harmonious Relationship.* Canberra: ANU Press, 2011.

Jünemann, Annette, Nicolas Fromm, and Nikolas Scherer, eds. *Fortress Europe? Challenges and Failures of Migration and Asylum Policies.* Wiesbaden: Springer VS, 2017.

Kassam, Natasha. *Lowy Institute Poll 2021: Understanding Australian Attitudes towards the World, 2021.* Sydney: Lowy Institute, 2021.

Kierkegaard, Søren. *The Concept of Anxiety: A Simple Psychologically Orienting Deliberation on the Dogmatic Issue of Hereditary Sin.* Princeton: Princeton University Press, 1981.

Kolstø, Pål, and Helge Blakkisrud, eds. *Russia Before and After Crimea.* Edinburgh: Edinburgh University Press, 2018.

Kukathas, Chandran. *The Liberal Archipelago: A Theory of Diversity and Freedom.* Oxford: Oxford University Press, 2003.

Laitin, David D. *Beached Diasporas. Identity in Formation: The Russian-Speaking Populations in the Near Abroad.* Ithaca: Cornell University Press, 1998.

Laruelle, Marlene. *Russian Nationalism: Imaginaries, Doctrines and Political Battlefields.* London: Routledge, 2018.

Lasch, Christopher. *The Culture of Narcissism: American Life in An Age of Diminishing Expectations.* New York: W.W. Norton, 2018.

Lawrence, Carmen. *Fear and Politics.* Melbourne: Scribe Short Books, 2006.

Lebow, Richard Ned, and Barry S. Strauss, eds. *Hegemonic Rivalry: From Thucydides to the Nuclear Age,* Boulder: Westview Press, 1991.

Lebow, Richard Ned. *Counterfactuals and International Relations.* Princeton: Princeton University Press, 2010.

Levin, Gail, Yasuo Kuniyoshi, and Hirose Naruhisa, *Kuniyoshi in Japanese Collections.* Okayama: Okayama Museum of Art, 2006.

Levy, Jacob T. *The Multiculturalism of Fear.* New York: Oxford University Press, 2000.

Light, Alison. *Forever England: Femininity, Literature and Conservatism Between the Wars.* London: Routledge, 1991.

Lilla, Mark. *The Once and Future Liberal: After Identity Politics.* New York: Harper, 2018.

Lippmann, Walter. *Public Opinion.* Saint Paul: Wilder Publications, 2018.

Lippmann, Walter. *The Phantom Public*. Saint Paul: Wilder Publications, 2021.

Lipset, Seymour Martin. *The First New Nation: The United States in Historical and Comparative Perspective*. New York: W.W. Norton, 1979.

Lukianoff, Greg, and Jonathan Haidt, *The Coddling of the American Mind: How Good Intentions and Bad Ideas Are Setting Up a Generation for Failure*. London: Penguin Press, 2019.

Mae, Ngae. *The Chinese Question: The Gold Rushes and Global Politics*. New York: W.W. Norton, 2022.

Markus, Andrew. *Mapping Social Cohesion: The Scanlon Foundation Surveys 2016*. Melbourne: Monash University, 2016.

Markus, Andrew. *Mapping Social Cohesion 2021*. Melbourne: Scanlon Foundation, Monash University, 2021.

Martin, Terry. *The Affirmative Action Empire: Nations and Nationalism in the Soviet Union, 1923–1939*. Ithaca: Cornell University Press, 2001.

Megalogenis, George. *The Australian Moment: How We Were Made for These Times*. Penguin Books Australia: Melbourne, 2017.

Meier, Christian. *The Uses of History: From Athens to Auschwitz*. Cambridge: Harvard University Press, 2005.

Milburn, Michael A., and Sheree D. Conrad. *The Politics of Denial*. Cambridge: MIT Press, 1996.

Miles, Robert, and Dietrich Thränhardt, eds., *Migration and European Integration: The Dynamics of Inclusion and Exclusion*. London: Pinter, 1995.

Mill, John Stuart. *On Liberty*. Garden City: Dover Publications, 2002.

Morrison, Toni. *Song of Solomon*. New York: Alfred A. Knopf, 1977.

Murrell, William. *Yasuo Kuniyoshi*. Woodstock: William M. Fisher Publishers, 2012.

Myers, Jane, and Tom Wolf. *The Shores of a Dream: Yasuo Kuniyoshi's Early Work in America*. Fort Worth: Amon Carter Museum, 1996.

Naipaul, V. S. *The Enigma of Arrival: A Novel in Five Sections*. New York: Vintage, 1988.

Newey, Glen. *Toleration in Political Conflict*. Cambridge: Cambridge University Press, 2013.

Noël, Lise. *Intolerance: A General Survey*. Montreal: McGill-Queen's University Press, 1994.

Norris, Pippa, and Ronald F. Inglehart. *Cultural Backlash: Trump, Brexit, and Authoritarian Populism*. Cambridge: Cambridge University Press, 2019.

OECD. *Perspectives on Global Development 2012: Social Cohesion in a Shifting World*. Paris: OECD, 2011.

Parens, Henri, Afaf Mahfouz, Stuart W. Twemlow, and David E. Scharff, eds. *The Future of Prejudice: Psychoanalysis and the Prevention of Prejudice*. Lanham: Rowman & Littlefield, 2007.

Pietsch, Juliet. *Race, Ethnicity, and the Participation Gap: Understanding Australia's Political Complexion*. Toronto: University of Toronto Press, 2018.

Pietsch, Juliet, and Haydn Aarons, eds. *Australia: Identity, Fear and Governance in the 21st Century*. Canberra: ANU Press, 2012.

Popper, Karl. *The Open Society and Its Enemies*. Princeton: Princeton University Press, 2013.

Prodi, Romano. *Europe as I See It*. Cambridge: Polity Press, 2000.

Ramaswamy, Vivek. *Woke, Inc: Inside Corporate America's Social Justice Scam*. New York: Center Street, 2021.

Ranciere, Jacques. *On the Shores of Politics*. London: Verso, 2007.

Rawls, John. *A Theory of Justice*. Cambridge: Harvard University Press, 1999.

Robin, Corey. *Fear: The History of a Political Idea*. New York: Oxford University Press, 2006.

BIBLIOGRAPHY

191

Rosenblum, Nancy L., ed. <i>Liberalism and the Moral Life.</i> Cambridge: Harvard University Press, 1989.
Rothstein, Bo. <i>The Quality of Government: Corruption, Social Trust, and Inequality in International Perspective.</i> Chicago: University of Chicago Press, 2011.
Rist, Ray. <i>Guestworkers in Germany: The Prospects for Pluralism.</i> New York: Praeger, 1978.
Rozanova, Marya S. <i>Migration Processes and Challenges in Contemporary Russia: St. Petersburg Case Study.</i> Princeton: Woodrow Wilson International Center for Scholars & Kennan Institute, 2012.
Schenk, Caress. <i>Why Control Immigration? Strategic Uses of Migration Management in Russia.</i> Toronto: University of Toronto Press, 2018.
Shipman, Tim. <i>All Out War: The Full Story of How Brexit Sank Britain's Political Class.</i> London: William Collins, 2016.
Shklar, Judith. <i>Ordinary Vices.</i> Cambridge, MA: Harvard University Press, 1984.
Sternberg, Robert J., and Karin Sternberg, <i>The Nature of Hate.</i> Cambridge: Cambridge University Press, 2008.
Taras, Raymond. <i>Fear and the Making of Foreign Policy: Europe and Beyond.</i> Edinburgh: Edinburgh University Press, 2015.
Taras, Raymond. <i>Nationhood, Migration and Global Politics.</i> Edinburgh: Edinburgh University Press, 2018.
Tilly, Charles. <i>Trust and Rule.</i> Cambridge: Cambridge University Press, 2005.
Tolz, Vera. <i>Russia.</i> London: Hodder Education, 2001.
Tsakmakis, Antonis, and Antonios Rengakos, eds. <i>Brill's Companion to Thucydides.</i> Leiden: Brill, 2006.
van Evera, Stephen. <i>Guide to Methods for Students of Political Science.</i> Ithaca: Cornell University Press, 1997.
Wang, ShiPu. <i>Becoming American: The Art and Identity Crisis of Yasuo Kuniyoshi.</i> Honolulu: University of Hawai'i Press, 2011.
Watts, Tim. <i>The Golden Country: Australia's Changing Identity.</i> Melbourne: Text Publishing, 2019.
Webster, Wendy. <i>Englishness and Empire: 1939–1965.</i> New York: Oxford University Press, 2005.
Weiner, Myron. <i>The Global Migration Crisis: Challenge to States and to Human Rights.</i> New York: HarperCollins, 1995.
Wellings, Ben. <i>English Nationalism, Brexit and the Anglosphere: Wider Still and Wider.</i> Manchester: Manchester University Press, 2019.
Wolf, Tom. <i>Yasuo Kuniyoshi's Women.</i> Rohnert Park: Pomegranate Artbooks, 1993.
Woolf, Virginia. <i>Between the Acts.</i> London: Mariner Books, 1970.
Woolf, Virginia. <i>A Room of One's Own.</i> London: Penguin Books, 2000.

INDEX

www.ingramcontent.com/pod-product-compliance
Lightning Source LLC
Chambersburg PA
CBHW030650270326
41929CB00007B/288